'This wonderful addition to the field offers an informed and helpful insight into the world of personal development groups. The collaboration of contributing authors, all experienced practitioners, supervisors and academics, provides an engaging and valuable resource to trainee counsellors and therapists and others interested in their own personal development. The rich integration of theory, practice examples, case studies and reflective exercises creates a well-informed companion guide, signposting the reader seamlessly through the often complex, challenging and ultimately rewarding experience of personal development groups.'

– **Anna Playle**, Psychotherapist, Supervisor & Programme Director
and Senior Lecturer, Canterbury Christ Church University

'It is acknowledged that personal development groups, although essential to therapeutic education, can be experienced with some trepidation—not only by students! This book, produced by five experienced and committed practitioners will be welcomed by trainee therapists, their teachers and supervisors. It is a 'go-to' handbook that helps to demystify the purposes and processes involved in PD group membership where the need for good facilitation and active participation is a given. This book is definitive in its broad-spectrum coverage and it is presented in a very accessible format.'

– **Marjorie Ashdown**, BACP Fellow, PD Group Supervisor,
Clinical Supervisor and Therapist

'I would thoroughly recommend this book to anyone who works with people, as it has certainly enhanced my capacity for reflection and broadened my personal development. The exercises were often transformative and encouraged me to look at things from a slightly different perspective. They encouraged self-reflection and I felt my capacity for personal development deepened through the experience. I especially appreciated the vignettes throughout which allowed me to put my learning into context.'

– **Margo Fourman**, Special Education and Learning Development
Tutor, University of Huddersfield

GW00771322

Personal Development Groups for Trainee Counsellors

Personal development (PD) groups are a key feature of many counsellor training programmes. *Personal Development Groups for Trainee Counsellors: An Essential Companion* is a comprehensive and accessible study guide written by experienced tutors and lecturers to support students with their PD group work and other personal development activities, helping students to get the most out of these experiences.

This essential resource is aimed primarily at those who are new to counsellor training. It will also be useful for anyone who wants to understand more about the nature of PD groups and how these can be used effectively. Case studies, questions and activities encourage readers to reflect on different topics and on themselves, including looking at how to improve self-care and how mindfulness can help. The book looks at the historical background to PD groups; how they can be used effectively, and also real-life experiences from both tutors and recent students. Other chapters invite the reader to develop their self-awareness through gaining an understanding of how ethics, relationships and identity are developed. There is a discussion about the merits or otherwise of mandatory personal therapy for trainees and also a discussion about the use of supervision. Finally, other important aspects of personal development are discussed including personal therapy, supervision, self-care and mindfulness.

Personal Development Groups for Trainee Counsellors will be of use to counsellor trainees on undergraduate and postgraduate diplomas to introduce them to PD groups and other essential activities. It will also be highly informative to those who are on counselling certificate courses to introduce them to aspects of personal development, as well as for tutors to support them in their work as PD group facilitators.

Jayne Godward is a Person-Centred Counsellor and Supervisor, who has been teaching and leading counselling courses in HE and FE since 1993. She has facilitated personal development groups since 2006. Jayne is a co-director of Yorkshire Counselling Training, working with students on the CPCAB L3 Certificate, L4 Diploma and L6 Certificate in Supervision courses.

Heather Dale is a Senior Practising Counsellor and Psychotherapist and is a Fellow of the British Association for Counselling and Psychotherapy and the Higher Education Academy. Alongside her private practice she has taught counselling courses at all levels, from complete beginners, to those studying for postgraduate degrees. She also writes and presents on ethical issues within the profession, such as the making of contracts, fitness to practice and charging for counselling.

Carole Smith is a Gestalt Psychotherapist working in private practice and a Senior Lecturer at the University of Huddersfield. She has been a counselling and psychotherapy trainer, supervisor and consultant for many years, and is currently working as UKCP Trainer/Supervisor for the Manchester Gestalt Centre.

Personal Development Groups for Trainee Counsellors

An Essential Companion

Jayne Godward, Heather Dale and Carole Smith

Routledge
Taylor & Francis Group

LONDON AND NEW YORK

First published 2020
by Routledge
2 Park Square, Milton Park, Abingdon, Oxon OX14 4RN

and by Routledge
52 Vanderbilt Avenue, New York, NY 10017

Routledge is an imprint of the Taylor & Francis Group, an informa business

British Library Cataloguing-in-Publication Data
A catalogue record for this book is available from the British Library

Library of Congress Cataloging-in-Publication Data
A catalog record has been requested for this book

ISBN: 978-1-138-47926-5 (hbk)
ISBN: 978-1-138-47928-9 (pbk)
ISBN: 978-1-351-06614-3 (ebk)

Typeset in Times New Roman
by Newgen Publishing UK

Contents

Contributors

Heather Dale is a Senior Practising Counsellor and Psychotherapist and is a Fellow of the British Association for Counselling and Psychotherapy (BACP) and the Higher Education Academy (HEA). Alongside her private practice she has taught counselling courses at all levels since 1985, most recently as a Senior Lecturer at Huddersfield University. She is an experienced PD group facilitator having facilitated groups both for counsellor training and for other groups, including, under a different name, for five-year-olds. She writes and presents on ethical issues including the need for making good contracts; fitness to practice issues; and charging for counselling. She was the editor of the Ethical Dilemma page in *Therapy Today* for several years.

Tara Fox is a lecturer in the school of Psychological Therapies and Mental Health at Leeds Beckett University and a relationship/young people's counsellor in private practice. She is a Registered Member of the BACP and a HEA Fellow. She has been teaching on counselling courses for 18 years and facilitating PD groups for six years. She advocates the relevance of mindfulness and self-compassion in counselling training and has a special interest in spirituality in counselling and psychotherapy. Research for her Master's looked at how the therapists' spirituality manifests in the therapeutic relationship.

Jayne Godward has been teaching counselling skills and counselling since 1993 and has taught on counselling practitioner courses in FE colleges and universities since 2006. Jayne is now a partner in her own company, Yorkshire Counselling Training, working with students on the CPCAB L3 certificate, L4 Diploma and L6 Certificate in Supervision courses. Her MA research interest was the conflict between students and tutors on counselling training courses and how this links in with personal development. She has written several articles for *Therapy Today*. Her modality is Person-Centred with an interest in psychodynamic processes in group work. She is a registered member of the BACP.

Tracy Hitchcock is a member of the BACP and has been training students in counselling and psychotherapy since the early 1990s. She works at Leeds Beckett University where she is the Course Leader for the BSc Honours Degree in Therapeutic Counselling. Her modality is psychodynamic and relational psychotherapy. She is currently studying labyrinths in higher education and their effectiveness for personal development and meditation

Carole Smith is a Gestalt Psychotherapist working in private practice and a Senior Lecturer at the University of Huddersfield. Her background was originally in nursing and midwifery. She initially trained in the Person-Centred Approach, did a Master's in Integrative Psychotherapy at the University of Nottingham and then trained as a Gestalt Psychotherapist at the Metanoia Institute and the Sherwood Institute. She has been a counselling and psychotherapy trainer, supervisor and consultant for many years, and is currently working as UKCP Trainer/Supervisor for the Manchester Gestalt Centre. Her PhD interest is in personal development groups and how self-awareness is used in client work.

Preface: How this book came about

After many years of teaching counselling, I began to notice how few women were publishing books, compared to the numbers of female students on my courses. For some reason women were not writing about their therapeutic work, and especially their work as tutors.

The area I had specialised in was personal development and in particular the personal development (PD) group. This was often quite misunderstood by both students and other tutors who were not involved. I think it is quite hard to understand the demands of running this kind of group without having experienced the particular demands it makes, on both students and facilitators. So I decided to write a book on personal development with a focus on the PD group. There were very few books on this topic that I could recommend to my students, so the aim was also to fill this gap.

I see the personal development aspect of counsellor training as one of the most important activities, if not the most important. If as a counsellor you don't have self-awareness and self-understanding, I believe that you will not be as effective as a practitioner and will also be less effective in helping a client to develop their understanding of self.

I also see the PD group as the hub of the training where students can piece together their learning and development and become aware of the processes they are going through.

I did not have the confidence to write this book alone and wanted to collaborate with colleagues who had an interest in the subject area or were experienced counselling lecturers. A key aim was to encourage other unpublished women to write as well.

Some of the reactions to this were quite interesting. Not everyone I approached was keen – one reaction was 'What do I know?' or 'I don't know how to write'. There was generally a lack of confidence from some very experienced therapists and senior lecturers I approached.

Heather and Carole were already researching for their PhDs and had topics that they were interested in sharing with the wider world, and we had worked together before in different capacities. So we then formed the editing team as well as deciding to write some individual and joint chapters. This has been challenging at times, but always stimulating

So it was a female enterprise, which has been hard work but also rewarding. I have enjoyed the discussions and the research and the collaboration, meeting in cafes, working things out. It is interesting in a book that has a focus on group work that we have gone through stages where we have both formed and stormed but hopefully performed well enough for this book to be useful for both students and tutors who are engaged in PD group work.

I am grateful to Routledge for accepting the proposal and for giving us the chance to write and be published.

Jayne Godward

Acknowledgements

To Margo Fourman, who patiently read through all my chapters and who, with great tact, commented on much-needed changes, and who believed in my writing. Also to Roger Cowell, who brought me coffee, chocolate and comfort in equal measures when the going got tough, and who was a sounding board and confidante throughout.

Heather Dale

To Mark, my dear partner for bearing with me and for listening to my moans and groans; to Davida Lumsden for her support when times were tough and to Tara who read my first chapters and encouraged me to carry on writing.

Jayne Godward

To Phil for his tolerance, love and patient ears; to Heather who inspired my PhD and to Vicki for her sensible advice when I was floundering

Carole Smith

A big thanks to Hannah Holden at the Artlink, Hull who produced some of the diagrams for the book.

We would like to thank all our students over the years, but in particular those who submitted personal accounts/experiences to us to be included in this book.

Introduction

Aim of the book

What sets counsellor training apart from other professional training is the need for trainees to look closely at themselves and dissect their traits and experience. No matter how well-prepared trainees are, this can be a draining and difficult experience.

Therefore, we have written this book as a resource or companion to support you with all your personal development work but with an emphasis on the PD group as this can be where students struggle most. A common analogy linked to personal development is that it is like peeling the layers of an onion, as you learn about yourself and discover more about how you have become who you are. We hope that reading the personal accounts from previous students will give you examples of this and might help you to understand what you are about to undertake and how personal development in counselling training may affect you.

All the writers are involved with counsellor training, and part of the thrust of the book is to address common issues brought to us by students over the years.

The book is divided into three parts, which are described in the overview below.

You may wish to read through this book before starting your counselling training or at the beginning to help you prepare for the demands involved. Or you might prefer to read the chapters that interest you in no particular order. The chapters are all stand-alone, so it is easy to move through the book at whatever pace you like.

The personal development work you do on yourself directly links to your effectiveness as a practitioner and the type of therapeutic relationships you are able to form with your clients. This book aims to help you get the most out of your personal development group work and other personal development activities to become the best possible counsellor you can be.

Focus of the book

Rather than just talking about personal development and personal development groups we have aimed to bring the subject alive by looking at student and tutor experiences. We use these to look at the nuts and bolts and give you useful tips and advice to help you to use your groups and other activities. We have also included relevant theory and recent research to support some of our writing, as we wanted to encourage you to look at the research around this area.

Using this book

As a learning resource, the book contains activities, case studies and questions to help you look at yourself and to support your development further. Some chapters are more practical than others and will include more of these, while others are more academic in nature and present research findings and discussion. The latter are aimed at encouraging you to think about the evidence base for personal development groups and other personal development activities. As tutors we want you to be looking at yourself and also questioning what you are doing as part of your training. We feel it is important for counselling students to be both analytical and reflective.

Terms used in our book

- We have used 'counsellor' and 'therapist' interchangeably.
- The initials BACP stand for the British Association for Counselling and Psychotherapy. This is the largest UK counselling and therapy body and all the authors are obligated by its *Ethical Framework*.
- The initials PD are used to prevent repetition of 'personal development' throughout.
- Most of the chapters contain *case studies* – which are fictitious characters or scenarios based on our experiences.
- We have included *activity* boxes at times, which contain longer reflective exercises than just answering questions. An activity suggests that you pause and think about something in more detail.

Overview: A look inside

Section A: Understanding personal development

We start with an introduction to personal development and personal development groups generally. In Chapter 1, Carole Smith introduces what personal development is and starts to look at the PD group and why it is important in counsellor training. Then in Chapter 2 Carole goes on to looks at the historical background of PD groups. This is followed by Tracy Hitchcock's personal account of the different groups she experienced as a trainee in the 1990s, followed by Chapter 4 where five different students share their recent personal development journeys.

Section B: The personal development group

In the next section our aim is to help you understand a personal development group, using the experiences of participants and tutors to explore this. We have done this because often students are confused about what the PD group is about or how to use it. The aim here is to clarify areas which are confusing. In Chapter 5, Jayne Godward looks at what you can expect from this process and what is expected of the trainee.

Carole goes on to look at her research into PD group experiences drawing on her primary and secondary research findings in Chapter 6. In contrast in Chapter 7, Jayne looks at the PD group from a tutor perspective, sharing her experiences of running PD groups and examining what a PD tutor's role is during the life of a group.

In Chapter 8 Jayne's focus turns to conflict and difficulties in PD groups drawing on her research into tutor–student conflict to look at why conflict occurs and how it can be managed.

Section C: Developing self-awareness to enhance practice

We will then go on to look at important topics related to self-awareness which relate to what is being explored in the PD group.

An important aspect of personal development that is often overlooked is the cultivation of the student's core ethical belief system and a focus on their personal moral qualities. These are addressed in two specific chapters in this book by Heather Dale, who has worked with ethical dilemmas and issues for many years and who both writes and speaks on the subject of ethical practice. In Chapter 9, Heather discusses ethics and how these relate to the work in the PD group. She then goes on in Chapter 10 to look at personal moral qualities and how these may be played out in the PD group. A detailed case study is used to help examine the issues involved.

The next area we write about is to do with our attachment styles and relational patterns. Our earlier attachments and patterns will have an impact on how we relate to our clients and to our peers. In Chapter 11, Tracy Hitchcock looks at different attachment styles and how these may manifest in PD groups, inviting the reader to look at their patterns of relating.

Finally in this section Tara Fox and Jayne Godward explore the concept of identity and look at how the PD group can be used to become more aware of ourselves and our reactions to other people.

Section D: Other aspects of personal development

In the final section of the book, we focus on other essential aspects of personal development that are either required or necessary for trainees to develop as effective practitioners. Many counsellor training courses stipulate a certain amount of personal therapy and all training courses need students to be supervised for their practice with clients. So in Chapter 13 we introduce a debate about the usefulness of mandatory personal therapy. The chapter starts by looking at existing research and then moves into a debate written by Heather and Jayne.

In Chapter 14 supervision is the focus. This chapter discusses, first, the purpose of supervision and then how trainees can gain the most out of it for their personal development.

Both personal therapy and supervision are important methods that students use to take care of themselves, but Chapter 15 takes this further and looks at what self-care really means. It also addresses why this is particularly relevant to trainee counsellors. This is a useful and practical chapter to help you plan out your self-care activities.

Tara Fox has gradually been introducing some mindfulness work on the courses she teaches on and has been studying this in relation to self-compassion. In Chapter 16, she shares her views and findings on this area in this book. This will be a useful introduction for students who find it difficult to be 'in the moment' with clients and who suffer from anxiety about their performance as fledgling counsellors, tending to be overly self-critical.

Finally personal learning needs to be captured and written about to help both students and tutors assess the development that has taken place. Our short Chapter 17 has a look at this with some examples to help you.

We hope you will enjoy reading this book and that you find it useful for your studies and development.

Section A

Understanding personal development

Chapter 1

What is personal development?

Carole Smith

Introduction

Personal development (PD) is a difficult notion to define, but there is a suggestion that growth or improvement is involved in some way. However, the word 'personal' complicates matters as this alludes to a very individual concept. Historically, personal development has been a large umbrella term covering numerous aspects of process including the personal used interchangeably with professional, and literature has seemed to struggle in its classification. The subject is complex and this chapter begins the voyage of demystification by introducing:

- an explanation of the complexity of definitions;
- a focus on self-awareness, which is at the heart of personal development;
- some exercises to help you personally define your own aims of PD;
- questions about whether the PD group is the right format for your development;
- an insight into expectations for PD;
- potential difficulties you may experience.

Defining personal development

This chapter may leave you with more questions than answers, but that's good because you are an individual and each person's needs and outcomes in their personal development path will be different. This 'path' is also a way of mystery, imagination and enquiry, which will leave you sometimes frustrated, surprised and perplexed and other times, puzzled, indignant and even outraged!

To start off, write a sentence or two about what experience you have of personal development groups so far (and it is OK if you have none) or what you imagine personal development will entail for you.

Activity

What is personal development for you?

1.
2.
3.

So, you might have written down things like – 'developing my self- awareness', 'learning about others', 'exploring my feelings', 'raising my knowledge of theory' or even 'learning to be assertive or challenging'. It is all these and much more, but self-awareness would be a holistic definition.

Personal development groups are almost always incorporated as a core component in counselling and psychotherapy training courses and are known by various terms, such as process groups, development groups, personal growth, self-awareness groups or personal development groups. Normally there is no planned theoretical input; the process is purely experiential and 'in the moment', although occasions may lend themselves to some exploration and cross-referencing into theory. Generally, your contributions are not formally assessed, but you will be urged to keep a reflective journal or diary recording your thoughts, feelings and experiences. The assessment will usually be in the form of a summary or a reflective report highlighting your development.

Facilitators of these groups will vary in their style; some will be challenging, others may prefer individuals in the group to be more autonomous, yet others will take a more passive role. There is learning to be had from all of these role models, both for your client work and for future groups you will inevitably take part in, so journal as much as you can. When you are in the later stages of your training, tutors may even suggest the group runs without a leader, where there will be rich learning about group roles we most naturally adopt in our lives.

A generic definition of personal development encompasses the encouragement to reflect on experiences from differing perspectives, which can then provide options for action or decision-making, as well as offering insight and understanding about our own human motivations and behaviours. Personal development can also be awareness of one's thoughts, feelings, beliefs, behaviours and attitudes and an understanding of how they are shaped by historical experiences. However, alternative definitions have surfaced over the years, ranging from the development of cognitive understanding (Irving and Williams, 1999) or self-communication to the development of metacognitive skills (Fauth et al., 2007) or skills in self-reflection (BPS, 2007). Avoiding personal blind spots and being confident of the relationship with the client with differing perspectives also seems crucial.

Self-awareness

Self-awareness is, in my view, the ethical and most central nub of becoming a counsellor but is also probably the trickiest. Part of this is because self-awareness is never complete; we continue on a lifelong journey of self-discovery, learning about ourselves in relation to others, including our clients. Self-awareness forms a large part of personal development. However, self-awareness does enable us to be more fully accepting of ourselves, which is essential if we are to wholly accept the client in our therapeutic work.

The use of self as a tool in this relationship is particularly important in the Person-Centred model of counselling but the importance of the relationship between client and counsellor is becoming increasingly better recognised and researched. As far back as the 1950s, Carl Rogers offered discussions about the importance of the therapeutic relationship. There is a body of evidence that suggests that the quality of the client/counsellor relationship is one of the key factors in client outcomes (Cooper, 2005; Knox, 2008). Cooper (2005) explored trainers/therapists experiences in working at relational depth with clients. The results highlighted the importance of engagement with the client, particularly in the use of empathy, congruence and acceptance.

Also, Knox's (2008) study of clients demonstrated similar results of the value of interconnectedness with their therapists. In fact, all participants identified at least one moment of 'relational depth' with a therapist. Similarly, Smith et al. (2010) ascertained the importance of the therapeutic alliance in client outcomes and concluded that counsellors who had an ability to relate were more likely to achieve good outcomes, with this ability to relate being linked to self-awareness.

So, how are you going to arrive at this state of self-awareness? Regrettably, there is no arrival at an end result; self-awareness is an ongoing process that is constantly stimulated by our new experiences every day, such as our interactions with others or our reflections on actions. It is about the distance we have travelled from the point we have started. The personal development group is designed to help you in this ongoing progression.

Case study: Holly

Holly sits in the PD group feeling nervous about making a contribution, as she feels that others in the group are more articulate and confident than her. She is so nervous, she is unable to say what is happening for her. Another group member, Beth, whose anxiety is manifesting in an aggressive way, confronts Holly and says 'I notice that you haven't said anything at all this morning, it doesn't seem fair that you get to opt out!' Holly's response is to shrink further into herself and stutter 'I'm just tired today, so I'm observing, that's all'. This isn't helpful for her as she feels unable to voice her anxiety and also is unable to confront Beth. Others in the group, Jenny and Fran, jump to support Holly and confront Beth for her as they are also feeling nervous but are more able to say what they think as the confrontation has not been directed at them. Fran finds it slightly easier to step in as Jenny has spoken first. Holly is very relieved to have this support.
Discuss the following:

 What is the learning for Holly? For Beth? For Jenny and Fran?
 How could the group facilitator help this situation?
 How could Holly support herself to be more congruent?

There is no textbook to relay the knowledge and skills of self-awareness as each person contains their own insight into wisdom, understanding and vision, although the ability to access this is often something of a challenge. However, the key to obtaining an unbiased view is in receiving feedback from others. This may involve bringing unconscious motives and drives into the conscious parts of ourselves for processing. There are differing ways you can do that, with support and help from training facilitators, and this book is designed to show you some of those ways and to encourage you in this very crucial part of your development. Our individual blind spots can cloud objectivity and leave us with a less than satisfactory judgement of ourselves, which can lead us into a level of avoidance of this important process. It seems, therefore, essential that we have ventured into an exploration of these to some extent, before working with clients' experiences, actions and drives.

How can we recognise our self-development?

Diagram 1.1 illustrates the Johari Window (Luft and Ingham, 1955), which is a model developed to help you understand the gradual unfolding awareness of yourself and others. The idea behind this is to increase the 'blind' area, through feedback from others (this is like becoming aware of your blind spot in your driving mirror), and to discover areas of yourself that are as yet unknown to you or in your subconscious. The hidden areas are places that you can choose to reveal or equally keep hidden.

Activity: Exploring your Johari Window

Make a list of ten statements about yourself (you can later choose to either share them with others or not). For example, 'I have an absolute dislike of busy places' or 'Sometimes I eat more than I should'.

Now highlight those statements that you would be happy to share with others

---

Try to monitor any changes in your self-development, using the Johari Window. You will at times, feel vulnerable even sharing aspects of yourself *with* yourself but this is the first step to sharing with others. You can now think about how a client might feel when confronted by a stranger and having to tell you.

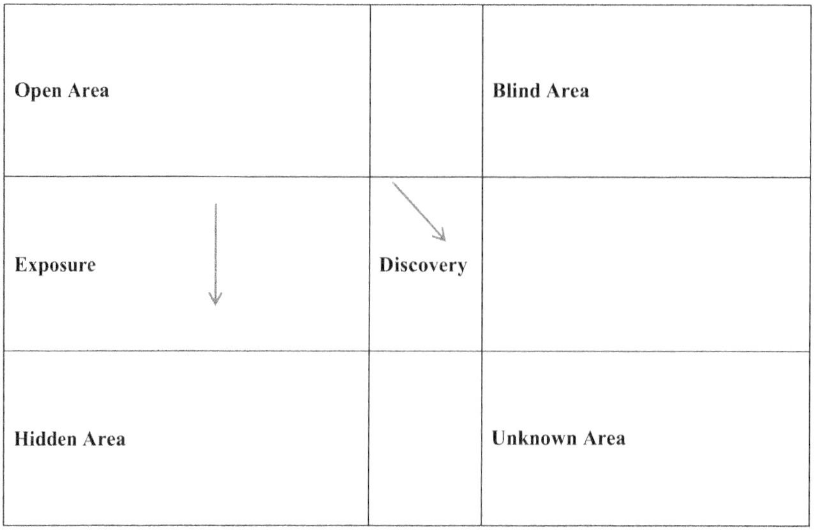

Open Area		Blind Area
Exposure	Discovery	
Hidden Area		Unknown Area

Diagram 1.1 The Johari Window
Source: Adapted from Luft and Ingham (1955)

Activity

Make a list of features in the environment such as lighting, warmth, etc. that would help you feel safe in sharing information about yourself:

1.
2.
3.
4.
5.

Now make a list of the characteristics of others that would enable feelings of safety:

1
2
3.

During my own training in counselling and then in psychotherapy, I took part in compulsory personal development training, in the form of PD groups or what is sometimes known as 'group process'. I initially found myself sitting on the edge of groups, being afraid to share too much of myself in my confusion about what this practice entailed and not knowing how much support I was going to get. The aims of this activity remained a mystery to me and to many participants on my course for a large part of my early counselling training. We were informed by lecturers that it was important that we 'got to know ourselves better in order to be able to work with clients safely', but the actual process of what we were meant to do, or what this consisted of, was not clarified. As a trainee I never really knew whether I was contributing to the PD group process in the correct way as little feedback on our participation in the group was offered. Similarly, I did not know or understand what tangible learning I was making at the time. Some years later I came to understand that contribution was individual and that facilitators of this personal development process were observing us closely for any underlying 'issues' that might interfere with safe client work. I also eventually realised that personal growth confirmation comes from a retrospective or reflexive stance. In other words, it is going to be important for you to keep an ongoing document of your personal reflections during your training, which you can add to as you go along.

Robson and Robson (2008, p. 371) suggest that the PD group, for some students, is 'the most powerful experience of their training' but for others, 'they never really seem to understand or engage in its purpose'. Rose (2012) suggests that the counsellor has a responsibility to understand her/his part in the therapeutic relationship, which in effect is an ongoing process with each contributing to the change mechanism. This reflects a particularly relational model of working therapeutically, although it could be argued that every theoretical approach involves some form or level of relationship.

Is the PD group the best way to develop?

Perhaps first we need to consider whether learning in groups generally is beneficial. We need feedback from others to learn about ourselves, interrelationships, relating styles and differing levels of communication, including the non-verbal. Within a group setting, we can observe and partake of all of these at once if we so choose. However, you will need to be aware that the PD group can raise negative feelings such as irritation with others, jealousy, anxiety and powerful occurrences of transference and counter-transference – the downside of intensive and experiential groups. There may even be a mirroring of your historical family position in the PD group. There will certainly be a plethora of differing values, expectations, backgrounds, sexualities, social classes and personalities, which may clash. There will also be individuals who are louder and more controlling than you or who display prejudiced opinions and beliefs that outrage you.

Some people have reported a triggering of past parental or sibling dynamics playing out in the group. These are very normal manifestations, but the PD group is particularly a source of these reactions as often the aims and structure of them are flexible, so boundaries are a little more elastic than in an ordinary group. Facilitators will sometimes allow interactions to 'run' in the hope that there will be powerful learning when connections are made with emotions. This is believed to be useful for client work in that we can minimise any surprises in ourselves when in the therapy room.

The evidence for PD groups

In the context of counselling training, while much 'evidence' on the advantages and limitations of group dynamics has been discussed, through examples such as the work of Yalom and Leszcz (2005), they have been based on experiences of group therapy, not on PD group settings. Nonetheless, the anecdotal evidence is that they can create corrective emotional experiences, significant personal learning (for some) and inter-personal learning if the environment is safe. As can be seen in Yalom and Leszcz's work, group process contributing to interpersonal learning relies on the group being a constructive learning environment (Yalom and Leszcz, 2005). This is dependent on many factors, including the skill of the group facilitator. Bloch et al. (1979) and Mahrer and Nadler (1986), support the notion of group process having therapeutic impact on its members. Similarly, Dima and Bucuta (2012) in their study, found that therapeutic group factors contributed to a more authentic and stronger self, which seems a necessity in the face of some difficult client work you are bound to encounter in your career.

So, why do we need self-development to work with clients and why are personal development groups used to help us do this, particularly in the light of Johns' view that personal development has not been acknowledged enough (Johns, 2009)? Personal development could be described as a vague and undefinable concept. This is because each 'journey' of development is an individual one and is taken at discrete paces, levels and stages for each unique person. If this is the case, then it follows that providing aims and objectives for personal development is virtually impossible.

Mearns and Thorne (1997) suggested that one of the reasons for the emphasis on PD group work in counselling training is that it is believed to provide more personally challenging encounters than does a single therapeutic contact with another. There are less than extensive studies on PD groups, other than anecdotal, although Lennie's (2007) empirical study on PD groups suggests that the complexities of group roles and group dynamics complicates learning. However, Bloch et al. (1979) and Mahrer and Nadler (1986), all support the notion of group process having therapeutic impact on its members. In fact, Yalom and Leszcz's observations that group process contributed to interpersonal learning is dependent on the group being a constructive learning environment (Yalom and Leszcz, 2005), so it is important that you feel relatively comfortable and able to contribute in the group generally.

Up to now, there is little evidence on the effectiveness of PD groups; much of what is written is around individual perceptions of their value and, as you can imagine, there are subjective pros and cons. However, my own research (unpublished) is a retrospective study of how experienced counsellors/therapists believe PD groups in their past training contribute to their client work (see Chapter 6), which identifies the absolute value of the PD group, but also recognises the difficulties and stressors of this journey.

Part of the problem seems to be that there is no universally accepted definition of what personal development is and the term is often used interchangeably with professional development in the counselling and psychotherapy world. An explanation for this may be that personal development is not a single entity (McLeod and McLeod, 2014). As Hughes and Youngson (2009) state, there is a vast literature on personal development, which in itself covers a wealth of issues, such as 'quality of life, meaning and understanding and positive thinking and goal setting' (p. 25).

Another factor to perhaps consider is the overlap between personal therapy and your group experiences. Sometimes group participants seem to be confused about what to take to the PD group and what to keep for therapy. Your group facilitator will guide you on this (don't be surprised if s/he challenges you on this).

Defining your objectives

To help you define your own objectives for your PD group, the following is a list of, *in my view*, important aspects to aim for, but remember you will achieve your own development and learning in specific ways distinctive to your own self:

- Understand more about yourself and others, e.g., your style of relating to others.
- Recognise how your past history affects you in certain situations, e.g. your attachment style.
- Identify particular life events that have had an impact on you.
- Be aware of certain personality traits in others that 'push your buttons'.
- Learn how to accept and empathise with others situations even when your values are in conflict with the other.
- Explore the use of core conditions in yourself and others.
- Discover more about group dynamics than you ever knew existed.
- Learn how to support yourself and others.
- Investigate, and even try out, numerous forms and styles of communication that you have never tried before.
- Be open to taking some risks (as long as you are supported in this) and entering into experiential forms of learning in the group.
- Reflect on your development as a counsellor.

You should expect to have support from your group facilitator as well as from some of your peers; if you don't, you can ask for it, and this is better done in the moment if you are able. You can also assume you will receive challenge in some form or other, so reflect on how you normally deal with dispute and questioning. Challenge should be offered with a bedrock of kindness, but sometimes it is difficult to perceive this when we are confronted. It is perfectly acceptable to say 'let me have a few moments to think about that', which will give you time to step back and consider how safe you feel and how you want to respond. On the other hand, you may feel perfectly fine to respond in the moment – both methods will offer you some learning on your own and others' styles of relating. Reflecting on process has a developmental trajectory, where 'lightbulb' moments can occur some long time after the event, so you may also want to take your reflections back to the group at a later date. Use your personal journal to help you with this expansion of your awareness.

Support in processing your PD experiences

Whether or not your course requires or recommends personal therapy while you are training, it is a good idea for you to access this for a number of reasons (see Chapter 13). It is important for your development, as well as your sanity, that you allow yourself some one-to-one talking support in order to untangle your group experiences and help you to make sense of them. An experienced therapist will have had similar experiences and will be able to offer you feedback in an objective way. Hughes and Youngson (2009) also advocate the use of other support systems such as buddying, mentoring and clinical tutors. There is, of course, reflection through clinical supervision and your regular entries in the personal journal, which can be a sound source of support if used productively and honestly.

Your experience of PD will be very individual to you and it will be up to you to take your own personal responsibility for your learning, but your perceptions, interpretations, perspectives and stage of learning will inevitably be different to that of your peers. However, the PD group should be a safe space for you and difficult experiences should be supported by the group facilitator. It is the unknowing that may feel threatening, but trust your own learning process and take some risks with the experiential work. If you engage fully it will be a satisfying and revealing journey.

Conclusion

Undoubtedly, taking part in a personal development group in counselling training can facilitate personal growth and awareness *for some*, but seems essential for practising counsellors and psychotherapists working with clients. Moreover, as seen from these studies, there is an increasing awareness of the dynamics of the interpersonal relationship, essential knowledge, said to be crucial for the therapeutic relationship. For example, Dima and Bucuta (2012, p. 676) in their study, found that therapeutic group factors contributed to a more 'authentic and stronger self'. The group experiences were found to offer different perspectives on the human experience and offered preparation and ability to be empathic towards others.

In the words of Hazel Johns (2009, p. 118):

'Development' implies learning and potential change and reminds us that trainees on a course are engaged essentially in a learning process, while 'personal' reiterates that the self of the counsellor and the personal relationship implemented by that self are crucial to the effectiveness of any counselling exchange.

Every one of your experiences will offer you learning about yourself and others, so be open to this in each moment and reflect on it within the context of your previous personal and professional history. All of it will add to your self-awareness and will be valuable when working with clients, as they will also bring their life experiences as a holistic entity; the two together will create a whole.

References

Bloch, S., Reibstein, J., Crouch, E., Holroyd, P. and Themen, J. (1979) A method for the study of therapeutic factors in group psychotherapy. *British Journal of Psychiatry*, 134, pp. 257–263.

British Psychological Society (BPS) (2007) *Criteria for Postgraduate Courses in Clinical Psychology*. Leicester: British Psychological Society.

Cooper, M. (2005) Therapists' experiences of relational depth: A qualitative interview study. *Counselling and Psychotherapy Research*, 5, pp. 87–95.

Dima, G. and Bucuta, M.D. (2012) The experience of therapeutic change for psychologists preparing to become psychotherapists. *Procedia: Social and Behavioral Sciences*, 33, pp. 672–676.

Fauth, J., Gates, S., Vinca, M.A., Bowles, S. and Hayes, J.A. (2007) Big ideas for psychotherapy training. *Psychotherapy: Theory, Research, Practice, Training*, 44(4), pp. 384–391.

Hughes, J. and Youngson, S. (2009) *Personal Development and Clinical Psychology*. Chichester: Blackwell Publishers.

Irving, J.A. and Williams, D.I. (1999) Personal growth and personal development: concepts clarified. *British Journal of Guidance & Counselling*, 27(4), pp. 517–526.

Johns, H. (2009) *Personal Development in Counsellor Training*. London: Sage.

Knox, R. (2008) Clients' experiences of relational depth in Person-Centred counselling. *Counselling and Psychotherapy Research*, 8, pp. 182–188.

Lennie, C. (2007) The role of personal development groups in counsellor training: understanding factors contributing to self-awareness in the personal development group. *British Journal of Guidance & Counselling*, 35(1), pp. 115–129.

Luft, J. and Ingham, H. (1955) *The Johari Window: A Graphic Model of Interpersonal Awareness* Los Angeles: University of California.

Mahrer, A.R. and Nadler, W.P. (1986) Good moments in psychotherapy: A preliminary review, a list, and some promising research avenues. *Journal of Consulting and Clinical Psychology*, 54, pp. 10–15.

McLeod, J. and McLeod, J. (2014) *Personal and Professional Development for Counsellors, Psychotherapists and Mental Health Practitioners*. London: Open University Press.

Mearns, D. and Thorne, B. (1997) *Person-Centred Counselling Training*. London: Sage.

Robson, M. and Robson, J. (2008) Explorations of participants' experiences of a personal development group held as part of a counselling psychology training group: Is it safe in here? *Counselling Psychology Quarterly*, 21(4), pp. 371–382.

Rose, C. (2012) *Self-Awareness and Personal Development*. London: Sage.

Smith, S.A., Thomas, S.A. and Jackson, A.C. (2010) An exploration of the therapeutic relationship and counselling outcomes in a problem gambling counselling service. *Journal of Social Work Practice: Psychotherapeutic Approaches in Health, Welfare and the Community*, 18(1), pp. 99–112.

Yalom, I.D. and Leszcz, M. (2005) *The Theory and Practice of Group Psychotherapy*. New York: Basic Books.

Chapter 2

A historical overview of personal development groups

Carole Smith

Introduction

Personal development (PD) groups have an interesting history and have survived as a method of increasing self-awareness in counselling training for a long time, particularly in the light of their lack of evidence-based research. Related to the history of the PD group is the encounter group defined by Colman (2015) as a form of experiential therapy or group therapy with an aim to increase self-awareness and encourage greater understanding of others through expression of feelings and verbal confrontation and contact. The 'T group' also shares this history, classified as a group who meet to investigate patterns of communication among themselves, as a technique of group therapy as well as training. These were developed in the 1940s by the German-American psychologist Kurt Lewin (1890–1947). They were also called *human relations groups* or *sensitivity training groups* (Colman, 2015).

In this chapter, I will:

- briefly define the concept of a group;
- introduce the need for self-awareness in counselling training;
- outline the history of encounter groups and T groups in the 1900s;
- summarise the development of PD groups in counselling training;
- explore some of the early works on group dynamics.

What is a group?

First, it is important to define the nature of a group as they are a norm of society; without groups, we would be unable to learn diversity, alternative perspectives or use combined strengths and interdependence to reach achievements. The ways we define a group are diverse and debatable, but generally a group is a number of people who come together with a working aim.

However, a PD group does not fit with this description as the working aim for each individual will not be the same and this is clouded even more by the concept of 'being in the moment' within each group interaction. This here-and-now model makes it essential that discovery about the self or self-awareness needs to be in relation to others.

It could be argued that without the learning from others, as well as the learning about dependence and independence, in groups, it would be impossible to work empathically and with acceptance of others. Using collaborative groups in education has long been debated with varying results. Johnson et al. (1989) asserted that they resulted in improved student relationships and better retention of material; Launer (2015) discusses collaborative learning in groups in relation to case study examination for doctors and asserts that communication skills, group dynamics and parallel process (in conjunction with client work) can benefit clinical work. He refers to the concept of Balint groups, which are small experiential-type groups used to explore clinical cases and highlight interaction between medic and patient. Presenters often chose to present patients who have elicited strong emotional responses in them. Any exploration is designed to raise self-awareness, introspection and for the group to develop skills including empathy (O'Neill et al., 2016). This emphasises the educational value of '*in the moment*' encounters between group participants.

What kinds of groups are you involved in in your life and what are the purposes of them?

Why do we need to develop self-awareness?

Cozolino (2016, p. 103) said 'safety is at the heart of positive change' and in order for clients to have a safe relationship with their counsellor, it is necessary for the counsellor to bracket their own needs, motives and personal difficulties in the therapeutic moment. To do this, a great degree of self-awareness is inevitably needed to prevent the unexpected arising in the counselling session, and so hindering a full and relational contact. Rose (2012) similarly suggests that the counsellor has a responsibility to understand her/his part in the therapeutic relationship, which in effect is an ongoing process with each contributing to the change mechanism.

Pieterse et al. (2013, p. 191) define self-awareness as 'an understanding of one's values system and relationship process', which suggests that learning takes place through relationships with others, feedback and differentiated experiences. They also document an awareness of personal reactions (to others), which can be transferred into relationships with our clients. The 'psychological openness' they refer to coincides with Rogers' (1969) work at the time. The encounter groups initiated by Carl Rogers in the 1950s were designed to facilitate personal growth through interpersonal relationships; the facilitator of the group aimed to communicate qualities to the group without being prescriptive (Rogers, 1970).

In his book *Freedom to Learn* (1969) Rogers documents a set of interesting vignettes from his first encounter groups, in which he demonstrates how freedom of expression can be meaningful and life-changing for some. In fact, he identifies the goal of education as the facilitation of change and learning. The set of principles that Rogers (1969) laid out as being essential for learning probably still holds firm today and can be applied to your PD group experiences; these included:

- Significant learning takes place when the subject matter is perceived by the student as relevant for his own purpose.
- Learning that involves a change in self-organisation – in the perception of oneself – is threatening and tends to be resisted.

- Those learnings that are threatening to the self are more easily perceived and assimilated when external threats are at a minimum.
- When threat to the self is low, experience can be perceived and learning can proceed.
- Much significant learning is acquired through doing.
- Learning is facilitated when the student participates responsibly in the learning process.
- Self-initiated learning that involves the whole person of the learner including feelings as well as intellect – is the most lasting and pervasive.
- Independence, creativity and self-reliance are all facilitated when self-criticism and self-evaluation are basic and evaluation by others is of secondary importance.
- The most socially useful learning in the modern world is the learning of the process of learning, a continuing openness to experience and incorporation into oneself of the process of change.

Activity

Reflect on your own group experiences and if possible, discuss with others:

- whether you agree with these statements
- whether these conditions are present in your learning

History of PD groups

Carl Rogers wrote about the group movement:

> It would, in fact, be surprising – and perhaps worse – if we were all that sure all this soon about what they are, because the group experience is so new. It is a potent new cultural development, an exciting social invention, a truly grassroots movement that has grown out of personal, organizational and social needs.
>
> (1969, p. 27)

This was an interesting comment in view of the fact that Moreno began the encounter group movement, generating the term 'encounter' as far back as 1914 (Treadwell, 2014). Moreno's first published journal, *Sociometry*, was published in 1937 and in 1942, the Institute of Sociometry was established, which still operates under the name of International Network for Social Network Analysis.

The word 'encounter' can be translated as a meeting with some relational depth, as described by Buber (1958) as an 'I-Thou' experience. Sociometry was a concept focusing on interpersonal relationships in groups (Treadwell, 2014), examining their varying forces and led to the first reported group psychotherapy. So, it appears that there are some conflicting reports of the chronology and history of the PD group, even though the principles of group discussion and dialogue are as old as time.

Moreno and Fox (1987), writing about Moreno's work, highlighted both the belief in the nature of groups having an internal life of their own and the conviction of the intensity of learning through engagement in the moment with another. Nonetheless, and certainly in the initial stages of training, plenty of support, encouragement, empathy and clearer aims are needed to survive and learn from the PD group.

Treadwell (2014) illustrates the rise of Kurt Lewin (1890–1947), a trainee of Moreno who developed Sociometry further. Lewin studied group dynamics, including conflict, scapegoating and group authority and is thought to have been responsible for the first 'T groups' (training groups). Lewin's field theory emphasised the importance of context asserting that a group or individual studied in isolation loses its holistic meaning; that everything is interdependent, which parallels the gestalt philosophy that no individual functions in isolation (Connors and Caple, 2005). The 1960s and 1970s saw a rapid growth of the group movement in North America, which was a new conception following the previous psychotherapy and psychology practice of one-to-one.

The PD group as we know it today evolved from encounter groups, and was developed by Carl Rogers (1970), among others, at the University of Chicago in order to train counsellors to help veterans of war reintegrate into society in the post-war era of 1946. Trainees met daily in intensive experiential groups (Brison et al., 2015) with the aim of increasing their self-awareness. There is little doubt that these groups were successful and as Rogers (1970) ascertained, they enabled group participants to explore themselves through intra- and interpersonal interaction. From their early beginnings, these groups increased in popularity and began to be used all over the world. Within a Person-Centred modality, the group aims are to foster a live experience of the core conditions of empathy, unconditional positive regard and congruence (Brison et al., 2015). More recently, studies have clearly demonstrated that a group process can increase self-awareness and self-acceptance (Jorgensen, 2016). This echoes the work done by Yalom (1980), Yalom and Leszcz (2005), Mearns and Cooper (2005) and Cooper et al. (2013).

Encounter groups, which consisted of clients in therapy, were thought by Rogers to foster awareness by enabling participants to explore themselves and others. Treadwell (2014, p. 98) discusses the notion of an encounter as 'a meeting of two with the opportunity to reverse roles' as long as the relationship is equal and both have equal amounts of spontaneity – the 'here and now' concept.

My own experience of 'the encounter' as a trainee was of fairly direct 'here and now' confrontations that sometimes resulted in tears and emotional disturbance as well as some laughter and learning. The confrontation style was designed to help the person develop self-learning but often left individuals in the group shamed and distressed because, of course, human nature being what it is, a perceived 'attack' can cause our normal defence systems to crumble. Group dynamics can also create power struggles and projections that can be less than helpful and can lead to individuals leaving training if not enough support is given to the process. However, over the years the PD group has probably evolved into a less intense, more supportive structure, although the original principles of the encounter are still there.

Wilfred Bion (1897–1979) now needs to be introduced in history at this point as he was a key figure in the history of groups, group theory and group culture. Bion was a medical doctor who became interested in psychoanalysis and trained at the Tavistock Institute, working with Melanie Klein from 1946, before going on to work with traumatised soldiers in the Second World War. His thoughts on groups are outlined in his *Experiences in Groups* (1961), which contributed to academic research, executive coaching, group work and management leadership development and group relations (French and Simpson, 2010).

Bion's three basic assumptions of groups were:

- Dependency when the group looks to the leader to lead and do the work for them.
- Fight/flight – when the group resists any attempt on the part of the leader or group members to structure the group by rebelling against them (fight) or ignoring them (flight).
- Pairing – 'when members pair off psychologically, hoping that the pairs will provide the structure they need to do the work and produce a solution to the work task' (Tudor, 1999, p. 19).

Activity

Write a few paragraphs about your own experiences in your PD group (if you have begun) or counselling course groups where any of these three things have happened.
  How was it resolved by:

  group members?
  tutor/ facilitator?

You could make a note of this in your learning journal.

Bion particularly documented dynamic forces in groups, noticing that interactions between group members can be heavily infused with emotion and imbued with collusion, but he also recognised that a group mentality can create a powerful working environment. His specific ideas related to group mentality and group culture and he built on Klein's ideas about projective identification, writing about the notion of countertransference. He also developed the radical (at the time) idea of the 'leaderless' group, which is used today in the PD setting – groups are 'facilitated' rather than led. This idea was aimed at exploring a person's ability to maintain relationships in a group setting without this being managed.

Both Yalom (2002) and Berne (1963) played parts in the history and dynamics of group functioning (see Tudor, 1999 for a comprehensive view of the history of group psychotherapy, factors necessary in groups and the functioning and stages of group development).

Much of the existing literature on PD groups identifies them as ambiguous, indefinable and having elusive outcomes (Irving and Williams, 1999; Payne, 2010; Donati and Watts, 2005; Moller and Rance, 2013). Acampora and Stern, (1994, in Broekaert et al., 2004, p. 232) described the process as (initially):

> a brief silence, a scanning appraisal as to that is present, and a kind of sizing one another up. Then, the group launches into an intense emotional exchange of personal and collective problems. A key point of the sessions is the emphasis laid on extreme uncompromising candor about one another.

Broekaert et al.'s (2004) study of encounter groups in addiction work aimed to high-light differences between 'old' and 'new' styles of groups and their findings indicate that more contemporary groups are more supportive, but interestingly, expressed emotions are more negative. They also noticed that supportive behaviour is associated with confrontation, suggesting that confrontation need not be destructive and essentially support should be in place when it is used. They recommended that the 'prominent tool' in the encounter group should remain that of confrontation and that 'negative feelings should not be pushed away but lived through' (Broekaert et al., 2004, p. 241).

Current PD groups

The PD group, sometimes called a self-awareness or process group, is a training method designed to increase self-awareness and self-acceptance (Jorgensen, 2016). Groups typically consist of 10–12 participants and are unstructured. Other than through facilitator interventions around group members' responses, Rogers himself would describe his interventions as directive, only in that his listening was focused and subjective, although avoidant of interpretation. It is undoubtedly a concept different to any other group activity and is a feature of many counselling and psychotherapy training courses, there is no set agenda, other than to enable personal development through individual autonomy and a mirroring of the intensity of the client/therapist relationship. The PD group is not usually assessed but participants are encouraged to reflect on the group and their individual process and development, which may have assessment connected to it.

Traditionally, PD groups emphasised self-direction and learning from experience, although today one might see a little more facilitator direction than of old. This is prob-ably due to the urge and necessity of shorter counsellor training and the assessment factors associated with this. There is still no evidence base to support the use of PD groups today or any confirmation of a link between personal development groups and client outcomes; although it does seem clear that the quality of the client/counsellor relationship can positively bring about therapeutic change (Rogers, 1970; Mearns and Cooper, 2005). Moreover, it is generally accepted that a counsellor/therapist who has explored aspects of her/himself in some depth will be better able to deal with any emo-tional triggers in working with clients, although, of course, it is a leap of faith to assume that a 'thoroughly' developed counsellor will have better therapeutic relationships with clients.

There is little doubt that the early encounter groups, which consisted of clients in therapy, fostered awareness and, as Rogers (1970) ascertained, they enabled group participants to explore themselves through intra- and interpersonal interaction. More recently, however, conceptual literature has demonstrated that a group process can increase self-awareness and self-acceptance (Jorgensen, 2016). This echoes the work done by Yalom (1980), Yalom and Leszcz (2005), Mearns and Cooper (2005) and Cooper et al. (2013). An earlier review by Smith (1975) found that participants of PD groups experienced long term benefits, but Hartman's (1979, p. 464) review discussed 'significant psychological injury', although admittedly there were limitations to the study. In the light of this, Broekaert et al.'s (2004) study points us in in the right direc-tion for current and future developments.

So, what has emerged from this history? Brison et al. (2015) document their thoughts on the lack of training methods in university training programmes that help students to develop their self-awareness and interaction skills. Hence their study on the use of Rogerian encounter groups, which confirmed their usefulness in the context of the development of emotional intelligence, personal growth, emotion perception and adaptability in their research participants. Self-development alongside specific helping skills such as advanced listening were also seen to be acquired.

Payne's (2010) study of PD groups in the Arts found a wide variety of powerful dynamics, such as rivalry and jealousy within the group, finding a stronger sense of self and projections of anger. The negative effects of Personal Development groups are well documented but, in Payne's words, 'The PD group remains a mystery, unquantifiable in aim and outcome but with hugely potent effects which surely need to be harnessed and harvested for the benefit of the trainee and their future clinical practice' (Payne, 2010, p. 209). These are compelling words highlighting the intensity and power of the PD group, an entity that has changed little in nature since those early years of encounter and which still as yet is relatively unresearched.

Conclusion

It can be seen in this chapter that the PD group has evolved from encounter and T groups, which were originally designed as therapeutic groups to enhance self-awareness through offering confrontation and feedback. Enhanced and heightened emotion was the norm in the hope that the interpersonal learning would contribute to change. The term 'sensitivity training' gave some clue as to the nature of this experiential and emotional learning. However, there is little evidence base for the use of them and whether there is any alternative to learning about ourselves through the interaction with others in preparation for client work. Chapter 6 outlines my research on this subject and attempts to redress this imbalance. The following chapter is a personal account of an individual's historical experience in PD type groups.

References

Berne, E. (1963) *The Structure and Dynamics of Organizations and Groups*. Oxford: Oxford University Press.
Bion, W.R. (1961) *Experiences in Groups and Other Papers*. London: Tavistock.
Brison, C., Zech, E., Jaeken, M., Priels, J.M., Verhofstadt, L., van Broeck and Mikolajczak, M. (2015) Encounter groups: Do they foster psychology students' psychological development and therapeutic attitudes? *Person-Centered & Experiential Psychotherapies*, 14(1), pp. 83–99.
Broekaert, E., Vandevelde, S., Schuyten, G., Erauw, K. and Bracke, R. (2004) Evolution of encounter group methods in therapeutic communities for substance abusers. *Addictive Behaviours*, 29(2), pp. 231–244.
Buber, M. (1958) *I-and-Thou*. Abingdon: Routledge.
Colman, A.M. (2015) *A Dictionary of Psychology* (4th edn). Oxford: Oxford University Press.
Connors, J.V. and Caple, R.B. (2005) A review of group systems theory. *The Journal for Specialists in Group Work*, 30(2), pp. 93–110.
Cooper, M., O'Hara, M., Schmid, P.F. and Bohart, A.C. (2013) *The Handbook of Person-Centred Psychotherapy and counselling*. London: Palgrave Macmillan.
Cozolino, L. (2016) *The Neuroscience of Psychotherapy: Healing the Social Brain* (2nd edn). New York: W.W. Norton & Co.

Donati, M., and Watts, M. (2005) Personal development in counsellor training: Towards a clarification of inter-related concepts. *British Journal of Guidance & Counselling*, 33(4), pp. 475–484.

French, R.B. and Simpson, P. (2010) The 'work group': Redressing the balance in Bion's *Experiences in Groups*. *Human Relations*, 63(12), pp. 1859–1878.

Hartman, J.J. (1979) Small group methods of personal change. *Annual review of Psychology*, 30(1), pp. 453–476.

Irving, J.A. and Williams, D.I. (1999) Personal growth and personal development: Concepts clarified. *British Journal of Guidance & Counselling*, 27(4), pp. 517–526.

Johnson, D.W., Stanne, M.B. and Garibaldi, A. (1989) Impact of group processing on achievement in cooperative groups. *The Journal of Social Psychology*, 130(4), pp. 507–516.

Jorgensen, L.I. (2016) Encounter group counsellor training with pre-service industrial psychologists: A pilot study. *Journal of Psychology in Africa*, 26(3), pp. 300–303.

Launer, J. (2015) Collaborative learning groups. *Postgraduate Medical Journal*, 91, p. 1078.

Mearns, D. and Cooper, M. (2005) *Working at Relational Depth in Counselling and Psychotherapy*. London: Sage.

Moller, N.P. and Rance, N. (2013) The good, the bad and the uncertainty: Trainees' perceptions of the personal development group. *Counselling and Psychotherapy Research*, 13(4), pp. 282–289.

Moreno, J.L. and Fox, J. (1987) *Essential Moreno: Writings on Psychodrama, Group Method and Spontaneity*. New York: Springer Publishing.

O'Neill, S., Foster, K. and Gilbert-Obrart, A. (2016) The Balint group experience for medical students: A pilot project. *Psychoanalytic Psychotherapy*, 30(1), pp. 96–108.

Payne, H. (2010) Personal development groups in post graduate dance movement psychotherapy. *The Arts in Psychotherapy*, 37(3), pp. 202–210.

Pieterse, A.L., Lee, M., Ritmeester, A., Noah M. and Collins, N.M (2013) Towards a model of self-awareness development for counselling and psychotherapy training. *Counselling Psychology Quarterly*, 26, pp. 190–207.

Rogers, C.R. (1969) *Freedom to Learn*. Ohio: Merrill Publishing.

Rogers, C.R. (1970) *Carl Rogers on Encounter Groups*. Boston: Harper and Row.

Rose, C. (2012) *Self-Awareness and Personal Development*. London: Palgrave Macmillan.

Smith, P.B. (1975) Are there adverse effects of sensitivity training? *Journal of Humanistic Psychology*, 15, pp. 29–47.

Treadwell, T. (2014) J.L. Moreno: the pioneer of the group encounter movement: the forerunner of web-based social media revolution. *Zeitschrift für Psychodrama und Soziometrie*, 13(S1), pp. 95–105.

Tudor, K. (1999) *Group Counselling*. London: Sage.

Yalom, I.D. (1980) *Existential Psychotherapy*. New York: Basic Books.

Yalom, I.D. (2002) *The Gift of Therapy*. London: Piatkus Books.

Yalom, I.D. and Leszcz, M. (2005) *The Theory and Practice of Group Psychotherapy*. New York: Basic Books.

Chapter 3

A historical and personal view of PD groups

Tracy Hitchcock

Introduction

The purpose of this chapter is for me to share my experience of groups during my psychotherapy training and to outline their importance for me. The groups I engaged in during my training in the 1990s were called experiential groups, where the focus was on therapeutic experience and encounter. Some groups would be led by a facilitator and other groups were more student-centred. In addition to the experiential groups I participated in as part of my training, I also embarked on other groups for my own personal development because the interest in personal learning and development had gripped me.

I should explain that most of these experiences were part of an intensive psychotherapy training supported by regular twice-weekly therapy and were not stand-alone groups available to any student or members of the public. I also need to stress that at the time these activities were conducted ethically by the trainers. I realise that in today's climate they may be seen quite differently.

In this chapter I will be looking at:

- my experience of engaging in psychodrama, encounter and rebirthing groups;
- my learning and self-awareness gained from taking part in groups;
- the usefulness of groups for personal development and increased self-awareness.

A word of caution

Therapies like psychodrama, encounter groups and rebirthing are usually experienced by people who have been or who are in extensive training accompanied by personal therapy. The group facilitators should be trained and experienced practitioners. Most reputable practitioners these days would undertake an initial assessment where it would be made clear to the individual what they would be expected to bring to the group and clearly outline expectations regarding participation in the group. Safety aspects should be emphasised so that group members can make an informed choice about their readiness and willingness for such an encounter.

My experience of therapy training

I remember when I was interviewed for my training course in London in the early 1990s. I was expected to have been in weekly therapy for two years prior to the course and then twice weekly throughout the three years of the course. My course was psychodynamic in origin, so this requirement was not totally unexpected. The question of whether personal therapy should be mandatory for trainee therapists is a question debated in Chapter 13.

My experiential groups were sometimes led by one trainer and others were co-facilitated. There was no agenda or structure, but the requirement was that we must participate and respond appropriately to each other. There was no hiding place. Both introverted, retiring types and more extroverted types were challenged and their intro-version or extroversion was exposed as a cop out or possibly a defence. The forfeit for not completely immersing oneself in the group could be repeating the year's training and hence the experiential group.

My psychodrama training day

It was a cold autumn rainy day in London in the mid-1990s and I was on my way to East London to embark on a psychodrama training day. Filled with excitement, nerves and apprehension, I entered the building where the course was held and found the therapy room. I was met with a sea of faces, about 18 people of all ages, cultures, male and female, sitting around on cushions. It was ten o'clock in the morning and when our cool, relaxed (or so he seemed to me at the time) male therapist entered the room, all eyes were on him. I wondered how we would be introduced to each other and what the ice-breaker activity might be.

While I was vaguely pondering this, the therapist suddenly shouted, 'Welcome to Battersea Dogs' Home' and threw a large pile of pink and blue rubber bones into the centre of the room. There were about 12 bones and there were 18 participants. 'You can snarl, growl, whine but no biting is allowed'. There was a long silence as we looked nervously around the group waiting for the first intrepid person to take the plunge and jump in. Within minutes we were rolling about on the floor barking, snarling, whining and snatching and grabbing bones out of each other's mouths with our teeth, spit and saliva ignored in the mayhem. After about 15 minutes of snarling, dogged encounter and subsequent exhaustion the facilitator said, 'you can stop there as you are probably a little more familiar with each other now' Then the serious work began.

This was an encounter certainly not for the faint-hearted or uninitiated into group work, which is why I stress the need for advance information. I was in my mid-thirties, in psychotherapy training and open to all types of therapeutic encounter. In fact, on a wave of enthusiasm I wanted to experience as many different types of therapy group that I possibly could.

Encounter groups

It was not long after the above workshop that I decided to enrol on two encounter group weekends in the east of England. It was intense, exposing and gruelling. On both occasions I spent 36 hours in a large room with 17 other participants, all sprawled out on cushions. In this environment the sessions were facilitated by a husband and wife team. It was very much a scenario reminiscent of 1960s Esalen in California. Esalen is a retreat centre in Big Sur, California that focuses on humanistic therapy and education. It was very popular in the 1960s when therapists such as Carl Rogers (Person-Centred therapy) and Fritz Perls (Gestalt therapy) would experiment with a wide range of humanistic and alternative therapies intended to free the individual from the shackles of their past.

The idea of the encounter group I attended was to bare your soul. Little sleep was had in this setting with 'work' continuing all night and into the early hours of the morning. There were breaks for meals and drinks but as I have said, little sleep was had. This was deliberate, the thinking being that when there is strain and mental exhaustion, defences are down and the person has less resistance and is therefore more open to change. It was certainly full on. At certain moments people would doze, only to be awakened from their slumber by cries of, 'I want to do some work. You over there, you remind me of my mother, father, partner, etc.... Enact the drama with me.'

Of course, the majority of us obliged and the screaming, shouting and periodic throwing up in sick buckets continued throughout the night and into the early hours of the morning. The exhaustion came to an end mid-morning on Sunday where we all moved and gyrated in a somnambulant state to Gabrielle Roth's trance dance music.

Why did I put myself through all this? In the name of what? Self-development, personal awareness, self-profligacy, masochism? No, it was because I hated being exposed and I hated being in groups. My first therapist said to me, 'You can only take your clients as far as you have come yourself'. I believed her and those words have resonated down the years.

For me, personal therapy and experiential groups were essential for my therapeutic training. The groups I attended asked me to challenge my assumptions and beliefs, which I found character-building and which strengthened my resilience and self-understanding. I would say that I am a better therapist as a result. However, please note, I was not just beginning my therapy training and had been in therapy for many years and had support networks to ensure this was a safe enough process for me.

Personal development groups

Through personally engaging in PD groups and experiential groups, I experienced deep therapeutic change and I felt equipped to work with clients at many levels. I fully trusted my group facilitators and I was aware that any issues that were raised by the group process could be thoroughly explored in my personal therapy. I remember that I used to feel very exposed in groups and would be quiet sometimes and at other times not participate. This would not go unnoticed and I would be regularly dragged back into the fold and be expected to say what was going on for me. Resistance was futile.

Experience of a rebirthing workshop

During my third year of psychodynamic training, I engaged in a weekend workshop as part of my course that held particular significance for me. This was the one on rebirthing. I was not looking forward to this workshop. I had heard from other students on my course that this could be quite traumatic. However, I knew that I needed to experience this to work through some personal issues in therapy relating to my birth. This had quite often been the theme during my eight years of personal therapy. I was the youngest of five children and my mother had me late in life at the age of 42. I know that she was seriously ill throughout her pregnancy and that she nearly died giving birth to me.

At various stages throughout my therapy, my therapist would often challenge my tendency to give up on myself and various projects that I had undertaken. I would present as not caring and say that I couldn't be bothered. I remember my therapist challenging me quite forcibly on more than one occasion by saying, 'What is your will?' She was challenging this conditioned response to give up on myself but the question confused and bothered me. It was as if I had no personal identity or and as I plunged further into my confusion, no separate identity from that of my mother.

I realised that at the time of my birth I was being plummeted into a state of non-existence with her. While therapy kept me in the shadowlands pondering on my dilemma, it was the rebirthing workshop that brought this to my full realisation. The activities in the workshop seemed quite straightforward. In turns we would lie on the floor and be asked to go into whatever position we wished. When we were comfortable students would pile cushions around us and on us, ensuring that there was some air ventilation.

When it was my turn, two students sat close by and transcribed everything I said and every movement I made. The other students sat on top of the cushions that were on top of me. The task was to try to wriggle my way from under the cushions into daylight. The 'activity' lasted over an hour. I was simply asked to be born. I remember pushing against the cushions with the students pressing on them. A voice asked me what was going on. I responded, 'I'm tired, so tired', and then would spend about ten minutes motionless. I felt like giving up. I realised that I did not want to come out of the womb.

Although I was in a state of deep regression, the adult part of me took over and after struggling for an hour I realised that I did in fact want to be born and eventually I came out, depleted in a state of exhaustion. All the work I had been doing in my personal therapy suddenly became crystal clear. I realised that I did have agency and identity apart from my mother. It made sense of the struggle I had endured throughout my life trying to separate from her psychologically, during her lifetime and after her death. I now knew when I was becoming merged with my mother and I had the awareness and ability to separate out and differentiate psychologically. I can therefore identify my attachment style as ambivalent and I can recognise my relational patterns (see Chapter 11 for an explanation of this). After my mother's death I was able to talk about my trauma without being diminished by her death. I learnt to become resilient and open to others' suffering without it clouding my own.

This was a very powerful experience for me but I recognise that there have been cases where participants have found rebirthing workshops harmful and dangerous. This workshop was facilitated by experienced therapists/facilitators and we were third-year psychotherapy students with a certain amount of resilience and personal therapy. We were carefully briefed on how to conduct the rebirthing experience and at any point could say 'stop' or opt out.

Eastern philosophies

The module I studied on Eastern philosophies also enthused me with the need to explore religious practices. I therefore studied various schools of Buddhism and Sufism. For me, there is nothing like a silent retreat to still the mind and I have been on three of these, two Buddhist and one Sufi. In the Western world we tend to believe that the greatest communication is through speech but for me, there is no greater communication than that experienced in silence. To move away from the general chatter that needlessly fills the space and just be with others in silence and communion is the most beautiful experience in my opinion. Some people are afraid of being in silence and will do everything to fill up the void. Rather than being avoided, it is something to be celebrated.

Mindfulness meditation has suddenly become very popular, even though people have been doing it for thousands of years in many different religious traditions. Meditation and practising being in silence can lead to greater attunement with self and others and it can also deepen greater empathy, along with a deeper sense of self and others.

Conclusion

This chapter has focused on my experience of different types of personal development groups during my training in the 1990s and what I gained from engaging in them. I have given some examples of my own personal journey and I have expressed the discomfort I felt from participating in them, but also the benefits of increased personal awareness.

Although personal development can be an uncomfortable process, it can also be significantly life-changing if facilitated and supported well.

As you can see I am an advocate of personal therapy and personal development groups. I concur with my therapist's statement that 'you can only bring your client as far as you have come yourself'. I have outlined my personal experiences of experiential groups and training weekends. I hope my personal journey will provide food for thought and personal reflection on the importance and significance of personal development and training groups.

Chapter 4

Personal development journeys
Student experiences

Edited by Jayne Godward

Introduction

In this chapter, five students who have completed counsellor training share their experiences of personal development and change, while undertaking their courses. Here they record their progress and describe the processes they went through and the effects personal development groups and personal therapy had on them. All the students have qualified within the last few years and are all women. The students come from a range of backgrounds including age, culture, class and ethnicity. They were all from different occupational backgrounds.

Contributors have used pseudonyms and accounts have been shortened, although still using the contributor's words. The first paragraph of each account, in italics, gives a potted biography of the contributor.

The aspects covered by the writers varies, but include:

- the value of personal therapy and the importance of the therapeutic relationship with their counsellors;
- personal development group experiences and the value of these;
- learning about themselves through the PD group;
- the link between personal therapy and the PD group in self-development work;
- the similarities between how personal development occurs in PD groups and this process in personal therapy;
- how personal therapy was used to work through past experiences and relationship issues;
- the power of personal therapy;
- the value of hearing different experiences and worldviews within the PD group;
- the value of working through relational issues within the PD group.

Experience 1: Zaara

I'm 32 years old and I'm female. I'm Middle Eastern by birth, but still carry on my Indian ethnicity and have settled in England. I come from a middle-class family, both my parents are of Indian origin but are British citizens now and so are my siblings. I completed my schooling in Kuwait and moved to England to study accounting at university. I gained employment by doing voluntary work as I didn't have any prior experience. My first paid job was in retail and I still work for the company up to this day.

There was quite a strong element of control in my family. Most decisions were taken by my parents and this made me very angry. I lost out on a lot because of them and tried to make up for it in the following years but by then I had become an adult but with childish habits, which wasn't received well by people around me. Because they were always making decisions, at one point in my life it was 'mommy and daddy know best, I'll listen to what they say', there was no internal locus of evaluation as a dependency had developed there. I didn't trust my inner self at all.

As I sit and reflect on that whole process of my personal development, I realise there were many factors that helped me grow and change. The most important one was going for personal therapy. I went with the mindset 'I need to change and I need help doing that'. I was very lucky to have a therapist who had many years of experience and I couldn't have asked for a better one. In our work together she was my 'cushion of support' throughout my therapeutic journey. The way we worked went on to shape how I work with my clients.

My therapist is one of those people who you can have an instant connection with, upon our initial meeting I knew she was someone I would like to work with. We had a very good therapeutic relationship built on mutual trust and respect, she was with me throughout my journey, she gave me the space and time to talk and for once in my life I felt I actually had somebody I could open up to and talk about my vulnerabilities without being judged and totally accepted for who I was. Our work together resulted in many toxic layers being peeled off just like you peel an onion and get to its core. I felt naked, but that nakedness was probably the best I ever felt, it was like starting over again on a clean slate. Bit by bit I rebuilt my life, taking on the positives and going with the flow rather than rushing into things. What also helped a lot was support from close friends and most importantly peers and tutors on the course.

The combination of the right support in a positive and nurturing environment changed my life immensely. I took back control of my life, I put myself first. I decided what I wanted not my parents. I trusted myself more than I had ever before and I didn't look for any approval from anyone.

Experience 2: Judy

I am a female born in Bradford in 1960 into a traditional working-class family, the eldest of three children. While in senior school, both family and school became a problem, and I left as soon as I could at 16 with no qualifications and, according to my deputy headmistress, no future.

Fortunately I had a Saturday job and bosses who could see my qualities, and I was offered a full-time position. I spent the next 34 years working in sales and marketing, gradually developing my skills and experience and working up the career ladder culminating in a senior management position.

Before starting my diploma training as a counsellor, in a discussion about the course one of the tutors described the personal and professional development aspect of the course as 'life-changing'. I remember thinking 'what on earth is this person talking about? A university course is not going to change my life.' I knew myself well. I had experienced the ups and downs of life and felt strong, resilient and secure in my relationships with others and felt comfortable with who I was. Or so I thought.

I never had in my life questioned who I was and more importantly why I behaved in the way I did. I just accepted that I was 'just me', no explanation required and while I recognised that the group PD sessions and personal therapy sessions were mandatory, some part of me held the belief that I knew everything there was to know about myself and couldn't really understand how the group PD sessions, in particular, could be beneficial.

How would sitting in a group consisting of 14 strangers who were a mixture of ages, gender, sexualities and cultures help me understand myself? Additionally, I questioned, as did others, the size of the group and how could we feel safe in such a large group. The question of confidentiality was another concern. We had agreed on a contract, but how did I know that these people would maintain confidentiality?

On reflection, I realise now that these were defences, ways of protecting myself from my vulnerabilities and fears of being judged as not 'good enough'. Even realising that I felt vulnerable was a new experience, as I realised quite soon that my lack of formal education was something that often left me feeling not quite 'good enough'. Yet here I was in world where the language consisted of words such as *phenomenology*, *ontological* and *epistemology*, words that were not only unknown but which left me feeling that I did not 'measure up' in a group where most of the members were postgraduates and therefore, according to my belief system, much better than I was.

The initial group sessions were, for me, a mixture of uncertainties and anxiety about not understanding the purpose of the group. I, like many, prefer to be prepared, but nothing in my past had prepared me for our group PD sessions. In the first few sessions, we often sat in uncomfortable silence, and it was a relief when someone eventually decided to speak.

Gradually, however, over the weeks, there was a shift within the group sessions. Relationships were formed, and these strangers were now my peers, and I realised that they were experiencing many of the same thoughts and feelings regarding personal development as I was. The group became more structured as the weeks progressed and I began to relax and feel safe. As a result, I became more willing to take risks and share some of my thoughts and feelings. I began to take ownership of my feelings and reflect on what I was learning academically, and I started to examine my life and question who I was and how I had become this person.

A significant turning point for me was realising that I am a 'rescuer' and 'people pleaser', and that these relational patterns had developed during childhood. I had developed a view that I was not acceptable and internalised these feeling as not been good enough, hence my need to please others so that they would like me. I had developed a 'false self', pretending and denying my true feelings as revealing these could result in rejection, which as a child had been my biggest fear. This new knowledge frightened me and was painful to accept and left me feeling angry and incredibly emotional. However, when I had shed all my tears, I realised both how my relational patterns had developed. More importantly, I recognised that I no longer needed to be tied to the constraints of keeping others happy to feel safe.

I took what I had learnt in the group sessions to personal therapy and brought back to the group what I had discovered about myself in individual therapy. The group sessions had become an integral part of my self-development. I learnt more about my relational patterns in two years than I had learnt in my entire lifetime. I discovered, from my therapist, how to listen to the messages my body was sending me and how to name the felt sensations. I know that if I feel anxious, for example, I hold my breath and clench my teeth. This self-awareness has been invaluable and enables me to have honest conversations with myself about the actual cause of my feelings and how I can deal with these feelings from an adult perspective.

The group sessions provided an opportunity to listen to the different experiences of the other group members and to understand their emotional pain without having to find a solution. I learnt how therapeutic it was to sit in silence and reflect on what I had said or what I had heard from others. Rather than fear the personal development sessions I began to look forward to them. Additionally, the group sessions provided a safe space to be able to take risks with others in the group while having the secure presence of a competent facilitator. I learnt how to give honest, constructive feedback to my peers while at the same time being aware of the damage that criticism has played in many of our lives.

My experience of personal development has been so similar to the process of counselling and the fundamental viewpoint that to understand the personality of a client it is essential to understand the development of the personality through childhood and the family environment. Having this understanding and being able to express my feelings has enabled me to acknowledge my inner child and remove the shackles of shame. Rather than spending valuable energies in the quest to have others like me, I discovered that all that was required was for me to learn that the acceptance was all about me accepting me.

My previous fears of rejection from others initially hindered my expression of feelings, but I learnt how empowering it felt to express my feelings more honestly and confidently without fear. I am aware that my relational patterns will not disappear; they are part of who I am. My need to rescue is entrenched within me, but having an awareness of this prevents me from activating this reaction and provides me with the opportunity to address my own needs before the needs of others.

The PD sessions and my continued professional and personal development have provided me with the self-awareness and courage to live life as thoroughly as I am able. For me, the experience has been invaluable and, despite my protestations at the start of the course, I support the statement of the tutor who said the experience would be life-changing.

Experience 3: Sheila

I am a mature woman and live in a seaside town with my husband and two teenage daughters, four cats and one dog. I come from a working-class background, went to university at 18 and haven't stopped studying since, with the Level 4 diploma being my most recent accomplishment at age 51. Currently I have two part-time counselling jobs.

The idea of personal development and self-analysis was not necessarily an alien concept to me at the start of the course, I believed I was at a point that I had a sufficient understanding of myself and needed little 'work' to do. How wrong I was.

In my final personal development presentation, I summed up my journey thus;

- Still dealing with losses, even though I thought I had done so much.
- Looking calm on the outside but being overwhelmed with questions on the inside.

- Beginning to understand that I was laden down with particular stuff.
- Then working through a mix of emotions by getting a helping hand and using a trusting gestalt therapeutic relationship to 'go in deep'.
- Re-evaluating teasing out and looking at things differently.
- Changing in essence a huge pile of muck into a much smaller one.

I now see that my understanding of my own 'self' has evolved and changed through group process and personal counselling. My own experience of counselling enabled me to explore the patterns of negativity I had internalised, much of this coming from a negative and destructive relationship with my dad.

It felt as though I had managed to work through aspects of my grief for my partner and my mum, and even be OK about coming through my cancer. The biggest driver that affected my patterns of relating and that hung over me like a cloud weighing heavy on my shoulders was the stuff tied up with my dad.

During an exercise in personal development work in the early days of the course I was able to explore my own conditions of worth. By sharing those conditions of worth with the group – although I was aware of them on one level, to see them written down and stand back gave more clarity – it was quite shocking. I knew that most of my conditions of worth that inhibited my self-development of real self came from my dad. What I hadn't realised was that they were all about money and ambition, values he held high to the detriment of a quality family life. Looking at these conditions of worth – 'I should be financially independent', 'I should be ambitious', 'I should be careful with money' – were all clearly imposed upon me by my dad, to whom 'money was king'. It was actually quite a liberating exercise where I could see how my dad had 'missed the point' of life and that I really didn't want to; I wanted to enjoy my family without work and money interfering at that level.

My own therapy seemed to be quite difficult and slow in the first ten sessions, but after that it felt as though I was getting somewhere and I was able to be more honest. A turning point may have been the 'empty chair' work I did about my dad. It enabled me to tell him how I felt and see him differently – having less impact on me.

But then after 20 sessions I took a short break from counselling and in some ways I missed the opportunity to keep the momentum of exploring my own issues; in essence I was hiding, there was still some fear attached to what might emerge. So I went back for two more sessions to confront my ongoing issue with my dad. These two sessions were highly powerful and gave me a strategy to move forward.

Although I had worked through much of this, the relationship I had with him, was still affecting me and I wanted to stop it impacting on my life. With my therapist we explored what might be achievable, looking at making this part of me smaller and more manageable. He suggested that it was about dismantling parts of a machine that were no longer required. But that did not resonate with me; however, it enabled me to visualise my own metaphor. I suggested that it was a big pile of muck that I was slowly but surely clearing away, and it was becoming smaller. The whole session worked around how I felt about my dad and if I loved him and what that actually meant. There was a realisation that there had been some love for him at a very low level and because it was not nurtured by him it didn't grow, but I grew bigger alongside that, in spite of him, with love from and for other people. In a sense, one of my conditions of worth was to love my dad, and to be loved I needed to love him, yet what has become apparent to me is that I don't need his love or to love him to be valued and I can trust my own internal locus of evaluation.

In some ways the journey has been tough then at other junctions a breeze, but never a straight path. Personal therapy for me was essential and now on reflection I can see how at various points I believed I was 'done', but in reality it took 22 sessions to feel a sense of ease and self-acceptance that I do today.

I am grateful to myself that I decided to do the course in some ways knowing that it would be somewhat exhausting and time-consuming but not quite realising to what extent. So thank you me!

Experience 4: Liz

At the time of taking my Level 4 course I was a 45-year-old woman working in an administrative role in and occupational health unit. I had worked there for 15 years. I was raised by a mum who was a school teacher and a dad who was a book keeper. I have a brother. I was adopted. My husband is a police officer. I have two children of my own and two step-children who are all adults. I also have a little Labrador dog who keeps me fit and active.

Part of the course is an obligation to attend 20 sessions of personal therapy, which I was certain would be straightforward and simple. I had been through some events in life, like everybody, but I was over them. I wondered what on earth I could possibly have to say. What a challenge personal therapy turned into. What a heart-wrenching, thought-provoking, strenuous process. One of the first lessons I learnt on my course was never to underestimate the power of therapy. I promised myself that I would never forget how it feels to sit in the client chair. I also learnt so much about myself, my boundaries, my relationships with others, how to deal with my pain from the past, how to accept that I have darkness and anger, how to be kind to myself, how to accept a compliment and believe in myself. I eventually had 26 sessions of personal therapy and hold an awareness that I would return to therapy at any time to work things through.

At the same time as the personal therapy, things began to start happening in group process too. Our studies progressed steadily and the group became close. At first I was tentative about sharing things from my life. Trust has to be earnt and knowledge is power. Why would I expose my innermost thoughts to a group of strangers? However, to be able to sit with a group of people who had been open and honest with each other and discuss my conditions of worth, my light and shade, my inner and deepest thoughts knowing that they would be held in confidence and that no judgement was being passed was an amazing experience.

Group process was a major part of the course, because even when I was struggling to believe I could do this, the others were there encouraging and supporting me. Sometimes I felt OK and I was able to support others. During these sessions we could grow and learn from each other. Everybody had a chance to speak, to be encouraged and to encourage others. I was never left feeling silly about some of the things I said, more often it was explored. On one occasion we looked at what we were afraid of about ourselves and I said I was afraid of being strict. This simple statement led to so much personal growth. I had never faced this part of myself before and yet once it was out in the open it changed me completely as a person. All my past history about being punished, all my fears around what strictness led to, the way I had never had boundaries in place because of what I feared would happen once people became angry, the harm I had done in so many aspects of my personal and family life due to being unable to be a bit firmer with others, so much growth from this one statement. Group process was dark and powerful and sad and took so much bravery but there was also laughter and joy. These were the hope-giving moments. Rays of sunshine through the clouds. Moments to treasure and another way of seeing life. Sometimes it's not all harrowing, and growth is about happiness as much as anything else.

Looking back over my personal development I can see only growth. At the start of my course, as a woman in her forties, I thought life was alright and I pretty much knew who I was and what I was doing. During the course I smashed myself into a 1,000-piece jigsaw and started rebuilding. Now I feel like there is always room to know more about myself but I feel more comfortable with myself than I have ever been. I am no longer afraid of the things that I didn't even know I needed to be afraid of. I believe in the counselling process with all my heart. I trust the process. I have never been happier that I trained to be a counsellor and understood what it means to be self-aware.

Experience 5: Shanaya

I am a woman in my early thirties, of Indian nationality and I moved to the UK a year before I started the diploma. I completed a Bachelor's and Master's in Psychology in India and underwent counselling training there. However, the style and content was very different from my training in the UK, which is what I initially found very challenging. I was practicing CBT [Cognitive Behavioural Therapy] before joining the course and Person-Centred therapy was new to me. I remember feeling overwhelmed with a totally new educational setup, group of people and accents, and I struggled with these during my diploma, as well as while counselling clients. I am hoping the short piece below will elucidate my experiences and personal growth on the course.

I initially found personal development groups quite a strange experience as not only was sharing my feelings and personal experiences unfamiliar to me, the group setting made it even more awkward and challenging. In the first few weeks, I did not feel like sharing anything at all, and instead listened to others' stories and how they expressed their feelings. I felt pressured to speak about my feelings because of the fear of not being included and desire to fit in. I also had a lot of assumptions and beliefs related to myself and the idea of sharing emotions. For example, I felt it was selfish to talk about myself and I felt extremely uncomfortable doing so. However the fact that most people in the group were speaking about themselves made it easier and more natural for me. I tried to venture outside my comfort zone no matter how difficult it was. If I had assumptions such as those I have mentioned above, I tried to express them and see what my peers thought of it. It was comforting and assuring to know that a few others had similar feelings, and I also noted that their views on sharing feelings were different from mine. It was refreshing to hear about people's varied thoughts, and I could see ways in which my early childhood experiences shaped how I viewed my current relationships. The great differences in the personalities and worldviews of each individual in the PD group gave rise to immensely rich discussions and reflections. These were very helpful in my development as a trainee counsellor.

I believe the PD group had elements of both personal therapy and supervision as we would be listened to, empathised with, as well as given suggestions or feedback related to counselling practice, if asked for. Since we were all trainees, a lot of us shared very similar experiences with respect to professional issues and growth. It also was a more natural situation and people were free to share their views. I think this is a unique aspect of PD groups and I doubt I would have experienced something like this elsewhere. I agree that a lot of sharing depends on one's perceived safety in the group. This, I believe, depends on group members and their relational patterns. To elucidate with a personal example, I recall feeling intimidated by one or two members in the group and I attempted to share this with them, which led to many useful insights about my own relational patterns as well as subconscious feelings towards my caregivers. Such exploratory discussions have had a positive impact on my confidence and self-esteem.

As I was undergoing rapid changes internally, it was useful to test out my predictions in the PD group. For example, my issues with trust and rejection came to the surface while doing the course. I attempted being vocal about this when I felt rejected by a group member as she did not maintain eye contact with me. However, it turned out that she felt anxious and therefore looked away sometimes. I realised that my conclusion was more due to my own issues and perception, and that others interpreted the group member's reduced eye contact differently, which was interesting to see. Incidents such as this have influenced my way of looking at people and the world in general. I believe I am more flexible now, and attempt to understand others' perspectives. I am more open to criticism and constructive feedback from others, and willing to look at doing things differently, whether in my personal or professional life.

> Having read these accounts, what reactions do you have?
> How does this mirror your experiences of personal development?
> If you are new to training, were there some surprises?

Conclusion

It is clear from reading these accounts that these students gained a great deal of self-awareness by engaging in the personal development aspects of their courses and as Judy clearly states, it has been life changing to undergo this process.

For Zaara and Sheila the personal therapy aspect seems to have been the biggest factor, but all writers mention the PD group as being useful in their development.

The value and power of personal therapy was highlighted in most accounts with the therapeutic relationship between student and counsellor seen as important.

Although sometimes difficult and uncomfortable, the value of the PD group for increasing self-awareness and understanding of patterns of relating is reflected upon here.

Similarities between the PD group and the counselling process were identified, particularly by Judy.

It is obvious from these accounts that students gained important insights into themselves that would aid their professional development as counsellors.

Section B

The personal development group

Chapter 5

Understanding the personal development group

Jayne Godward

Introduction

Students often struggle to understand the purpose of the personal development group – a group where you sit together each week for possibly two years without having a clear agenda. Students often ask 'what are we doing here?'

In this chapter I will look at:

- what a PD group is and its purpose;
- experiential learning in the group and what experiential learning is;
- how it is different from a therapy group;
- what the group can give you;
- what to expect when you begin the process;
- how to begin the process or participate;
- your role as a participant;
- what can hold you back;
- driver behaviours in PD groups;
- PD group skills.

What is a PD group?

A personal development group is what it says it is: a group where you can look at your personal development and explore what is happening for you as you go through your counselling training. It is a space to reflect on what you are becoming aware of in yourself and to explore what you are learning about yourself. Unlike personal therapy where you can explore issues and emotional difficulties with a trained professional, you are with peers travelling along the same road who can bear witness to your learning and development. By hearing others sharing their experiences, this can trigger a realisation in you about your experiences and in turn, by you sharing, you may encourage them to look at their personal learning. So the benefits are mutual.

I see the PD group as a special space on courses where we are encouraging students to be themselves and to explore what they are learning about themselves. The majority of students I teach lead busy lives, where they are squeezing their courses in between work and family commitments, leaving little opportunity for reflection as to what is happening to them and their development.

Also on large courses this is a chance to be with a smaller group of peers to look at themselves and share worries, fears and realisations in a confidential setting. So the PD group, hopefully, becomes a safe base and provides stability during the personal and emotional changes that occur as a result of engaging in counsellor training.

Case study: Jonathan

Jonathan had been a youth worker and was interested in working with disadvantaged young people. He was a very keen student and had flown through his certificate course in counselling studies. When he came on to the diploma level he thought it was just a case of doing another two years training to become a professional. He expected the placement to be demanding and the academic work to be a strain; however, when he started personal therapy and reading and applying theory to himself, he realised that he had real attachment issues that he had never looked at which affected his self-concept and current relationships. As a result he was bowled over and felt as if he was disintegrating inside.

By talking about this process in his PD group he was able to get the support he needed from his peers, particularly because they were also experiencing similar processes. It was not possible to get this support from his partner as she did not really understand it, and although he could examine the process in therapy, it really helped to have his group alongside him. It is possible that without his group he would have found it hard to cope and would have given up the course.

So the PD group is an important facility on a training course. It is a space where you can step back to look at what is going on for you personally with peers who understand what you are talking about. The beauty of the PD group experience is that it can help normalise feelings and processes and prevent students feeling alone while experiencing strong emotional changes or realisations. It can also be a safe space to become more aware of personal processes rather than getting into client work and having issues triggered by something a client says or does.

Another key purpose of the group is that it is a place where you can make connections between different aspects of the training. I see it as the core of the training or the hub of the training wheel (see Diagram 5.1 on p. 41). In the PD group you are able to connect your learning from different experiences and link them together.

The experiential aspect

In counsellor training we talk a lot about experiential learning, but what exactly does that mean? Experiential learning is a chance to learn from the experience you are having and it is a chance to experiment with different ways of being. It is active learning rather than passively listening to a tutor telling you about something or how to do something. Here you have to use your own knowledge and experience and reflect on what is happening to you. This values the abilities of the student and relies on their full participation (Johns, 2012). So in the PD group you are going to experience being in a group with people who are different from you and who will express thoughts and feelings in a

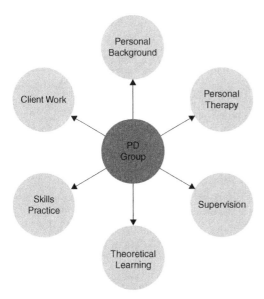

Personal
Background

Client Work

Personal
Therapy

PD
Group

Skills
Practice

Supervision

Theoretical
Learning

Diagram 5.1 The Training Wheel

real way. You will also be expected to express thoughts and feelings and will be learning from the reactions you get and the reactions you have to these. So the group gives you an increased awareness of social interactions and you may become more aware of personal and interpersonal issues you have due to the group process.

The group gives you a chance to experiment with relating to others in different ways, may highlight your strengths and protective strategies and may help you to see the ways you affect others through the feedback you receive.

The key thing here is that you must be really willing to be actively involved in the group experience. Sometimes this means being fully present listening to others or responding, while other times you will be encouraged to share in the group. It is useful to reflect on what has happened in the group and your reactions in order to learn from it. We will look more at reflecting on learning in Chapter 17.

Learning from the PD group experience: A group process example

Marie is in a PD group. She has been really quiet since it began a few weeks ago and feels uncomfortable speaking as everyone seems to have more important things to share than her. She becomes particularly uncomfortable when one member, Penny, says angrily: 'I'm fed up with this. Why should a few of us do all the work in this group? Why don't more people contribute?' Marie feels personally attacked and starts to cry. She leaves the group without saying anything but feels very uncomfortable. No one says anything about her crying and seems to be ignoring this. The facilitator is busy paying attention to Penny.

What would you do if you were in Marie's situation? What could you do to use the PD group to help your personal development?

Martin is in the same PD group. He has also been a quiet member. He feels uncomfortable as there are some very articulate people in his group and he has not felt good enough to share some of what is going on for him. He feels that Penny was rather out of order and lacked empathy. He talks to his personal therapist about the experience. He looks at his feelings of not being good enough and the difficulty he has with dominant people due to a father who constantly put him down. He makes some useful connections between then and how he feels being in the group now. At the next group session he decides to challenge Penny about her comment. Having discussed his issues and feelings with his therapist he can calmly say how he felt last week and talk about the connections he has made. He is able to give Penny the feedback that her comments felt sharp and critical to him and then she is able to realise that she was being insensitive.

So both Martin and Penny learn from the experience. As a result of Martin's challenge, Penny makes a connection between her experience in the group and that of her early childhood where she had been the one in the family who had been expected to help out in the home while her brothers and sisters didn't have to because they were younger. It had felt like 'here we go again I have to do the work for others'. She also changes her behaviour in the group as a result and stops filling the gaps left so that other people can contribute.

Marie also realises she isn't alone and that her feelings of being upset were valid and is then able to share these.

This is an example of how the group process works to help individuals learn about themselves and develop; however, if no one had been honest and had taken a risk to share, there would have been no development. If Martin had not spoken about his experiences, Marie would have probably retreated further into herself and might not have used the group at all.

This is how the PD group works with people's views and feelings bouncing off each other. In the group it is often as if there is an imaginary ball that is passed around, which is sometimes caught by group members or just bounces off on to someone else. In groups that are at an early stage or those that have become a bit stagnant, sometimes the ball just drops on the floor waiting for someone to pick it up and start the process again.

What can we talk about here?

Students bring their lives and personal experiences, placement work, personal therapy, supervision, aspects of theory, skills work and any other learning to the groups and can make sense of these in relation to themselves and their development as a counsellor. It is a place where these can all connect together.

When students ask: 'What can we talk about here?' Or say 'I don't know what to talk about here', my answer would be 'you can talk about anything so long as it relates to your personal development'. Sometimes students begin by talking about things 'out there', like a theory they are learning or another person, such as a client, supervisor, or therapist. Then my role is to help them focus on themselves and their part in this experience. In this way, while the PD group may be close to being in personal therapy, the purpose of the group is not personal therapy. This is where it can be confusing, as being in a PD group can be very therapeutic and can have similar effects to therapy, e.g., increasing self-awareness, helping you gain insight into your behaviour and patterns, being cathartic (helping you release emotions) and promoting development. Facilitator styles will vary and whereas some are active in this group process, others may take a more passive role – but whichever style is used, you can learn from both.

So how is it different from a therapy group?

For a start, PD groups are often a lot larger than therapy groups. The role of the tutor is not to give therapy (see Chapter 7) and the role of the student is not to be a client in therapy in the group. If you were to use the group for therapy, it would take up too much group time as well. However, the PD group might highlight areas that need to be looked at in personal therapy or supervision. It also gives you the chance to review how your personal therapy is going and what issues are being raised for you. The aim of the group is to give you a safe space to unpack and explore what is happening for you. The group can provide a sounding board where you can get different views, opinions and feelings on your experiences rather than being left alone with these.

Here it is presumed that you will feel safe enough in the group to share, but this may not always be the case (see Chapter 7).

What does the PD group give you?

Activity

It might be useful at this point to think about why you are on the course and what has brought you to counsellor training in terms of your personal history and background.

What are your needs?
What do you want to get out of being in the PD group, which is there to help your personal development?

What the group can give you is the opportunity to offer the core conditions (Rogers, 1957) of congruence, unconditional positive regard and empathic understanding, and also the opportunity to experience these in action in a group setting.

I put congruence first, as the more congruent and real people are in a PD group, the more an environment of honesty and sharing is created and the deeper the group can go. However, along with this there needs to be a real respect for each individual in the group and a willingness to listen to the different views expressed without judgement, so unconditional positive regard (Mearns and Thorne, 2007) is terribly important.

As soon as you feel judged in a group or in any relationship you are likely to become defensive and closed off. Third, it is important to be able to empathise with people in the group. I am cautious about this in that the group is not like counselling practice sessions where we have to put our thoughts and feelings to one side and empathise with the person speaking. We might empathise, but we are also there to share our own thoughts and feelings, which might be different.

I think you can learn a lot about yourself by being in a group and by becoming aware of your reactions to others as in the example below.

Case study: Transference

Maarya was in a PD group. She kept having strong reactions to an older woman, Sobia, a fellow Muslim in the group. Sobia appeared quite stern and to Maarya she looked disapproving whenever Maarya spoke about her difficulties of balancing the coursework with that of bringing up her young children. At one point Sobia made a comment about the mother's role and Maarya felt that she had been told off and became very angry.

At the next group session Maarya said she had been sitting on something all week and wanted to bring it in to the group. She was able to express how she had felt and was able to say that she had felt criticised and told off by Sobia.

Sobia was shocked by this and could not remember what she had said that fitted this description. The group and the facilitator were able to help Maarya unpick it. It turns out that Sobia reminded Maarya of her mother-in-law who had been very critical of her in her first few years of marriage and did not approve of her doing the course. Maarya had never felt good enough or felt that she could get it right. A simple comment had triggered lots of memories and feelings in Maarya. As she explored, she realised that Sobia was very different from her mother-in-law and that she had experienced a negative transference towards her peer.

Being able to examine her reaction in the group led Maarya to further exploration of herself and self-understanding.

If the PD group is a safe space, it will give you the opportunity to explore reactions to a range of people and for other people to respond to you. The following often occur:

- **Transference** – as in the Maarya example above, we associate a person with another person in our life and transfer feelings we had for them to that person (Short and Thomas, 2015).
- **Countertransference** – where we react to the transference from the other person as if we had become the other person. So in the example if Sobia had started acting in a critical way with Maarya she might have been having a countertransference response.

By unpicking our *transferences* (how we are associating others with people we have known and transferring the feelings we had for them to someone in the group) and *countertransference* (our reactions to the way we are being treated by the person who has a transference to us) and *projections* (our internal dialogues and feelings that we think other people are having) we have the chance to understand ourselves a lot more and this may lead to us understanding our relationships with others in our work and personal lives.

Although these terms come from psychodynamic theory, which you may not study on your course, they are useful ways of reflecting on our responses to a range of people. The theory used on your course may use alternative concepts. Also, being aware of these reactions will help us prepare for client work where we are likely to have strong responses to some of the people we are supposed to be helping. See Short and Thomas (2015, pp. 176–182) for further explanation of these theoretical concepts.

The early stages of the PD group

Being in a PD group is a very personal and individual process. No two students will experience it in the same way, just as no two groups are the same. Students enter the PD group experience in different ways. I have often compared this to a pool of water. Some students dip their toes in then quickly come out again. Others dip in and gradually get further in. While some boldly wade in and keep going, other students jump straight in with no toe-dipping. And some sit on the side for a while to emotionally prepare.

No one way is correct as each person has their own needs and has to take care of themselves. The toe-dippers may have difficulty trusting others and may be wary of opening up to relative strangers, especially if they have never shared feelings with others before or they have had previous negative experiences of groups. Those who ease themselves in may share a bit more each week and go deeper and be determined to use the group to personally develop. The plungers may be used to being open and to expressing thoughts and feelings or they may not be taking adequate care. The people who dip in and out might not feel ready to share or may have real difficulties being in the group.

Some group members may just stay on the side watching and listening but not actively participating because it is so alien to them and does not feel safe at all.

> If you think of this imaginary pool, where do you think you were when you began your group?
> Or if you are beginning where do you think you are now?

Your role as a participant

Given the experiential nature of the learning of the group, all participants have a role to play in the group process. Even if you do not speak you are having an impact on the group; but as someone who has signed up for the course and wants to develop, it is your role to try to enter the pool and participate in the group process.

Recognising that it might not be easy or may seem strange is part of the process. Reflecting on this will help you understand what is going on for you and how your previous relationships and group experiences are impacting on this new experience.

Engaging with the PD group is as much about an attitude or a way of being as about doing the work. It is a willingness to come each week or each time and share experiences, feelings and reactions without holding back too much. It is a willingness to be interested in others in the group and the actual group process, i.e., what is actually going on here?

It is also a willingness to go with the flow rather than needing a structure. I acknowledge this is not always easy but the process in a PD group mirrors what goes on in a counselling session in that you never really know what is going to happen and usually you have to go with the flow of your client like rafting down a river. So, to participate in a PD group you need to come with an openness to the process without a fixed agenda in your mind as the challenge is that there is no agenda for the session usually.

Part of your role in the group is that you are helping provide the right conditions for others to personally develop – as mentioned, these are usually the core conditions of empathy, unconditional positive regard and genuineness (Mearns and Thorne, 2007). So it is a team effort to do this and it only takes one person in a group to not be providing these for the group to become 'unsafe' – like a boat with a leak.

What holds you back?

The difficulties students face in starting to engage with the group process will be due to numerous factors but will usually be connected to past experiences including previous group situations, e.g., early family group, school groups, peer groups, work groups, etc. Whether these groups were positive or negative experiences will affect how we enter new groups and how we participate in these. The factors that prevent students joining in include:

- lack of trust of others, which may relate to past experiences;
- being unable to express oneself emotionally;
- lack of confidence when speaking in groups or in front of others;
- low self-esteem/negative self-worth;
- negative attitudes to the PD group and process because it feels very alien;
- negative attitudes to people in the group or the facilitator which may be due to negative transference or prejudice, etc.;
- negative attitudes towards self – not feeling you have anything worth saying or that people will be interested in you;
- fear of taking up too much time;
- fear of becoming too emotional if you speak;
- fear of being judged;
- unhelpful, unsupported or negative past experiences in groups.

Activity

Look at the above reasons why a trainee might find it difficult to engage in the PD group.

Which if any apply to you?
Are there other factors which are making it difficult?
What can you do to overcome these?

Ironically it is the very factors that prevent students engaging in the PD group which are areas that can be worked with in the group or used. I have found that the group process can help students develop trust in others, gain confidence in speaking in groups and increase their self-worth and self-esteem through being in a group of supportive, accepting and genuine individuals. However, without the right support, the opposite could occur. Students, who like to *do* rather than *be*, find themselves being able to be in the moment and those who are quite self-critical and critical of others can become less judgemental of self and others through the work.

How our drivers might hold us back and prevent us making use of the group

You may have studied some transactional analysis (TA) theory on your courses so far, if not you could have a look at this to help you understand the group process and your behaviour more (see Short and Thomas, 2015 for an overview).

In TA theory there are five drivers that explain ways in which we may operate at certain times. These are behaviour types or traits that someone may show (Stewart and Joines, 2012). I have noticed when working with groups that some of these tendencies appear. It might be worth thinking about these here. This will also make you aware of what you do outside the group.

'Be perfect' driver – I am only OK if I get everything right

When you are in your PD group, is it important for you to get it right and say the correct things and be the perfect student? Are you being really careful how you say things? Behaving in this way may be a real block to spontaneity and it might stop you contributing for fear of getting it wrong.

'Please others' driver – I am only OK when I please others

Do you feel that you have to behave in a certain way to please others or the tutor? It is likely that if you are doing this in the group, it is a common trait in your everyday life. With this driver you aren't going to want to upset anyone by being challenging or saying what you think if it goes against the consensus of the group. You are also going to put other people before yourself, so might be worried about taking too much time in the group. The downside is that you might not get your needs met or achieve as much personal development in the group.

'Hurry up' driver – I am only OK if I am busy and quick about it

Have you noticed that you are looking at the clock or that you are thinking I could be doing something more useful if I wasn't here? Are you finding it a waste of time? Are you finding it difficult to just sit and be and want to be doing? Are you feeling impatient with people? This might be manifest by finger- or foot-tapping, moving in your chair rather than being able to sit still. The PD group gives you the chance to become more comfortable with silence and slow down and be still, which is very important in counselling where we have to allow space and silence to our clients and also where we need to be calm and centred.

'Be strong' driver – I am only OK if I hide my feelings and needs from others; I must not be weak

Can you allow yourself to be upset and affected by other people? How easy is it for you to share your vulnerabilities in this group? Do you find it hard to express feelings in the group? What would happen if you wanted to cry in your group?

The PD group will be very challenging if you have this driver as tutors are expecting you to be open and honest and share aspects of yourself that are vulnerable. In the group you might physically protect yourself by crossing your arms and legs. People with the 'be strong' driver tend to talk about their feelings like they are outside themselves and blame external factors for their feelings. So instead of saying 'I felt angry when you said that to me in the group' they might say '*you* made me angry when you said that'. Over time you may become more comfortable with expressing feelings depending on the genuine acceptance there is in the group.

'Try hard' driver – I am only OK if I keep trying to do things

It might be that each week you come to the group and you think 'today I'll try to contribute something', but don't actually do so or you try to say something but don't say it properly or completely. Students with this driver may say 'I am trying to understand what this group is about but I still don't get it, I need to build my confidence up before I can contribute anything'. The downside is that it might stop you getting the most out of the group or you might give up on the group process or the course and not achieve what you started out to do.

To sum up, becoming aware of your main driver behaviours could be a key to personal development and experimenting with being different. All these driver behaviours can be useful at times in our lives but in counselling practice they may be barriers to being effective.

PD group skills and qualities

Having looked at what PD groups are, their purpose and the trainee's role, this final section will summarise the skills you will need to enter fully into the group's work.

Not surprisingly the skills required are those that you are already using in your counselling or counselling skills practice sessions, except here you are providing these for others in the group and they are hopefully providing these for you.

So you will be using counselling and active listening skills and, as mentioned before, will provide the core conditions (Rogers, 1957) to a certain degree with an emphasis on acceptance, respect and congruence.

You will also need to be able to give feedback to peers on how they are in the group and also you will need to be able to receive feedback.

Self-awareness may be seen as a quality; however, it requires a number of skills. First you need to understand what is going on for you and then you need to be able to express this and then learn from this.

There will be times when you have to be assertive as you may not always agree with others in the group or may need to put yourself forward to speak and take the spotlight.

Perhaps this highlights another skill – being able to speak in front of a group, which can be very nerve-wracking. So the skills here might be about handling your nerves, breathing and keeping calm as well as overcoming personal censure.

Conclusion

In this chapter we have recognised that the PD group is a special space on counselling training courses where students are encouraged to be themselves and really reflect on their personal learning with peers who are going through a similar process.

In the PD group you can reflect on your learning from the different experiences involved in the training and link them together to enhance your personal and professional development.

Learning is experiential and is about taking part and learning from the group process and interactions in the group. Even if you do not take an active part initially, it will be important to reflect on group happenings and your feelings towards these. To participate you need to be open to this process and be able to go with the flow, as there is usually no specific agenda for the session.

The PD group works with different members sharing their views and feelings, leading to reactions from others and further sharing

Everyone has a different way of coming into and being in the PD group but it is useful to examine these patterns, as working on these may help you to be more effective in client work.

We need a range of skills to participate in the PD group, including counselling skills, feedback skills, self-awareness skills, assertiveness and the ability to speak in a group.

References

Johns, H. (2012) *Personal Development in Counsellor Training*. London: Sage.

Mearns, D. and Thorne, B. (2007) *Person-Centred Counselling in Action*. London: Sage.

Rogers, C. (1957) The necessary and sufficient conditions of therapeutic personality change. *Journal of Consulting Psychology*, 21(2), pp. 95–203.

Short, F. and Thomas, P. (2015) *Core Approaches in Counselling and Psychotherapy*. London: Routledge.

Stewart, I. and Joines, V. (2012) *TA Today: A New Introduction to Transactional Analysis*. Nottingham: Lifespace Publishing.

Chapter 6

Experiences of personal development groups

A research base

Carole Smith

Introduction

In this chapter, I have drawn on my research findings to highlight the usefulness of PD groups in the context of personal self-awareness development and help in client work.

By now, you will have come to the conclusion that personal development is not a single entity (McLeod and McLeod, 2014) and this makes it difficult to define and consequently for the trainee to identify what they need to do to develop.

As Hughes and Youngson (2009, p. 25) state, there is a vast literature on personal development which covers a wealth of issues, such as 'quality of life, meaning and understanding and positive thinking and goal setting'. Also, individual experiences in PD groups are vastly different depending on numerous factors, such as our past experiences, learning styles, personality and the group dynamic itself.

In this chapter I aim to:

- give an overview of the literature surrounding the pros and cons of PD groups;
- briefly explore how groups can enhance learning;
- offer an insight into my empirical findings on experiences in PD groups;
- highlight factors identified in the process of learning in PD groups;
- pose conclusions on the value of PD groups.

The motivation for the research

My motivation for doing a PhD was triggered by an event that happened many years ago when I was doing my Master's training in the integrative approach. I studied at a university not very close to home and made friends with a peer on the course who generously offered to let me stay overnight at her place when we were at the university one day a week. It was while we were having dinner one evening after a study day that she became upset over something that had happened in the group that day. She declared that she had felt 'traumatised' from the experience and I very unsympathetically challenged her on the depth of her emotion. I believed at the time that she was exaggerating her experience.

It was some years later, having forgotten all about it, when I began to facilitate PD groups, that the memory came back to me as I worked with group participants' (sometimes) very difficult emotions, that I began to wonder if 'traumatisation' was possible.

The meaning of trauma is 'a powerful psychological shock that has lasting effects' from the Greek word for 'wound' (Colman, 2014, p. 98), or disturbed, an ordeal, or distressed.

I wanted to find out more about individual experiences in PD groups so I began to search the literature and came across some narratives based on authors' experiences and observation (Bion, 1959; Lieberman, 1981, in Bates and Goodman, 1986; Nitsun, 1996), which supported the notion of individuals being traumatised or 'damaged' through negative group experiences.

Irving and Williams (1999, p. 139), suggest that 'not only do some individuals fail to benefit from the PD experience but may even be damaged by it', and Robson and Robson (2008) questioned the safety of groups for participants. In fact, some of my research participants did talk about feeling traumatised by some PD group experiences, and that was often linked to lack of support or poor facilitation. The literature does seem to indicate that experiences in PD groups are enhanced by a feeling of safety, but safety may be an individual perspective.

Activity

Make a list of things that are important to your learning and help you feel safe in the PD group, for example:

Do you like to be challenged fairly quickly, or do you like to initially observe before you take part?
Do you learn best from role play and experiment or do you like to read the theories?
Are you a 'people pleaser' or is that unimportant to you?
How might the environment help you?

Is self-awareness best learned in an experiential group?

As you will have seen in other chapters in this book, self-awareness is extremely important so that we can recognise any potential triggers when working with clients. The focus of my research was on how participants used and still use their PD experiences in their client work. This was based on an assumption that individuals *can* learn in group situations, particularly in an experiential group, consisting of techniques such as role play or demonstrations of skills. The learning that participants mostly referred to was emotional learning, often described as being linked to a bodily experience such as anxiety or fear.

Emotions can be heightened in the group collective and can both enhance and detract from learning. Also, emotions will be felt individually and differently in group situations, depending on the support on offer within the group. My own experiences, both as a participant in PD groups and as a trainer and facilitator is 'the greenhouse effect' where a wide range of emotions will bloom bigger, more colourfully and more speedily, like an exotic bunch of lilies. Facilitators are important in their role of managing the speed of this flourishing, slowing it down or allowing it space and making sure that the blossom does not wither before maturing.

Case study: Penny

Penny was in her first year of counsellor training. She liked all aspects of the course so far except the PD group because she wasn't sure what the aims were. The facilitator kept saying that each person's learning was individual and that their learning was what they made it. She didn't quite understand this and her feelings of insecurity were increasing as she was a person who liked certainty and structure in her life.

In the Monday PD group, several of her peers were expressing their fears over the upcoming assessments and Penny was becoming anxious just listening to them. The facilitator noticed Penny's withdrawal and her tense body language, so asked her what was going on for her. Penny felt herself becoming angry as she was put on the spot and didn't want her anxiety to be exposed. She looked around and saw 12 pairs of eyes watching her which made her feel worse. Her face was tingling and she knew she was breathing too fast. She just wanted to run out of the room. Then the facilitator said, 'I can see you need some support right now so I want you to breathe more slowly and listen to me talking'. She then proceeded to clarify how they all would be able to get some help with their assignment, now that she knew people were worried.

Penny began to calm down, feeling the support offered and noticed how the emotion in the room was diffused.

Now look at the learning for Penny and the others in the group:

> What aspects of Penny's self-awareness could she reflect on here?
> What can you see about the 'hot house' effect of group emotions?
> How might this help in client work?

Dewey (1933) first promoted the concept of reflective thinking, encompassing the 'what' and 'why' of the application of knowledge, and numerous reflections since then have been written, as well as empirical studies carried out, which illuminate the benefits of discussing clinical critical incidents in small group settings (Schon, 1983; Boud et al., 1985; Mezirow, 1990).

There are many opportunities for learning even in one single event in the PD group and this learning is enhanced by the many differing perspectives and interpretations that are inevitably brought into the group setting. We all bring a host of varied experiences, attitudes, values, beliefs and history into groups and as long as we are open to learning, with and from others, the group will be a place of rich discovery. However, it is important to self-reflect or mull over your experiences, journaling actual and potential outcomes and giving consideration to what you might do differently next time (see Schon's reflective cycle, 1983), as learning is complex and takes the form of a trajectory or a developmental pathway.

Calleja (2014) reviews the literature and history of Mezirow's (2003) 'transformative learning', highlighting the importance of experience and prior learning and the importance of self-reflection, through interacting with others. Diversity exists within the PD group (like any other group) but the emotional challenge created in the group through concepts such as projection and transference and countertransference (see Chapter 5 for definitions of these) challenges individuals to self-examine, assess assumptions and explore roles and relationships with others.

Case study: Rosemary

When Rosemary was challenged by her facilitator in the PD group, she experienced feelings of shyness, insecurity and some fear, which caused her to close down her feelings and avoid any direct interaction.

When she examined this with her therapist, she realised that the facilitator reminded her of one of her secondary schoolteachers who was a bully. Once she recognised this, she was able to separate her earlier feelings from what was happening in the current group. Her feelings of 'closing down' were an avoidance tactic to help her to feel safer in the past.

Experiencing this in the group helped her to recognise the potential of this happening with a client.

Mezirow (1990) asserts that the process is spiral and cumulative but could have regressive aspects too: 'Transformative learning … is often an intensely threatening experience in which we have to become aware of both the assumptions undergirding our ideas and our emotional responses to the need for change' (Mezirow, 2000, p. 67).

This underlines the emotional aspect of this type of learning as the challenging of assumptions, meaning and relationships that can be threatening and overwhelming through the questioning of long-held beliefs. This also includes the notion that learning will occur when we are confronted with either new and unfamiliar experiences or with what we do not know (Morrice, 2012) but could create more discriminating, open, inclusive learners with better ability to emotionally change.

The PD group experience has the ability, in the right conditions to generate a very different but richer learning than simple theory acquired in classroom conditions.

The pros of PD groups

It is important for us to have a sound sense of the self in order to keep our boundaries separate to those of the clients. Cozolino and Santos (2014, p. 168) called this 'safe and attuned connections', which this depth of self-awareness can support. Cozolino and Santos assert that this joint self-reflection can lead to successful therapeutic outcomes. In order for this to take place; it is necessary for the counsellor to bracket their own needs, motives and personal difficulties in the therapeutic moment. To do this, a great degree of self-awareness is inevitably needed to prevent the unexpected arising in the counselling session, and so hindering a full and relational contact. The PD group process may be the only medium that can provide this degree of self-awareness development. Rose (2012) supports this, writing from her own experiences with PD groups, suggesting that the counsellor has a responsibility to understand her/his part in the therapeutic relationship, which in effect is an ongoing process with each contributing to the change mechanism.

Self-awareness will not happen overnight, however; nor should we imagine that we will ever finish the learning. This is a lifelong journey of discovery and every new experience will increase and develop our wisdom, as long as we remain open to it. Groups are a norm of society; without groups we would be unable to learn about diversity, alternative perspectives or use combined strengths and interdependence to reach achievements. It could be argued that without the learning from others, as well as the learning about dependence, interdependence and independence, in groups, it would be impossible to work empathically and with acceptance of others.

Launer (2015) discusses collaborative learning in groups in relation to case study examination for doctors and asserts that communication skills, group dynamics and parallel process (in conjunction with client work) can benefit clinical work. He refers to the concept of Balint groups, which are small experiential type groups used to explore clinical cases and highlight interaction between medic and patient. Presenters often chose to present patients who have elicited strong emotional responses in them. Any exploration is designed to raise self-awareness, introspection and for the group to develop skills including empathy. This emphasises the educational value of 'in the moment' encounters between group participants and can be allied to the use of the exploration of the 'critical incident' in the PD group.

There is much discussion on the pros and cons of group dynamics through examples such as the work of Yalom and Leszcz (2005), although it is often based on experiences of group therapy and its aims for corrective emotional experiences. As can be seen in Yalom and Leszcz's work, group process contributing to interpersonal learning is dependent on the group being a constructive learning environment (Yalom and Leszcz, 2005) and is clearly reliant on many factors, not least the skill of the group facilitator. Other chapters in this book have highlighted the importance of feeling safe in the PD group and sound learning being dependent, to some extent, on the skills of the facilitator.

In the following sections, I give examples of my research participants' discussions to highlight the pros and cons of PD groups. Pseudonyms are used throughout this section.

My findings

Self-awareness

Jenny talked about a role play in the group that she had volunteered to take part in:

> Suddenly something happened where I realised that I could start to just accept myself as I was, rather than feeling I had to live up to someone else's expectations and that acceptance of self was the start of my personal development… but it took a long time for that to really happen.

Jenny had had difficulties in talking about herself in the open group and when she finally did do this, the acceptance from group members was transforming for her.

My main focus for the research was how participants perceived they used their PD learning in their client work and the following is a selection of transcripts demonstrating this.

Using experiences in client work

All of my participants were able to clearly indicate examples of these, with some particularly focusing on how client work was enhanced by their development of self-awareness. Janet said:

> My view is that actually what the PD group does is exactly what it's designed to do and that is to, you know, bring forward the issues you might act out with your clients if you don't get them sorted.

Beryl also reiterated this with

> I spent a lot of time crying... but that was therapeutic as well, to go through that, and it helped me working with clients, not to be frightened of emotion.

Janet described a process of learning that had taken place over a whole year of PD groups, but a particular incident that evoked anxiety for her in the group brought her to a crystallised realisation of her work with clients:

> That helped me to work out about my attachment pattern, it helped me to go on to explore it in counselling... which is important, because when I'm working with a client, I need to be aware of my own attachment pattern and what other people can trigger in me because otherwise it's just a theory out there isn't it?

She had been encouraged to take a particular reaction to some challenge on her style of relating to others, to her personal therapy, which brought her to this learning about herself. They also talked about being able to work at relational depth.

Learning emotional depth from the PD group

The necessity of undergoing feelings experientially (i.e., actually experiencing at first-hand) was important to all of them; for example, Marge said:

> In the second session, something someone did [which was to offer her support through holding her hand] moved me, and I felt tearful... and that's the way I've chosen to work with clients – with a bedrock of kindness.

Marge had been in a previous PD group (see the negative side of Marge's experience below) in which peers and facilitator had not supported her process of learning how past experiences affected her and she ended up leaving her course at that point. She talked about a feeling of 'being missed' when she divulged personal details, which she put down to the inexperience of the facilitator.

The cons of PD groups

There are both benefits and challenges to students in small group work, which allows rich learning about others' backgrounds, cultures, experiences, values and beliefs.

Developing knowledge about differences and learning from others' knowledge and skills requires open-mindedness and acceptance, which can be risky to the novice learner but can also offer growth and enhancement for client work.

However, there are additional factors to take into account when bringing individuals together in learning groups; for example, Kurland and Salmon (2006), in their review of clinical work, reiterate the importance of a good facilitator to prevent poor role modelling and the dangers of such things as dual relationships. The latter might include friendships outside the group or, indeed, contracts with facilitators in other contexts such as the client or supervisory relationship. However, if ground rules are set and the group is facilitated well, these things should not be an issue.

In support of this, Robson and Robson's (2008) study of counselling trainees' perceptions in their PD groups emphasised participants' fears around safety particularly, as well as lack of trust between participants and the difficulties in group members having varying agendas. Also, Lennie's (2007) work on PD groups suggests that the complexities of group roles and group dynamics complicate learning.

Indeed, Dryden et al. (1995) argued that participating in the personal development group can help identify blind spots about the self that may impact on client work, but Moller and Rance's (2013) study demonstrated that for some, the PD group enhances learning about the self and clients, but for others it is a source of fear, creating negative emotional experiences that sometimes stem from a lack of clarity about the purpose of the PD group.

Almost all the participants described some form of emotional disturbance or disruption, or at least being emotionally affected by their PD experiences.

Emotional disruption

For example, Marge had revealed a past traumatic experience to a group, hoping for support and the facilitator did not pick it up, resulting in Marge leaving the training group.

> It was handled really badly by the facilitator... she never went back to it, she never picked it up... I felt so shut down and so let down by the facilitator, that I decided to leave, and I know now... that actually that was the wrong thing to have done, but I was really inexperienced. I mean now I would have addressed it... but not everybody has the skills and knowledge to do that.

She eventually joined another training course, but the experience has affected her in other groups, causing her to be reticent in sharing.

Some of the participants' learning came from physical reactions that were often anxiety, teaching them about 'triggers' in certain situations. Janet experienced physical symptoms of anxiety in the group:

> Yeah, I wasn't aware that I could ask, but also that, in those Awareness Groups, or PD Groups, whatever you want to call them, that's when I realised how anxious I was, because all of a sudden, in a room full of people, I think there was about no more than nine or ten in each group, you know, they used to split us all off into

these different groups, that's when I realised how anxious I was because I just felt this intense burning or anxiety all around me and I just couldn't speak, I couldn't do anything. So that's when I realised how anxious I was, which I wouldn't have sussed out, I don't think otherwise.

Impact of past experiences

Group interactions can often bring up memories of difficult past experiences, e.g., anxiety at school or a clash in a past relationship. The PD group may elicit these historic encounters but will not only give us an insight into how, what and why we have these feelings, but also how we might deal with them in the here and now, particularly when working with clients.

Janet's difficulties involved being able to integrate into the group, as she had had past struggles with bullying, which had resulted in social anxiety for her:

> I'm an only child, quite isolated, so the group was overwhelming. It was really difficult, really overwhelming.

Arthur also revealed his difficulties in talking about himself and his past within the group, which related to him being shunned as a teenager after disclosing his homosexuality:

> There was a lot for me because of my childhood, there was a lot of shame.

He eventually, with peer support, personal therapy and skilful facilitation in the PD group, came to a point of acceptance of himself which he linked to his client work through his use of core conditions.

A final theme emerged which relates to Mezirow's (1990) theory of 'transformative learning' (see discussion above). Most participants described feeling a need to 'tolerate' the difficulties in the group, such as the emotional disruption, as they instinctively felt it was important to work through the emotions in order to arrive at some learning and development. They talked about what helped them to 'stay with' the trajectories of learning, such as kindness and support from the group, an open space to talk things through, the need for acceptance and core conditions, and a supportive facilitator and good role modelling. They also discussed how they were able to use counselling/therapy and clinical supervision to help them through the difficult times in the PD group.

Tolerance

Amelia highlighted the process of staying with the experiences to 'translate' them into learning when she said:

> I think it's, what immediately springs to mind for me of the learning in that is assertiveness to actually be able to support myself and stand up for myself verbally maybe and to stay, to be able to stay with discomfort and witness others' discomfort, not to try to change it or fix it… and to stay is the overall massive learning for me.

Amelia was the youngest child of six siblings and had been overwhelmed by them growing up. She had also been looked after by both them and her parents and had difficulties with resisting turning to someone else to sort things for her.

Jackie also emphasised the value of patience in the process of learning:

> It's just about the being and staying with [emotions in the group], that's not easy, that takes time to develop and without that, you're not going to work at relational depth.

Here she was talking about learning the skill of staying with a client's process and not trying to hurry things up too quickly.

One other concept arose in the research which was associated with the concept of tolerance, this was 'reflection'. You will see from my writing and others in this book, how important it is to reflect on our experiences. Reflection will help your learning to develop and also it will give some structure to it.

Reflection:

The research participants discussed the magnitude of using continuous reflection within the PD group and after sessions, in a number of ways including self-reflection, (by using one of the reflective cycles such as Schon, 1983), journaling, discussion with others and personal therapy and supervision.

Mike, for example, said:

> It [the group] was a very intense place and then you would go home after it and just talk about how it had been, and process it on the journey, but it was quite important to come down, and then by the time I got home... I'd kind of come around from it or I could reflect on it in a journal or something. It was quite powerful doing that.

Dave also said:

> I knew straight away that important things were coming up for me and others and that I would need to make notes, I've never been one to do that, but it has helped me enormously and sometimes I take my journal to my therapist to discuss it.

However, it must be remembered that if you are going to discuss the group afterwards, you should maintain confidentiality and only talk about yourself, not others.

Summing up the findings

Several themes emerged, the overarching feature being the generation of emotion, particularly anxiety, but other strong emotional responses related to childhood triggers were prominent. Many emotional responses were negative at the time of experiencing them in the group, corresponding with literature highlighting the distress sometimes generated in groups. However, most of the interviewees identified that they had processed these emotions (some with help from therapy and/or clinical supervision), going on to explore the ways they used their learning in their client work. The key theme was the need for tolerance and, associated with this, reflection. As long as the person can 'stick with it' and access support to process the learning, then development and self-awareness will be valuable, particularly for client work.

There was a central theme of acknowledgement of the importance of personal development group experiences, and almost all talked about it being a challenging experience either positively or negatively. Group facilitators were largely referred to as either helpful and supportive, playing a part in facilitation of learning, or as a factor in 'traumatic' experiences.

Based on these findings, it seems logical to conclude that there is emotional learning to be had from the PD group; something that would not be found in the classroom. Although a small study, the disclosures divulged were very rich experiences and the participants were able to recall those experiences as though they were recent events. It was clear to see that their PD journeys had had great impact on them and although their descriptions were at times emotional and tapped into their intense discomfort at the time, every one of them recounted how meaningful and how worthwhile the PD group is for sound and safe client outcomes.

Conclusion

So, it seems that the development of self-awareness and an in-depth knowledge of our responses to others is more than desirable for therapeutic outcomes in client work. It may be that the PD group suits some learning styles, such as the activist style, (learning by doing), much more than others and it seems logical that an activist might learn better in a group providing experiential factors (Honey and Mumford, 1983). However, so far, there is little research on experiences in PD group, differing learning styles and particularly any indications of their usefulness in client work, in terms of improved outcomes for clients.

The PD group is full of complexities and holds a vast unknown for trainees both in encounter and outcome. This leads us back to the question of whether PD groups are a good learning vehicle for all participants. It is difficult to find an alternative medium in which trainees can experience the depth of emotion that seems vital for client work, as my research findings suggests.

At the very least, groups can be anxiety-provoking, particularly when an experiential style is used and when there is an expectation that individuals need to take part for their own developmental process, as had happened to my friend all those years ago. This sometimes pressurises both the novice and the more experienced practitioner.

Much of the literature confirms that the personal development group in counselling training has been and continues to be a difficult area of work for the counselling trainee and hopefully this book will shine some light on the PD group generally for you. Undoubtedly, there can be difficulties (some of which are highlighted in my findings) in the PD group for a whole variety of reasons, but if those difficulties are tolerated and supported in some way(s), then learning can be very rich, rewarding and beneficial.

However, learning is not always immediate, so it is important to process events and experiences, using a reflective structure such as Schon (1983) and bear in mind that the process of learning is built on through experiences. It also must be recognised that there is currently little evidence base for using PD groups in counsellor training, other than anecdotal and experiential. My research was an attempt to redress this balance.

References

Bates, B. and Goodman, A. (1986) The effectiveness of encounter groups. *British journal of Guidance and Counselling*, 14(3), pp. 240–250.

Bion, W.R. (1959) *Second Thoughts*. London: Tavistock.

Boud, D., Keogh, R. and Walker, D. (1985) *Reflection: Turning Experience into Learning*. London: Routledge.

Calleja, C. (2014) Jack Mezirow's conceptualisation of adult transformative learning: A review. *Journal of Adult and Continuing Education*, 20(1), pp. 117–136.

Colman, A.M. (2014) *Oxford Dictionary of Psychology*. London: Oxford University Press.

Cozolino, L.J. and Santos, E.N. (2014) Why we need therapy – and why it works: A neuroscientific perspective. *Smith College Studies in Social Work*, 84(2–3), pp. 157–177.

Dewey, J. (1933) *How We Think: A Restatement of the Relation of Reflective Thinking to the Educative Process*. Boston: D.C. Heath.

Dryden, W., Horton, I. and Mearns, D. (1995) *Issues in Professional Counsellor Training*. London: Cassell.

Honey, P. and Mumford, A. (1983) *A Manual of Learning Styles*. London: P. Honey.

Hughes, J. and Youngson, S. (2009) *Personal Development and Clinical Psychology*. Oxford: Blackwell Publishing.

Irving, J.A. and Williams, D.I. (1999) Personal growth and personal development: concepts clarified. *British Journal of Guidance and Counselling*, 27(4), pp. 517–526.

Kurland, R. and Salmon, R. (2006) Making joyful noise: Presenting, promoting, and portraying group work to and for the profession. *Social Work With Groups*, 29(2–3), pp. 1–15.

Launer, J. (2015) Collaborative learning groups. *Postgraduate Medical Journal*, 91(1078), pp. 473–474.

Lennie, C. (2007) The role of personal development groups in counsellor training: Understanding factors contributing to self-awareness in the personal development group. *British Journal of Guidance & Counselling*, 35(1), pp. 115–129.

McLeod, J. and McLeod, J. (2014) *Personal and Professional Development for Counsellors, Psychotherapists and Mental Health Practitioners*. London: Open University Press.

Mearns, D. and Cooper, M. (2005) *Working at Relational Depth in Counselling and Psychotherapy*. London: Sage.

Mezirow, J. (1990) *Fostering Critical Reflection in Adulthood: A Guide to Transformative and Emancipatory Learning*. San Francisco: Jossey-Bass.

Mezirow, J. (2000) *Learning as Transformation: Critical Perspectives on a Theory in Progress*. San Francisco: Jossey-Bass.

Mezirow, J. (2003) Transformative learning as discourse. *Journal of Transformative Education*, 1(1), pp. 58–63.

Moller, N.P. and Rance, N. (2013) The good, the bad and the uncertainty: Trainees' perceptions of the personal development group. *Counselling and Psychotherapy Research*, 13(4), pp. 282–289.

Morrice, L. (2012) Learning and refugees: Recognizing the darker side of transformative learning. *Adult Education Quarterly*, 63(3), pp. 251–271.

Nitsun, M. (1996) *The Anti-Group: Destructive Forces and their Creative Potential*. London: Routledge.

Robson, M. and Robson, J. (2008) Explorations of participants' experiences of a personal development group held as part of a counselling psychology training group: Is it safe in here? *Counselling Psychology Quarterly*, 21(4), pp. 371–382.

Rose, C. (2012) *Self-Awareness and Personal Development Resources for Psychotherapists and Counsellors*. London: Palgrave Macmillan.

Schon, D. (1983) *The Reflective Practitioner: How Professionals Think in Action*. New York: Basic Books.

Yalom, I.D. and Leszcz, M. (2005) *The Theory and Practice of Group Psychotherapy*. New York: Basic Books.

Chapter 7

Experiences of running personal development groups

The facilitator role

Jayne Godward

The aim of this chapter is to share some of my experiences of running personal development (PD) groups over the last 12 years.

I want to clarify what students can expect in general, from their PD group facilitators and during the life of the group at different points; this will vary as tutors are all individuals with their own styles and methods of working, but there are some fundamental issues that will remain the same. The chapter will have a linear progression and will discuss my experiences and the role of a tutor at different points in the group's life. The metaphor of a sea voyage has been used to emphasise some aspects and Tuckman's theory of group development is referred to (Tuckman, 1965).

In this chapter I will look at:

- the importance of preparation for the PD group work and relevant considerations;
- beginning work with a new group;
- how the PD tutor role is different from other roles;
- encouraging participation;
- the PD tutor role during group process;
- facilitating groups during different stages.

The importance of preparation

For me, running a PD group can either be like stepping onto a floating raft or boarding a ship that is fit for a voyage. If I have been involved with the planning of the groups, it feels like a safer enterprise rather than going into a group without any prior involvement or planning.

Where possible it is important to prepare for running a PD group and consider the following:

Timing: How long the group session lasts may depend on the size of the group or the course requirements. I have worked with different models of PD groups from working regularly for up to 1.5 hours each week to having a regular PD slot sometimes monthly with other personal development activities slotted in on the other weeks. The time of day for the group is an important consideration as often students *and tutors* are very tired at the end of a long day training but may not be at their most alert first thing in the morning. For us tutors going straight on to another group after running a PD might not be a good idea due to the emotional content that can arise in these groups.

Size: This has been a big issue in some of the groups I have run. Where the group has been large – e.g., more than 12 people – students have often complained that it is too big for the personal development work to take place. This was cited as an issue linked to safety in Robson and Robson's study (2008). Group members do not feel safe to share when groups are large and they don't know the other members of the group. My experience has been that groups of between five and nine feel like an optimum size, with enough people for sharing of experiences but not so many that they are fighting for a space to share.

Place: This also links into safety as the room used needs to be private and confidential and not a space where students can be overheard, overlooked or disturbed. It helps if the room is not in a noisy place where outside sounds will distract from what is going on in the room.

Single or double tutoring: The ideal is to have a co-tutor running the PD group with you. This is usually supportive and helpful but in some organisations this is too expensive and not viable.

Support for staff and students: It is important to consider what support is available for you if you are running PD groups, as this can be personally demanding work, but also what support is available for students outside the PD group time if issues arise.

Although I look forward to the challenge of working with a new group, there is always trepidation that something will go wrong and no certainty that it will work out. All these group members have been selected to come on a demanding counsellor training course and hopefully are committed to doing personal development, but are they really? Selection to counsellor training is really important and will vary according to the tutors selecting and the demands for numbers of training organisations to fill the course spaces. Many of the counselling trainees I have met have experienced serious personal issues and/or have been affected by their life histories and they will be bringing these to the PD group. In the group it is likely they will play out their personal patterns and manner of relating to others. Their attitudes to others and to me as the facilitator will correspond to those played out in the past. I think it is realistic of me to expect some conflict within a PD group rather than expect it to be plain sailing and an easy ride to personal development.

Lennie in her study of PD group participation says:

> It is naïve to assume a harmony and inherent cohesion when a group of potentially different individuals get together in a personal development group setting. The suggestion that trainees in psychotherapy are more able to cope with the dissonance thrown up by heterogeneous group might account for the more negative experiences reported by trainees.
>
> (Lennie, 2007, p. 126)

In Chapter 8 I will discuss conflict in PD groups in detail and look at how this can be resolved.

So from the beginning my role is to be vigilant as to what is going on and to look beyond the surface behaviour of individuals. I need to be conscious of diversity in the group and of attitudes and opinions that are being expressed. There are actions

I can take at the beginning to lay the foundations for the group process and to make it easier for group members to use the personal development group. I need to aim to be accepting of individuals even if this is challenging.

Beginning stages

In recent years I have spent more time preparing the group for the PD time rather than launching straight into it. This has included introducing the idea of the PD group, its purpose, and addressing hopes, fears and expectations.

Having a shared focus or purpose for the group was shown to provide safety for PD group participants in Robson and Robson's study, whereas when the group did not have this, people felt unsafe (Robson and Robson, 2008).

This period of preparation for the more free-flowing group process seems like a good idea, especially when working with large groups as it provides some ice-breaking and time to get to know each other; however, sometimes I have questioned whether it would be better to just get started, as the delay might fuel some students' anxieties as to what it is going to be like. Although I think at least some introduction is always useful. In addition, I am also trying to avoid the mystique about the purpose of the group, but at the end of the day the group has to work out what it means to them.

The common ground is that learners have come because they want to be counsellors. I can't presume that they have come because they want to personally develop. Often I have found that the personal development aspect is a bit of a shock to people and that there is a resistance to it.

However, I have found that even when there is clear rationale for the group and why we have it on counsellor training courses, students may still continue not to understand why they are there or the real purpose of it. Sometimes it seems that individuals have to experience its value and purpose viscerally before they can understand it. By this I mean that there needs to be an emotional or deeper reaction before it can be appreciated.

Case study: Jan

Jan was very resistant to the PD group and could not really see the point of it. She sat in it scowling, with her arms crossed, week in and week out. This was very difficult for the group tutor who felt frustrated with Jan and experienced her as antagonistic and critical.

It was only towards the end of semester one when she came into the group upset after a skills session and was able to offload to her group colleagues in the safety of that space that she started to reflect on what had happened to her and saw the value of the group.

In this arena she was not being judged and could acknowledge feelings of being a failure in her skills practice. The tutor role here involved being patient and trying hard to empathise, even though it was a real challenge to do so.

Robson and Robson's study (2008) emphasises the key theme of safety and how important this is in PD groups. They highlight the need for contracting. Even if a course has already had a group contract for the learners, it appears that a clear contract is needed for the PD group. Rather than it just being an empty exercise where people throw out the words – e.g., respect, non-judgemental, confidentiality – these authors suggest it should be linked to the personal experience of the students and be negotiated between the facilitator and the group – more about a way of being in the group. Prior to the actual contracting I might get students to consider: how do you want it to be in this group? How do you expect group members to behave? What do you need in order to feel safe in this group?

Another thing I would ask the group would be: what do you expect of me as the facilitator? This would open the door for discussion into what my role is and what it isn't. Also I am part of the contract, as I am contracting with them as to what I will and will not be doing when facilitating the group.

The role of the PD tutor

Having spent quite a lot of space here looking at what I might do to prepare for the group work and at the beginning, I think it is important to make it clear how I see my role as facilitator of the PD group generally.

My role as a facilitator is not to do teaching in the didactic sense, to lead the process or to do therapy. Neither is my function to assess or judge people, although if I had real concerns about a student, I would have to raise this with the individual or the course team, so there may be a limit to the confidentiality I can keep, which needs to be stated at the contracting stage of the group.

Often students seem to want and expect all of these, so it is worth examining what it would be like if the PD tutor did these.

- **Teaching:** If the tutor started doing some kind of teaching in the PD group time this would probably disempower the group members as they would be relying on the facilitator's expertise. Also, time would be taken away from the group process and the students' space to explore and dialogue with each other.
- **Leading:** There will be a bit of leading and encouraging, especially at the beginning, but if the tutor led each session then this would take away the spontaneity of people sharing and would mean it was their agenda rather than the group members' agenda.
- **Doing therapy:** Although the PD group tutor will be a therapist, she will not be running a therapy group here and will not be trying to counsel individuals even though this might be tempting at times – this is not the place for that as this is a training group (see Chapter 5, which clarifies this).
- **Assessing:** If the tutor's role was to assess each student's behaviour and contribution in the group, this would mean that they would probably feel very self-conscious and not able to share for fear of being judged. Or they would be putting on an act to impress the tutor but not being themselves. I have found this aspect problematic, as there is often an assessment element linked to PD group work and it is very difficult for students not to see you as an assessor; however, generally, we are not assessing participants on their contributions in the PD group as such. I will look at this difficulty more in Chapter 8.

It is worth noting here that each PD group and each individual within each group will have different needs and may expect something different from the group facilitator, and it can be very difficult for the tutor to get it right all the time or most of the time. Whatever your expectations of the PD group tutor remember that they are human and fallible – we make mistakes like everyone else!

Activity

It might be useful for you to pause and to reflect on what you expect from your group facilitator.

What does this say about your needs?
How is this coloured by your previous group leaders / significant others / authority figures?
How realistic is this?
Have they made it clear what their role is? Have you checked out with them what their role is?

My role is to facilitate the personal development process through the group work that takes place. A big part of this role involves helping to create a safe space at the beginning and to continue to maintain this. My aim is to involve the group participants in this endeavour too.

Clarifying the boundaries and also the boundaries of the facilitator's role is also essential here.

Boundaries can be tricky with PD groups, as students see each other outside the PD group and often are friends and colleagues on placement. The bottom line is that issues discussed in the PD group stay in the PD group rather than being discussed outside. The exception here is that students can gain support in personal therapy as this is also a confidential and boundaried space, with the therapist not being involved with the course. See the Melinda case study in Chapter 10 for an example of a breach of this rule.

Setting off: Encouraging participation

Once the group has started, my role is to encourage different participants to take part. Sometimes I have done this by doing a round of how people are feeling to encourage all members to speak and share something in the group. This may be useful particularly in large groups where students might struggle to come in at first, but it is time-consuming and may take the whole of a first session in larger groups.

My preference is for the group interactions to be free-flowing so that people speak when they want to and where it is not tutor-led, but this may not be easy for members at the beginning. Students who are used to rounds on their previous courses may be happy doing this at first, but this can be really uncomfortable if you are a reserved person and you are anxiously waiting to have to speak.

I would be really vigilant as to how each member of the group is doing in these early stages. I do feel relieved when people start sharing spontaneously in the groups but I have to watch out for quiet members who feel they aren't able to do this. I understand how intimidating groups can be, especially when some students appear to be very articulate or confident or more intelligent than yourself. My dilemma in a group where some people are just not participating verbally would be: do I ask X and Y how they are or what is going on for them? Or will I be singling them out and putting them on the spot? Is it better if members of the group do this rather than the tutor? My temptation would be to leave the quiet people for a while before asking – allow them to come into the group

This is where the ground rules and contract for the group are important and I would want to make sure that we include some clauses to say that everyone's contribution will be valued and that people will not be judged. I would also encourage participation by all members and that the group will take some responsibility for involving everyone.

Some students find it painfully difficult to speak in a group, particularly when it is large but even when it is small they may find it hard to share personal information. This is when the group does really need to feel safe and trustworthy, which may take time just as it takes time in counselling for the client to feel able to share more personal information with a therapist.

Another way of dealing with a lack of contribution is to reflect back what is happening in the group without singling anyone out, showing that I am aware of it but not pointing a finger at anyone. This may lead to the group actually discussing this or talking about it. So I am passing over responsibility for the group process to the group.

The facilitator's role during group process

Chris Rose (2004, p. 29) uses a metaphor of 'a boat that has to be rowed and everyone has an oar, except me and I am at the tiller. If no one rows, then we are stationary. If half the group are rowing we might be going around in circles.'

I like this idea in that everyone has to get involved and it is up to the group whether we move or not and my role is to steer it through the choppy waters or to prevent us coming to harm. It is also to keep us on track in terms of focusing on personal development rather than letting the group talk about anything and everything but themselves. This is a form of flight when students start talking about things or people out there or theories rather than looking at themselves.

Another metaphor one of my tutors used when I was in a PD group was that of a gardener. This implies that the growing and work comes from the students but the facilitator keeps an eye on the overall situation and supports the growth of the plants. Provision of the right conditions and environment is important here.

The facilitator has to hand over some responsibility for growth and development to the students and make this clear. Just as in therapy the client is empowered to grow and develop through the right conditions and relationship being provided, so the facilitator is fostering relationships in the group that will lead to positive development. If no one feels safe in the group and relating is not open, honest and respectful, then people will not share and contribute and there will be no useful group process.

Facilitating groups during conflict

Over the years, I have compared the life of the PD group to a voyage of discovery. The first few weeks of a group may feel smooth, whereas with other groups the sea is choppy from the beginning, but most groups go through a period of conflict or times when disagreements or discomfort arise which would be termed 'storming' in the Tuckman model of group development (Tuckman, 1965).

This can take many forms including individuals disagreeing, students challenging the tutor as to what the purpose of the group is, people thinking they are being congruent but being aggressive to other group members or to the facilitator. Sometimes someone who is different in the group becomes the scapegoat and all the annoyances in the group are directed at them.

During the storming phase the group leader may be an easy target as s/he is not part of the course group or may be seen as a threat as an authority figure or assessor. I have seen students revert back to earlier behaviours in their life. So they may become very passive and timid or very angry or childlike. At this point the group can be a very scary place not just for the students but for the facilitator. The boat feels like it is going to tip over.

Gloster-Smith (2004) recommends that the group leader attends to sensations – their own, other people's, the group and relationships in the group. He says that the facilitator needs to be as fully aware as possible and needs to attend to the here and now. Perhaps the hardest thing for me in these situations is not to become defensive if under attack and also to stay objective rather than taking it personally. Staying grounded is an important part of the group leader's role, and being fully present to what is going on. This is often easier said than done, particularly when you are under attack on all sides or when there is an atmosphere of negativity. I have heard group leaders compare their PD groups to a pack of wolves who are after your blood! See Chapter 8 where I look at conflicts and difficulties that can occur.

Gloster-Smith (2004) speaks of the facilitator being an anchor. As a camper, I am thinking of myself like a tent frame that holds it all together in the wind and the storm rather than allowing the tent to collapse.

Conflict in groups can be useful, but it needs careful management by the group facilitator for survival and for people to learn from it. If you can navigate the boat through the storm then group members will have the confidence that it will be able to withstand other incidents. In terms of group safety, Robson and Robson (2008, p. 380) say: 'Trust is established by knowing oneself and others and through knowing others have the capacity to harm us but being confident this will not occur. It is established through congruence.'

If students express feelings and this has been handled in a safe way, members will feel safer participating in the group.

The performing stage

If the group survives conflict there may be a settling-down stage where people are working together and feel more comfortable in the group so that they can contribute more and understand what it is about. There is often a sense of identity where students talk about 'our group' and 'our tutor' as opposed to other groups. There may be a feeling of belonging and a cohesiveness that makes sharing and personal development easier.

As a tutor I would be experiencing some relief at this stage and might start to relax; however, from experience, I know I cannot be complacent as I don't know what is lurking beneath the surface like a shark in the sea. It is likely that some members of the group still find it hard to contribute or that there are unexpressed feelings. Some students never feel comfortable with the group while others embrace the opportunity from the beginning. Storming could easily reoccur and will challenge the cohesiveness of the group.

As a group matures, my work as a facilitator is less active and interventionist but more about keeping an eye on the process and sometimes offering observations on this if this isn't done by the group. I will also now try to involve people who are still not contributing. Just as in counselling where the client understands what is expected of them in therapy, students can use the space without being prompted. I still need to hold the boundaries, however, and attend to the well-being of the group. When the group, in Tuckman's (1965) words, is 'performing' and students are spontaneously sharing their personal learning or are responding to others, this is when it is most enjoyable for me as a group facilitator to see people discovering insights about themselves and learning from others.

Ending of the group

The ending of a PD group will depend on the life and personality of the group. Where there has been a lot of cohesion and sharing, this may feel more difficult and painful with members not wanting to let go. Here as a facilitator I would allow a few weeks to prepare the group for the inevitable by encouraging people to talk about it. Pretending it isn't going to happen is common, where students say they will keep in touch or they are staying on for another course. At this point I will emphasise that the group is ending and will never meet in this format or configuration again.

Sometimes groups are split between members who are really mourning the ending of the group and those who can't wait to finish and end their course. This is more difficult as a facilitator as some people have really valued the group but others still haven't got what it is about. In spite of this, it is important to acknowledge all feelings and to make sure there is an ending of some kind. I normally ask my groups what they would like to do to end and how they would like the final session to be and how I can facilitate this.

My group endings have normally included some reviewing, looking to the future and the formal saying of some final words or goodbyes. Sometimes I have used creative ways of doing this but my aim is to help the group have the best possible endings even if the group has had a lot of difficulties.

At times I have found endings very disappointing when people don't appear to have engaged, while other times there has been a real acknowledgement of the work that has been done and a sense of the distance travelled.

Where I have formed a positive and productive connection with groups, I can feel a sense of dread, sadness and loss that we are ending. These will be groups where people have been honest, delved deep and have shared a lot of themselves and where I have been able to build a good relationship with the group members.

On the other hand where groups have worked on a more superficial level or haven't bonded well with each other and me there will be less regret or difficult emotions for me to handle but I may feel some regret that the group did not achieve as much and will be questioning what else I could have done as a facilitator to enable the process. Here talking to my training supervisor and reviewing the life of the group is extremely important.

Conclusion

In this chapter I have shared my experiences of running personal development groups by looking at my role at the different stages of a group's development. I have particularly emphasised the importance of helping create a safe environment for groups to do the work and have referred to relevant research into this area.

I hope this chapter has given an insight into what is involved in the PD tutor role and its complexities as well as looking at the considerations that we have to take account of in our work. It is very difficult to get it right at times as all groups are different and life within a group is changeable over time. As tutors we have both a relationship with the whole group and a relationship with individuals in it. We are also in a dual relationship with students as their tutor and group facilitators.

The metaphor of the sea was used to show that it is not always plain sailing and that the facilitator has to be constantly alert to hazards and not become complacent when things appear to be going smoothly.

I hope I have shown that this work is both challenging and rewarding but at times can be emotional and personally demanding on many levels. In Chapter 8 I will look further at the difficulties I have faced as a PD tutor.

References

Gloster-Smith, J. (2004) Be here now – being present as a facilitator. *Counselling and Psychotherapy Journal*, 15(3), pp 44–46.

Lennie, C. (2007) The role of personal development groups in counsellor training: Understanding factors contributing to self-awareness in the personal development group. *British Journal of Guidance & Counselling*, 35(1), pp. 115–129.

Robson, M. and Robson, J. (2008) Exploration of participants' experiences of a personal development group held as part of a counselling psychology training group: Is it safe here? *Counselling Psychology Quarterly*, 21(4), pp. 371–382.

Rose, C. (2004) Using metaphor in groups. *Counselling and Psychotherapy Journal*, 15(4), pp. 29–31.

Tuckman, B. (1965) Developmental sequence in small groups. *Psychological Bulletin*, 63(6), pp. 384–399.

Chapter 8

Conflict and difficulties in personal development groups

Jayne Godward

Introduction

In the final chapter of this section I will look at some of the conflicts and difficulties which can arise in personal development (PD) groups. Conflict is not unusual in these groups and can occur between students and also between tutors and students. Based on my own research into tutor–student conflict in counsellor training (Godward, 2014) and personal experiences of conflict observed when facilitating PD groups, I will look at why conflict might occur and will explore ways in which this can be dealt with.

I will also touch on general difficulties which can arise which may affect the group process and the development of the group.

This chapter will explore:

* what conflict is and your reactions to this;
* the positive and negative effects of conflict;
* the reasons why conflict occurs in groups;
* research findings on dealing with conflict.

What is conflict?

Conflict can be defined as 'A disagreement and disaccord between two or more persons or groups due to several reasons and it surfaces when the needs, impulses and wishes of individuals do not correspond with those of others' (Argon, 2009, p. 1034). It is not surprising that conflict can occur in counsellor training where students are becoming particularly aware of their needs, may be vulnerable and are in usually a close working group with others, where there may be power differentials within the groups but particularly between tutors and students.

According to Corey and Corey (1997, p. 182) 'conflict is inevitable in all relationships, including groups, it is avoidance of conflict that makes it destructive'. They believe conflict is normal and say it is essential to deal with it so that groups can move on and develop. As we saw in the last chapter, storming is a stage that most groups go through in order to develop and mature (Tuckman, 1965).

If there were no conflicts or arguments in a group what do you think might be happening?

There are a number of possibilities including:

- The group has a norm of being nice to each other but individuals are not being honest about how they are feeling.
- It is not seen as acceptable to be annoyed or angry with someone and to express this.
- Dominant people in the group have their say but no one dares challenge them.
- One person is seen as a problem in the group rather than dealing with the group's difficulties openly. This is known as scapegoating. This person may end up leaving or becoming an outsider.

All groups develop greater intimacy and honesty through knowing that the conductor (group leader) and group members can accept and contain aggressive and destructive feelings. Otherwise the storm may be pushed into one person who becomes an outsider and leaves or the group may remain in a pallid place where no serious work can be done.

(Barnes et al., 1999, p. 74)

Our backgrounds and earlier relationships will have an impact on how we view conflict or disagreements. In groups, students often want to avoid this at all costs or do not think it is something that should happen. Another aspect which some people find hard to tolerate is other people's anger. In some households anger is not seen as an acceptable emotion so it is denied and may come out in other ways.

How do you feel about conflict?

Consider your earlier experiences of arguing or 'fighting' with others in your family.

What were these situations like? What feelings has it left in you?
What was it like for you when someone became angry with you?
What was it like for you when you became angry?
How did these situations affect you? How has it impacted on your view of conflict now as an adult and trainee counsellor?
What would you do if a client you were working with challenged you or was angry with you or expressed anger at someone else?

The positive and negative effects of conflict

Conflict can be seen in positive and negative ways. Although there is a lack of research into this area in counsellor training, in the research into supervisory relationships, it was found that conflict in these helped trainees learn how to manage difficult relationships with clients (Nelson et al., 2008).

Students who came through conflicts in these relationships learnt to accept feedback and improved their relationships with their supervisors. So it is possible that being able to work through conflicts with peers or tutors in a PD group will help students to be able to manage conflicts elsewhere.

Case study: The Wednesday PD group

The Wednesday PD group is made up of ten individuals who are in their first year of counsellor training. There has been good banter in the group and the atmosphere has been warm, with most people sharing something. One group member, Maria, has missed several group meetings and often arrives a little late for the group. People are starting to make comments about this like 'Where is Maria today?' 'She's late again.' Eventually one person, Rukhsana says something to Maria. 'How come you are always late Maria? I thought we had a group contract regarding boundaries and timekeeping?' Maria immediately becomes defensive and says she is sorry but she has a lot on at home and her bus is always late. Other people start to join in saying that they manage this, so why can't she and there is a lot of talking at once.

Maria is becoming visibly upset and feels as if the group is becoming a pack of wolves attacking her. The facilitator, Kate, has let this run for a while rather than jumping in but realises things are getting out of hand. She feels she needs to protect Maria. She has to assert her authority and steps in to ask the group to pause and observes that everyone is speaking at once. She invites each person to have their say but own it with 'I' rather than it being a 'you' and an attack against Maria. Things calm down and she acts as a mediator between group members and Maria. People are able to explore how they are feeling and Maria is given more space to explain her situation and her responsibilities at home.

In this case, the situation was resolved and the scapegoating of Maria was reduced. The tutor avoided defending and siding with Maria, and avoided the attack being directed at her. The incident had a positive effect on the group and people felt able to express how they felt rather than letting resentments build up or being passively aggressive.

On the downside, when a conflict does occur in a PD group, the whole atmosphere can be affected and this can cause a lot of anxiety and stress for both the group members and the tutor/s involved, particularly if this spirals out of control.

Nelson and Friedlander (2001) found that supervisees who went through negative experiences of conflict lost trust and felt unsafe, powerless and undervalued. If this is applied to the PD group and a conflict is not managed well then a similar situation may arise where people may feel unable to contribute or share personal experiences.

Case study: The Friday group

This is a counselling diploma group that has been meeting for nearly a year. Generally things have gone smoothly although people don't normally share anything too deep. The tutor, Kate is feeling frustrated with a group member, Simon, who never contributes and she feels he is having a negative impact on the group. She decides to challenge him about this. She does this in a fairly gentle way but he responds as if she is picking on him. Some other group members come to his defence and Kate becomes the target of criticism. She responds with a sharp remark and the discussion becomes quite heated. In the end she stops the group and says that they will finish there for the day. Kate feels upset and does not want to return to the group the following week. Many in the group are left disgruntled and unhappy. At the next session there is a deadly silence. People have got the message that it is not OK to express negative emotions. The group has reached an impasse. It is going to be very difficult to recover from this situation.

Kate, the group facilitator has taken this to her PD group supervision and comes in feeling calm. She models to the group by being honest about how she is feeling and then allows different people to speak without arguing with them and being defensive. She regains her empathy for individuals, including Simon. The group is shaken but gradually regains its composure and the work in future weeks is more honest and real rather than being superficial.

As we saw in the last chapter, students who went through conflict and were unharmed by it, developed confidence in the group's safety and were able to work more effectively (Robson and Robson, 2008). However, from my own experience, some conflicts are not resolved adequately and groups can become stuck in a stage where they do not go on to perform well and their interactions remain at a superficial level, which does not allow for real personal development. Or there may be a split in the group between group members who really use the group and others who feel unable to do so due to their fears over self-disclosure.

The reasons why conflict occurs in PD groups

In this section I will combine a look at the reasons for conflict with an examination of how this plays out in practice in PD groups using case study examples.

The key reasons why conflict occurs in counsellor training were identified by Connor (1994) and Thomas (1998) as follows:

- the personal issues and vulnerabilities of both the facilitator and the trainee counsellor;
- the need for trust and safety in trainees;
- interpersonal dynamics;
- power relationships;
- role conflict and ambiguity.

These can directly relate to what occurs in PD groups as follows below.

Personal issues and vulnerabilities of both the facilitator and the trainee counsellor

Moskowitz and Rupert (1983), writing about conflict resolution in supervision, found that conflicts involving personality factors were the most difficult to resolve because they involved 'the individual's characteristic styles of interacting or sensitive personal issues' (p. 640). Therefore individuals in a PD group may clash with each other due to their patterns of relating or because sensitive personal issues are stimulated by the other person. Perhaps here a lack of empathy is playing a part.

As a tutor, I have found that it is difficult to empathise with someone who is criticising me or suggesting how I can do something better, as I can experience this as a threatening situation. However, in this situation the group member is often feeling insecure and wants to control the environment or is covering this up by asserting their authority, as in the example below.

Case study: Vivienne

Vivienne had a difficult childhood and was brought up by an alcoholic mother. Her father left the family when she was six years old. She could not rely on her mother and had to take charge of her younger brother and make sure her mother was alright when she was drinking heavily. Her way of coping was to make sure she was in control of all situations.

She is now a social worker and has entered counselling training in order to be able to counsel alcoholics and support their families in a therapeutic way.

She finds the PD group very unsettling as there is no structure as such and the facilitator, Nigel, is not directing the session. She feels like she must take charge and be the 'responsible adult' as the tutor is not doing this.

When the tutor asks the group for feedback a few weeks in, Vivienne is quite scathing of what is going on. How are they supposed to learn if there is no direction? Can Nigel bring in some self-awareness exercises, so that they can get started? She says that when she is running groups at work she leads more and this seems to work.

It is not uncommon as a facilitator to be challenged in this way by students. What is required is to step back from it and pause and think about what might be going on for Vivienne. She is in unknown territory here. It feels unsafe for her and she is trying to make it safe. Although counterintuitive, instead of battling with Vivienne, Nigel needs to hear what she is saying and acknowledge this and maybe explore how she is feeling about being in this group. Vivienne needs boosting, not knocking down. Her way of coping has always been to take control. For all her assertiveness and outward strength, Vivienne's self-esteem may be quite low and careful handling is required.

However, if Nigel, the tutor is also feeling vulnerable, he may not find it as easy to respond in a measured way. For example, if he has just had a fall out with his partner or if he has just been turned down for a promotion, his self-worth may be low and this may feel like another knock to him and may feed into his insecurities. Here, his own supervision will be vital in helping him see what is his stuff and what is the student's material.

The need for trust and safety in trainees

This need for trust and safety has already been emphasised in this chapter and Chapter 7 when we looked at beginning the group. As with counselling, unless the PD group feels like a safe space to disclose, people will not share personal information. This is highlighted more here as it is not just a one-to-one situation but often students feel like they are under the spotlight.

Safety may be established but then broken because of breaches in boundaries which then causes conflict within the group. Examples are when students talk about what has happened in a PD group outside the group and other group members find out or when people don't feel safe in the group because they fear or even perceive judgemental attitudes. This links with people not being listened to or sensing disapproval.

Occasionally there is even more of an upheaval when a tutor leaves or there is a change in facilitator:

> What hasn't been helpful is a change of tutor part way through the course. It's felt disjointed and the group has had to form all over again with the associated discomfort of the storming and norming phases. This has resulted in the group going from feeling like a safe supportive space where development happens to a defensive place where communication is more difficult. This has given me a different perspective of PD groups and without the feeling of safety I feel my development and willingness to be vulnerable has been reduced.
>
> (Ex-diploma student)

Interpersonal dynamics

Within any one-to-one or group situation it is important to attend to the interpersonal dynamics that might occur. Becoming aware of these might help us understand how we can move forward with our personal development. According to Barnes et al., 1999, p. 74), 'the earliest childhood relationships have a profound effect on later personal development and this will, in turn, affect relationships within a group setting' (see Chapter 11 where we look at attachment styles).

As a PD group tutor I have experienced transference, countertransference and projection and have observed this happening in the groups I have been with. See Chapter 5 for definitions of these and an example of transference where a group member reacted to another group member as if she was her mother-in-law due to the way she spoke to her.

In one PD group, a male student snapped at me sharply after I had asked him something. Later he realised I reminded him of an ex-partner who had been abusive. It was something about how I looked or spoke. We were able to explore this and look at this more.

In another group, a student reminded me of a surly teenager who I had known at school, who kept causing trouble in class. Because this person was challenging me, I responded as if she was the teenager and this led to an exchange where she then saw me like her mother and she was like a teenage daughter. I realised I needed to step out of this to look at what was going on.

Between group members similar processes can occur. Frequently I have observed students projecting how they are feeling about themselves onto others, particularly if there is not a lot of open communication going on.

For example, Shanaya's experience in Chapter 4:

> my issues with trust and rejection came to the surface while doing the course. I attempted being vocal about this when I felt rejected from a group member as she

did not maintain eye contact with me. However, it turned out that she felt anxious and therefore looked away sometimes. I realised that my conclusion was more due to my own issues and perception, and that others interpreted the group member's reduced eye contact differently, which was interesting to see.

This could have led to conflict; if Shanaya had said nothing then there would have been no personal learning. So being able to explore interpersonal dynamics is the bread and butter of PD group work.

For tutors a common experience is to be seen as the authority figure no matter how much you are trying to facilitate or be democratic. Sometimes this goes a step further when a student's transference is to see you as an authority figure from the past with negative effects, e.g., a parent, partner, etc. This might lead to them being confrontational and to them not seeing you as you really are. We will explore this more below in the next section.

Activity

Think about your PD tutor or course tutors:

Do they remind you of anyone from the past or present?
What are your feelings towards them?
How do you behave when you are with them?
Is there any transference going on here for you?

Power relationships

Whatever I do to equalise the situation, as a PD tutor I have got some authority and power over the group members. I need to help set the boundaries and I am facilitating the session. I am also part of a course team. This may mean that any dissatisfaction with the course can be directed at me and also group members may decide to attack me because they fear something from me rather than waiting to be attacked. If their experience of authority figures has been negative, it is likely that their trust in me might be lacking. If as a child they were let down, then they may be highly sensitive to how I hold the group as a facilitator. This has happened to me with most groups I have facilitated where there has been a vulnerable group member who cannot trust they will be safe because their primary care givers were not reliable.

In terms of power relationships between group members, sometimes there are dominant group members who have an influence on the group and will argue with those who do not agree with them. Because of their dominance, they set the group norms and anyone who is different becomes the target for an attack, as in the Wednesday PD group example.

Role conflict

In my research involving nine experienced counselling tutors who were also therapists, a difficult issue was the danger of role conflict. Some became confused between their therapist role and the tutor role. While they really wanted to be therapeutic and supportive in the way they dealt with trainees, being a tutor necessitates carrying out assessments and making judgements about a student's work and ultimately deciding on passing or failing. The PD group particularly highlights these issues as we are encouraging students to share and offering therapeutic qualities and using therapeutic type skills, but at the same time we are tutors as well.

Students sometimes had strong reactions to tutors who did not live up to their expectations of what a therapist should be like. Tutors said:

> 'They have us on a pedestal and see us in a certain way and when we don't act in that way they can take it quite personally and be hurt and angry.' Another said simply: 'I can't always be the therapist they might want me to be.'
>
> (Godward, 2014, p. 20)

In the past, PD groups were often only facilitated by therapists who just had that role and did not have other teaching on programmes. But this is not always possible as courses and staff teams may be small and tutors have to be involved with other roles on the course.

In one group I experienced a lot of conflict with a student who did not trust me because she thought I would assess her negatively and that I could fail her based on her contributions in the PD group. This is a real issue where you are a PD group tutor with other roles and responsibilities on a course. In this kind of situation students are very unlikely to share personal details if they think these will show them up in a negative light.

Here the need for very clear contracting at the beginning of the group and an explanation of the PD tutor's role is needed. Students need to know what might be disclosed by tutors outside the PD group room and when a disclosure might be needed. Clear guidelines on assessment may be needed to show that students are not being assessed for their contributions in class but on other tasks they perform, e.g., written reflections, etc. From experience these need to be done early on to avoid misunderstandings.

Dealing with conflict

The main themes are:

* the tutor's approach;
* the professional trainer role;
* providing appropriate opportunity to share and discuss;
* using the group;
* reflection.

I will explore these below but will also make links to dealing with student–student conflict.

Tutor's approach: Hearing and understanding the student

This was seen as important by all participants that as a tutor you work hard to hear what students are saying if they are in conflict with you.

> When people feel aggrieved, what they want even more than a head on a plate is to feel heard in their distress.
>
> (Tutor)

Tutors felt that if the student felt listened to they would also then listen to the tutor's point of view. However, if a student can't hear the tutor or others in their group they are not going to take feedback and learn from this on the course and in their PD group and may not even be listening to clients with different viewpoints.

Many of the participants in my study really wanted to empathise and understand the student's point of view and to actively find out what was going on for the person through questioning them. To do this, you needed to avoid being defensive and to show a genuine interest in the person and even be prepared to apologise if they were at fault. It was seen as important to be non-judgemental and to be fair. This fit really well with the Person-Centred tutors who would be modelling the core conditions to students during a conflict situation.

The same principles above would apply between PD group members in conflict, where it would be important for group members to listen to each other, even if this was challenging, and try not to be defensive but hear the other person's point of view. Sometimes in groups there may have to be an agreement that it is OK not to agree with everything or for others not to agree with you but all views are respected. This can be contracted for at the beginning of the group to anticipate conflict situations.

The professional trainer role

We have spoken earlier about role conflict and what this raises for tutors and students. Sometimes it was very hard for tutors to accept the responsibility they have as a trainer and to take on the trainer role. Participants acknowledged that it was part of their role to manage conflict and model conflict management approaches. Tutors spoke here about the effort it required to do this job and the resilience required to remain professional. Tutors had to leave out their personal feelings and be assertive, not taking things personally. Hearing people talking about this and reading their accounts, it was clear that it did not come naturally for these therapists to maintain this role and it wasn't easy to bear the personal effects.

Many reported the difficulty of dealing with anger, projection, not being liked and feeling irritated and annoyed.

Similarly when students are in groups where there is conflict, it may be very hard dealing with the above and there may be effects on the group members that stay with them when they leave the group. Sometimes students cope with this by taking their reactions to personal therapy, on other occasions students book tutorials to look at how they are before they go back into the group. As a PD tutor I would always encourage students to bring their reactions back into the group and would support students to talk about how they are feeling there.

Providing an appropriate opportunity and environment for sharing and discussion

It was seen as important that students are given the opportunity to air their thoughts and feelings and that tutors are approachable. Some participants said that students were told that they could come and see them if they felt aggrieved in some way and they could talk to them about any issues. Sometimes I have met with students in tutorial who are struggling with other group members but I always encourage them to take their concerns or difficulties back into the group as what is occurring in the group needs to be dealt with within the boundary of the group, if possible.

Sometimes tutors have to mediate between participants in groups and this often takes place in the PD group as has been seen in some of the earlier examples in this chapter. Here the importance of letting everyone speak and not taking sides is important.

Tutors felt that you should not react on the spot to situations; however, it was not good to leave issues for too long.

Using the group

Linked to the above, most participants in the study felt that the course group or PD group should be used to resolve conflict and issues rather than the tutor trying to deal with issues on a one-to-one basis with students or outside the group. There were two parts to this point. One is to prepare students for dealing with conflict through contracting at the beginning and also by actually discussing how conflict would be managed if it arose.

Second, if there was conflict in the group, tutors wanted to put exercises in which would help or involve other students in managing the conflict rather than it being just focused on the individuals concerned.

The other thing tutors wanted to do was to encourage the group to challenge each other. It was seen as better for other students to challenge as this was from a peer rather than coming from a tutor, where it might be seen as 'top-down' and too powerful in a negative way.

There was a downside to trying to use the group to resolve conflict and that is in some cases, students wanted to rescue others and further conflict might occur, where the group becomes divided.

Reflection

The tutors in the study felt that reflection was essential in conflict management for all parties involved. The tutor and student needed to go away and think about their parts in the conflict. A tutor in conflict said she needed to 'separate her stuff from the student's stuff'. Another said they gave a student chance to reflect on what they (the tutors) had said.

Some tutors saw being able to reflect on one's own behaviour as one of the goals of training, so if a student was not able to do this, then they might be seen as not suitable to continue on the course or at least qualify.

This sounds stark but actually the whole theme of this book is about increasing self-awareness and being aware of our behaviour and relational patterns.

Reflection seemed to be a central theme in the research I did, as it is both a process and an end goal in counselling training

Successful conflict resolution

To sum up the findings of the research study, Diagram 8.1 is my pictorial representation showing the importance of both parties being heard, reflection taking place and then some personal development occurring or insight which enables the relationship to be restored and then the student is able to progress. Obviously this is the ideal and this is what successful conflict resolution would look like, whereas sometimes this might only be partially achieved with the relationship between the two parties not being fully restored but repaired enough for students to progress.

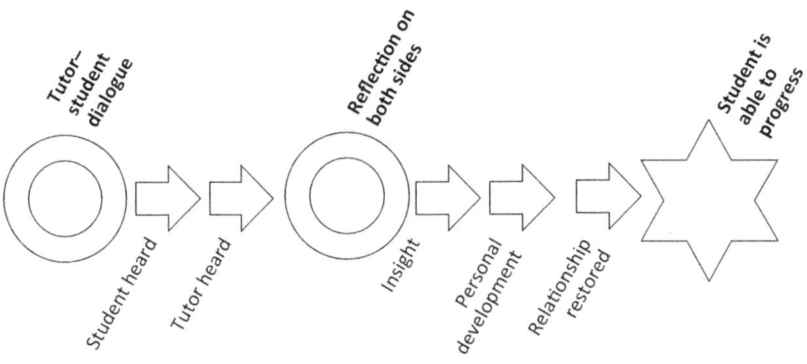

Diagram 8.1 Process of successful conflict resolution

In terms of PD groups where the conflict is between members the same principles apply of students hearing what the other is saying and both being encouraged to reflect on what is going on and hopefully gaining some insight to allow for progression and some resolution so that the students and the group can move on.

Conclusion

In this chapter I have discussed what conflict is and how it is a normal and inevitable factor in relationships and in groups. I have explored its usefulness and disadvantages using case study examples to highlight this.

I have discussed the reasons why conflict occurs and have related this to PD groups. Once again, as in other places in this book, the issues of trust and safety have been seen as important factors that, if absent, might contribute to conflict.

Aspects of transference, countertransference and projection have been touched upon when looking at interpersonal dynamics as these may contribute to conflict between peers and between students and tutors.

Power relationships and tutor role conflict seem to be linked together in that the tutor role brings with it real and perceived authority, which can cause difficulties and conflict in PD groups.

Finally, my focus was on how to deal with conflict based on my findings from the research I had carried out into tutor–student conflict (Godward, 2014) with a summary of some of the results from this, ending with a diagrammatic representation of how conflict can be resolved, which could be applied to student–student conflict as well as student–tutor conflicts.

References

Argon, T. (2009) The development and implementation of a scale to the causes of conflict in the classroom of university students. *Education Science: Theory and Practice*, 9(3), pp. 1033–1041.

Barnes, B., Ernst, S. and Hyde, K. (1999) An Introduction to Groupwork: A Group Analytic Perspective. London: Macmillan.

Connor, M. (1994) *Training the Counsellor: An Integrative Model.* London: Routledge

Corey, M.S. and Corey, G. (1997) *Groups: Process and Practice.* Belmont: Brooks/Cole.

Godward, J. (2014) Student-tutor conflict in counsellor training. *Therapy Today,* 25(8), pp. 18–21.

Moskowitz, S. and Rupert, P. (1983) Conflict resolution within the supervisory relationship. *Professional Psychology: Research and Practice,* 14(5), pp. 632–641.

Nelson, M.L. and Friedlander, M.L. (2001) A close look at conflictual supervisory relationships: The trainee's perspective. *Journal of Counselling Psychology,* 48(4), pp. 384–395.

Nelson, M.L., Barnes, K.L., Evans, A.L and Triggiano, P.J. (2008) Working with conflict in clinical supervision: Wise supervisor's perspectives. *Journal of Counselling Psychology,* 55(2), pp. 172–184.

Robson, M. and Robson, J. (2008) Exploration of participants' experiences of a personal development group held as part of a counselling psychology training group: Is it safe in here? *Counselling Psychology Quarterly,* 21(4), pp. 371–382.

Thomas, A., (1998) The stresses of being a counsellor trainer. In H. Johns (ed.), *Balancing Acts: Studies in Counselling Training.* London: Routledge.

Tuckman, B. (1965) Developmental sequence in small groups. *Psychological Bulletin,* 63(6), pp. 384–399.

Section C

Developing self-awareness to enhance practice

Chapter 9

Ethics and personal development
Understanding personal ethics

Heather Dale

Introduction

The very word *ethics* can make people yawn. I think this is because it appears to be one of those meaningless philosophical concepts that has very little do with our daily lives. However, ethics are very much part of our everyday life, as they are about what we consider to be morally right or wrong. Most people have a set of values and principles that they live by, whether or not these are conscious or unconscious, and, put together, this is all that ethics are – the lived experiences of our values and principles. Examples of ethical conversations may include discussions regarding the right to die (euthanasia); whether or not abortion should be legal or illegal; when a friend or colleague discusses leaving their partner; or whether to tell an employer that a friend and colleague is stealing from the office. These are ethical conversations because they involve making moral judgements based on one's own values. Another way of saying this is that each of these discussions involves a statement of an ethical position. So in this chapter you will be introduced to:

*   the concepts of ethics;
*   three of the most common types of ethical codes;
*   why an understanding of ethics matters within counselling and psychotherapy;
*   personal ethics and personal development (PD).

Ethics: A beginning

To start off, try the quiz in the box.

Activity

Consider this: What would you steal from the office?

Stationery?
Laptop?
Electricity? (by, e.g., plugging in a mobile)
Food?
Money?

For each answer jot down your thinking.

Most people would probably draw the line at stealing actual money from their work, but may take stationery, or use the work printer to print off personal material or plug in a mobile that is only used for personal calls. However, all these things will cost the institution money and could be considered forms of theft. (This does not apply to your training organisation – your fees pay for your use of electricity.) You might want to discuss this idea with your friends and colleagues and find out what your thinking is. Some people will argue that it is perfectly all right to do these things, and some might not. However, the discussion itself will be a discussion about ethics; that is, about what is right and what is wrong.

An ethical conversation involves considering moral values and judgements and ultimately concluding about what is a right course of action and what is a wrong one according to one's own judgement. Of course, not everyone will come to the same conclusion, so one of the fascinating complexities of ethical thinking is that there is no one right answer.

Activity

Can you think of any ethical conversations that have come up in the PD group? Examples might be:

Wondering what to do if a fellow member of the group appears too angry.
Another person saying something that you perceive as homophobic and deciding whether or not to challenge them.

The conversations mentioned above are all examples of personal ethics: that is, the ethical conversations we have in everyday life. Professional ethics, on the other hand, are concerned with the ethical codes that need to be adhered to in a working life. Sometimes these may clash but generally, in a working life, professional ethics trump personal ethics, although there may be cases where personal values are so out of sync with professional values that the only option may be to leave the job.

Personal ethics versus professional ethics

Can you think of some examples of where your personal ethics and professional ethics may clash? Examples might include: a client who wishes to go to Dignitas to end their lives whereas the counsellor feels strongly that suicide is wrong; a client or a colleague who express strong racist or homophobic views; a client who tells of having had an affair with a previous therapist. These are not always easy decisions to make, but the therapist has to decide whether they are able to maintain a position of non-judgemental unconditional positive regard or whether their personal ethics are so outraged that they cannot work with this client.

In short, personal ethics can be defined as a personal set of values that determine how individuals live their lives and how they might deal with situations that arise in everyday life.

Professional ethics on the other hand, are those which define professional or working lives, and are usually written in terms of a code.

What is an ethical code?

At its very simplest, an ethical code is a set of moral rules (Dale, 2010). Taken individually, these consist of values, such as being helpful or patient or assertive, being conscientious, hardworking or putting family first. Taken altogether, they become a set of rules or a code. So, an ethical code really just means a set of moral rules or imperatives.

Most of us will already have an ethical (or moral) code that we may have taken from our parents or caregivers and that we have probably added to as we come across more and different value systems. This may be outside of our conscious awareness or we may have made conscious decisions to change as we develop. In part, the aim of not just the PD group but personal development work in counsellor training generally is to allow students to become more aware of their ethical choices.

Case study: Jane

Let's look at the case of Jane, who grew up in a large family where everyone, including friends and relatives, drank immoderately and regularly used illegal drugs. In addition, petty crime as a way of making money was considered normal, and time spent in prison as a result considered an unfortunate by-product.

As a child and even as young adult, Jane took this way of life for granted, assuming that everyone did these things. In copying the behaviours she perceived as normal, she herself became addicted to various substances and later sold drugs herself, although only to other users; as part of her moral code she believed that it was wrong to start people on drugs. She also believed, as she had been taught, that drug- dealing was a legitimate source of income, and that it did not hurt anyone as no one was forced to buy, so only those who wanted drugs were buying and they would buy them anyway.

Effectively, Jane made a living in the same way she had seen members of her family do, seeing no harm in it and as a way to earn a living. She received short prison sentences along the way but accepted these as part of her career choice. In her forties, having developed her business into the international stage, Jane was caught with large amounts of drugs and received a considerably longer prison sentence than she had served so far. This time, as an older woman, she noticed that there were young people in prison who had been harmed by their drug use. Jane began to reconsider whether in fact her actions had harmed young people, and realised that in fact they may well have done.

While in prison, Jane was able to join some classes. In time, when she left prison, Jane decided to train as a counsellor so that she would be able to help others who had had similar earlier life experiences.

In the scenario, Jane was able to rethink her ethical position and gain a greater understanding of the impact of her actions on others. In order to do this, she had to reconsider her values and principles and rewrite her ethical code.

> - When you were a child, what values were you taught which were important? E.g., family first, keep secrets, look after others before yourself.
> - What have you learned in the PD group about other people's moral codes?

Organisational codes

An ethical code for organisations comes about when groups of people form a club, an organisation or an institution and decide which principles they share and would like all members of that organisation to sign up to.

Most educational institutions will almost certainly have a code like this which students are required to sign up to prior to starting their studies. I wonder how many students read this information before signing and if so whether they remember what they have signed up to.

Personal development groups can be seen as a mini-organisation and it may be that in your PD group, there is an established set of rules for the group. These might include arriving and finishing on time, issues of confidentiality and what can be said inside and outside the group, and listening to each other. These rules become the ethical code that all group members should abide by. If you have not started your course yet, notice whether these rules are imposed by the group leader or whether the group is invited to develop them. You can also notice your feelings and thoughts about the way in which the group rules are made.

In addition, all reputable counselling organisations have codes of ethics, and while there are some variations, these are often fairly similar to each other with an emphasis on maintaining confidentiality, clarity of information, and adherence to some basic principles (which will be discussed in a later chapter). Everyone who joins these has to agree to the relevant ethical code. Because the codes are public documents, this means that violations or breaches can be reported by clients and the practitioner can be required to explain themselves to the organisation. If the alleged violations are found to be correct, sanctions may be imposed with the strongest being the withdrawal of membership. In countries such as the USA, where psychotherapy is a regulated profession, this may equate to the loss of livelihood. In the UK, there is a system of voluntary regulation, which means joining a professional body such as BACP or UKCP is not essential. However, many if not most training organisations, as well as employers, ask as a given that employees are accredited or registered members of a professional body and losing that status may result in loss of job. However, for practitioners who are members of more than one organisation, care needs to be taken to ensure compliance with both codes.

I argue that not being part of a regulatory body such as BACP or UKCP is in itself unethical, as the client has no right of complaint or redress. However, before joining an organisation, it is a good idea to read their ethical code first to ensure willingness to comply.

Types of ethics

Ethical thinking (ethical mindfulness) can be traced back down the centuries at least as far as ancient Greeks such as Socrates, Plato and Aristotle. There are various philosophical ways of understanding ethical theories and ethical systems, which can be interesting to explore but for the purpose of this chapter I am going to focus on the systems most commonly used within the counselling and psychotherapy professions and look at their practical applications within the profession.

The types of ethical systems most commonly used in the profession are mandatory (deontological or duty-bound) and aspirational or virtue ethical codes. For example, the BACP currently has a code, called *Ethical Framework for the Counselling Professions* (2018) which is a mixture of mandatory and aspirational ethics. When you have finished reading this chapter, have a look at this framework, which you can find on the BACP website at www.bacp.co.uk, and decide which paragraphs are mandatory and which are aspirational.

What are mandatory ethics?

Mandatory or deontological (duty-bound) ethics are moral rules or codes that are imposed by an organisation or an authority. These codes consist of rules that must be adhered to. An early example of a mandatory code is the Ten Commandments from the Judaeo-Christo Bible. According to the story as told in the Bible, these are commandments given to Moses at a time when the Jews had been wandering around the desert for some years and were drifting into a state of anarchy. Moses climbed a mountain, called Sinai, and spoke with God who told him to hammer these commandments onto two tablets of stone. One tablet consisted of commandments regarding relationships within society and the other tablet relates to the relationship with a higher being.

The Ten Commandments, whatever one's chosen belief system, are a good example of mandatory codes as they consist of orders that were imposed upon a people with the intention of bringing discipline back into their lives. They are rules that must be obeyed, on pain of death in this case (Deuteronomy 11:13–21). In some societies today, breaking rules might still end in death.

> How many of the Judaeo-Christo commandments can you write down? (See the end of this chapter for a full list.)
> Do you think any of these are relevant today and if so, which ones?
> Are there any other mandatory values you would like to impose on society as a whole?

The big advantage of mandatory codes is their clarity: those who follow them have a clear and unambiguous set of rules for living their lives. There is no room for disagreement as these are rules that must be obeyed unquestioningly within that particular group. In many ways that makes life quite simple as it is just a matter of following the rules. For those who like to know where they are in life, and for those who like a clear statement of how to act, mandatory codes may work well.

However, the disadvantage of a mandatory or duty-bound code is the lack of flexibility. A set of compulsory rules that must be followed can be helpful, but they do not allow for any grey areas. The code is not to be thought about but merely followed.

Activity

Within a PD group, an example of a compulsory rule might be a rule that says members of the group must not discuss what happens in the group outside the group, in the same way that therapists do not discuss clients outside the group.

Can you see any issues that might cause for you?
If you are already in a PD group, think about whether or not you have ever discussed the material that comes up with anyone else, either within your training group or at home.
Consider how easy or difficult that particular rule has been for you to follow.
Was it easy because you are naturally a reticent person, or was it hard because your natural way of being is to want to talk things through?

For the trainee counsellor a clear set of rules is often appreciated; but later, as experience grows, a mandatory code may be confining rather than comforting. In any case, one set of proscribed rules rarely covers every situation: ethical dilemmas in therapy as in other areas of life, are rarely black and white but have many grey areas

Utilitarian ethics

This is a form of ethics developed by Jeremy Bentham (1748–1832) and John Stuart Mill (1806–1873). The idea behind this branch of ethics is that decisions should be made on the basis of what will bring the greatest happiness to the greatest number of people.

In a PD group, an example of utilitarian ethics may be if one or two people are taking up much time in the group, to the detriment of the larger number. In this case the group facilitator may make an ethical decision to silence the speakers in the interest of the majority of the group. However, it may be that the 'talkers' need to do so as it is their particular way of learning and understanding. In that case they may be severely disadvantaged by being silenced.

Again, what do you think of this?
Should individuals have to bow to the majority, or should the majority take up the needs of the individuals?

As always there is no one right answer, but hopefully the above gives you food for thought.

Utilitarian ethics can be summed up as 'the ends justify the means'.

Aspirational or virtue ethics

Aspirational or virtual ethics originate with Aristotle and continue with Jean Paul Sartre (1905–1980). Aspirational codes consist of ideals to be reached for with the understanding that sometimes practitioners may fall short.

Aspirational codes therefore are not lists of 'musts' or 'shoulds' but intended to encourage best practice. They ask the question, not 'what must I do?' but 'what is the best I can do?' Because this means that they are not solely about justice or the greater good, (and in therapy in particular), they can focus more on care and nurturing.

Aspirational ethics can be hard to follow as there is not a clear set of guidance to follow and they rely more on the innate qualities of the therapist. Because of this, they also require ceaseless self-examination, which may not be to everyone's taste. In particular they may be hard for trainees who may prefer set rules to follow.

Let's look at the PD group again. In this scenario, the rule that anything that is said in the group stays in the group is an aspirational rule not a mandatory one. Consider how that might change your behaviour and whether that is for better or worse. In this scenario, you might have to make a decision for yourself rather than follow or not follow a decision imposed on you.

In some ways this second scenario is harder as you must make your own decision rather than follow a set of proscribed rules, but it might make it easier to bring the issue back to the group at a later stage.

Why are ethics particularly important in counselling and therapy?

Unlike other professions, therapy is perhaps unique in the fact that one's personal and professional ethics are closely tied together. Most people enter counselling in order to be of help to others, to do good, but it is all too easy to confuse doing good with 'overdoing' and therefore allowing a slippage of professional boundaries that will probably be to the detriment of the client. Knowledge of the ethical code of your professional organisation can help appreciate where helping stops and inappropriate rescuing begins.

Within counselling or therapy organisations there are three main principles behind ethical codes or frameworks:

- To offer a frame, or a boundary that protects the relationship, in order to create a safe space in which helping can happen.
- To protect therapist and client from exploitation.
- To set a minimum standard for professional practice (below which standards should not fall (Corey et al., 2007; Dale, 2010; Bond, 2016).

Let's take these one at a time:

Offering a frame or boundary. The therapeutic relationship is a very special one. It is so special that the renowned psychotherapist Irving Yalom once wrote 'it's the relationship that heals'. This is a quotation that has been used many times since and most practitioners would agree that the relationship is key to change (Cooper and Lesser, 2011). What Yalom means is that it is the quality of the relationship between therapist and client rather than therapeutic techniques that determines whether the client makes their desired changes.

However, because the relationship is so special and intense, it is easy to confuse it with other forms of connections, particularly romantic or friendship relationships. Therefore, care has to be taken to make it clear that this is a relationship that can only take place within very specific boundaries of time and place, and where the focus of the time is completely on one person's (the client's) issues. It could be compared to the frame that surrounds a picture: there may be different types of frame but all of them enclose the picture tightly and make sure that there is no overlap. The ethical code is the manual that therapists use when thinking about the frame, and how they explain it to their clients.

Protect from exploitation. Within the counselling relationship, both client and therapist hold power, although this may be experienced differently at certain times. There may at times be a bid for more power from either position (client or counsellor) and it is therefore important to note that both need protecting from exploitation and manipulation.

A knowledge of the 'rules' that govern the relationship and adherence to a code of ethics on the therapist's part, allows boundary issues to be noted and dealt with. While this might sound obvious in theory, in practice it can become much harder. Common issues here include: the client who, in the last minutes of a session, discloses something important. Does the therapist give extra time, which might be seen as collusion, or stop on time, which might be seen as uncaring? Or the client who writes a long letter to the therapist between sessions: does the therapist read it outside of the session, in the session, or ignore it altogether? What does the therapist do if the client expresses sexual feelings that in fact are reciprocated? These are all common problems where exploitation on either side may happen and therefore examples of the need for a strong understanding of ethical principles, or a safe place to discuss them.

Set a minimum standard for professional practice (below which standards should not fall). Having a code of practice means that all members of that organisation adhere to certain standards. This does not mean that there is not a variation of working styles: of course, there will be, and that is not a bad thing. But ethical codes give basic standards that all members of the organisation agree to adhere to, which is likely to include some form of continuing professional development (CPD) each year. This means that practitioners have a duty to keep knowledge up-to-date.

As I write this, in the UK, changes are being made to data protection, which is something that practitioners need to be aware of, as it affects record-keeping, which, for BACP and other organisations, is a mandatory requirement, as is making these records easily available to the client (BACP, 2018). Not keeping accurate and accessible records may not only be a breach of an ethical standard but a legal one as well.

To summarise the above, adherence to an ethical code allows the setting of clear boundaries that can be acknowledged and agreed by all parties prior to work starting, and which means that misunderstandings later on are less likely to occur. It also means that practitioners can be held accountable both to clients and to the profession if their work drops below outlined minimum standards.

The argument against ethical codes is that they can be seen as squashing innovative ways of working and leave no room for pushing back of boundaries in the client's interests. This is true, but on balance the safety of the client is best protected with a clear set of guidelines.

Personal ethics in the PD group

So far, throughout this chapter, we have considered both personal and professional dilemmas. Remember that an ethical dilemma, whether personal or professional, can be defined as when there appear to be good, if contradictory, moral reasons for taking one or more course of action (Kitchener 1984). If there are not at least two equally ethical ways of solving an ethical dilemma it is not a dilemma but another issue altogether.

However, all practitioners, at whatever their level of training or experience, are faced with ethical dilemmas on a regular basis. Some may appear easy to solve and others more difficult, but all have to be thought about and a considered decision made, preferably in consultation with a supervisor or more experienced practitioners.

Discussing a dilemma, or a potential dilemma, out loud helps clarify the issue significantly more than any amount of self-talk. This is one of the very good reasons for the importance of regular supervision, again, at whatever level of experience. I notice in my own practice that it is more likely to be the experienced practitioners who recognise a dilemma and ask for a listening ear.

There are many examples of dilemmas both within the literature and within real-life practice, but some increasingly common ones might be: deciding whether or not to accept a client's invitation to connect on social media; whether or not to Google a client (remembering that there is a high chance they will have Googled prospective practitioners); or deciding whether or not to break client confidentiality.

Within training, the PD group goes hand-in-hand with supervision in helping trainees to begin to think ethically (ethical mindfulness) I wrote earlier in this chapter about the fact that PD groups often devise (or have imposed on them) group rules. It may be interesting and useful to look at these rules and decide whether they are mandatory (must be obeyed) or aspirational (best practice). What are the rules in your group? How were they decided? Did the group leader impose them on you, or did the group decide for themselves? The first way will take less time, but in the second way, the group may be readier to work to the rules and to call out anyone who does not adhere to them.

Activity

Take a moment to consider your group rules and how easy or hard it is to stay with them:

Are these rules you are happy to sign up to?
Do you ever break a rule? For example, discuss the group with friends or family?

Having considered the above, now consider what might happen if there were no rules at all. For example, many groups have a rule about punctuality. If that rule was not made explicit, it is possible that most group members would arrive on time anyway, in which case there being a rule makes no difference to behaviour. On the other hand, it is not uncommon, for example, for group members to break group rules despite having originally agreed them. Breaking the rule around confidentiality or keeping issues that come up in the group within the group can be especially troublesome. As discussed above, the rule generally states that what is said in the group should not be discussed outside the group. In more than 30 years of training I have never met a group where this rule has not been broken by one or more participants. In some groups, the numbers of people admitting to breaking this rule when asked outnumbered those who have not.

In part this is due to the dual relationships that group members find themselves in, where they are members of a closed group but also colleagues and perhaps friends outside of the group as well as working as each other's counsellors and clients during skills practice sessions. If something particularly emotive has happened in a group, it is human nature to wish to share it and the need to offload can be very strong. A common belief is that, in terms of confidentiality, be it the PD group or clients, it is somehow OK to discuss things with family or partners. Or, as I was once told 'I talk about it with my partner, because partners don't count'.

Deciding whether or not to discuss issues outside the group is an ethical decision and should be taken seriously

As trainees learn more about themselves, their beliefs and values and the origin of these, they will also be developing a personal ethical code as well as developing ideas of good practice. In terms of counsellor training, the PD group can be the place where theory and practice meet. Knowing about ethics in theory is fine but understanding how and whether you practice your ethics can be a different issue.

This means that having a good understanding of one's own ethical code helps us to see where other people fit with this. It may be that, in listening to others' stories in the group, it becomes easier to reflect on one's own codes and to consider whether or not it is still appropriate. The same is true the other way around: other people's codes may sound inappropriate and then this becomes a discussion topic within the group. For example, if a group member, in discussing their moral outlook appears to be stating an unethical position, each group member may need to consider their position. Alternatives might include doing nothing, using the group time to clarify what has been said, or going outside the group and discussing or reporting to a tutor or supervisor. Each of these scenarios is possible: each will have different possible repercussions to consider.

Part of the purpose of the PD group is to allow students time to consider their own moral position and to set this against that of others. In this way, it is possible to challenge your own beliefs or that of others in the group, and develop a broad base of ethical awareness. In a way, the PD group is a place where you can put what you have learned from reading about ethics into practice. It is also a place where you can test out theories and see if they stand up to discussion.

Conclusion

Now you have come to the end of this chapter, you might wish to go back and try out the exercises and see if your answers remain the same or differ. I hope you will have had a glimpse into the importance of ethics and ethical mindfulness, both in everyday life (personal ethics) and within counselling as a profession (professional ethics). There may be issues that come up in your PD group where a theoretical understanding of ethics will be a great help in explaining thinking around dilemmas.

While an understanding of theory does not necessarily equate to great practice, nevertheless, theoretical knowledge is an important tool in both thinking about and solving professional and personal issues. The decision itself is less important than having a clear rationale to support whatever course of action has been decided. That rationale needs to come from a deep understanding of professional ethics, and an understanding of their use in protecting the practitioner as well as the client.

The PD group, at its best, may offer a safe space to explore, among other issues, where the theory and practice of ethical behaviour meet and some of the dilemmas within that.

Ten commandments from the Judaeo-Christo Bible

1. Have no other gods but me
2. Do not worship idols
3. Don't swear
4. Keep one day a week for prayer
5. Honour your parents
6. Murder no one
7. Only sleep with your own partner, not someone else's (or anyone else)
8. Don't steal
9. Or lie
10. Don't envy what is not yours

References

BACP (2018) *Ethical Framework for the Counselling Professions*. Lutterworth: BACP.

Bond, T. (2016) *Standards and Ethics for Counselling in Action*. London: Sage.

Cooper, M.G. and Leeser, J.G. (2011) *Clinical Social Work Practices an Integrated Approach* (4th edn). Boston, MA: Allyn & Bacon.

Corey, G., Schneider Corey, M. and Callanan, P. (2007) *Issues and Ethics in the Helping Professions*. Belmont: Thomson/Brook Cole.

Dale, H. (2010) Can ethics be sexy? *The Independent Practitioner*, p. 11.

Kitchener, K.S. (1984) Intuition, critical evaluation and ethical principles: The foundation for ethical decisions in counseling psychology. *The Counseling Psychologist*, 12(1), 43–45.

Yalom, I. (2013) *Love's Executioner*. London: Penguin

Chapter 10

Personal moral qualities

Heather Dale

Introduction

In the previous chapter, I discussed the idea of aspirational ethics. Integral to this change is the idea of values and ethics. These are widely discussed within the therapeutic community (Palmer Barnes and Murdin, 2001; Bond, 2010), but the meaning of individual personal moral qualities is rarely discussed.

Even Tim Bond, in his seminal work on standards and ethics (Bond, 2015) does not specifically discuss individual qualities and their impact on the counselling relationship. Some of these qualities, such as empathy and respect, have been written about widely enough (Rogers, 1951; Mearns and Cooper, 2005) as examples, to be well-understood, but there are others, such as wisdom, humility and integrity, which are less written about and it is these that particularly interest me and which I will discuss in this chapter.

This chapter focuses on personal moral qualities (PMQs) and their importance for practitioners but also how they can be developed through personal development (PD) groups. It starts by defining PMQs and taking a close look at four of the least considered, but nevertheless important ones. These are: courage, humility, integrity and wisdom. Each of these qualities is defined and then analysed via a case study that is set in a PD group.

In this chapter I will:

- introduce the concept of personal moral qualities;
- define some of the most important PMQs needed for therapists;
- explain how PMQs and the PD group interrelate;
- discuss whether PMQs are innate or can be learned.

What are personal moral qualities?

Sometimes called virtues or principles, personal moral qualities are the traits that we consider as essential to who we are, such as a sense of fairness, honesty or compassion. There is not one definition that is universally accepted. Bond describes them as:

> internalised values that shape how we relate to others and our environment. They represent a moral energy or drive which may operate unconsciously and unexamined. This moral energy or drive is ethically more beneficial when consciously examined from time to time and used to motivate our ethical development or shape how we work towards a good society.
>
> (Bond, 2015, p. 7)

Are PMQs innate or can they be learned?

The philosophical issue is whether we are born blank slates or with an innate sense of PMQs. This is a question that has been debated for at least 2,500 years as it appears in pre-Socratic writing. Some argue that beliefs and values are innate, others that they can be learned or developed over time. Maybe the truth is in the middle: for example, practitioners without a sense of compassion may not be very good at their job, but empathy, as a higher form of compassion, is not usually innate and must be learned and developed, preferably to a high degree.

Wisdom can and must be learned; none of us are born wise and/or with common sense. I argue that common sense is only common sense once it has been taught. Think about crossing a busy road: common sense says to look all ways, but most of us will have been taught this at some stage in our childhood. In the same way, we can see that children have to learn resilience, and this too can be developed through training.

This point of view is not necessarily shared by practitioners as evidenced by Richardson, Sheean and Bambling (2009), who found that while practitioners valued PMQs such as warmth, empathy and compassion, only 32 per cent believed that integrity was important and only 13 per cent (less than one in seven) believed humility to be important. These findings suggest that neither honesty nor humility are considered important by many practitioners. While this was a small-scale survey (out of 92 potential respondents there was a 40 per cent response rate) it can still be considered a representative sample (Hamilton, 2009).

My story

In order to make this leap between theory and reality I include here part of my development of PMQs.

In my own experience, my PMQs were developed along the way. I come from a family in which certain traits – being articulate and achieving high grades in school – were prized over others. However, my parents valued different attributes. For my father, physical courage and humour were important; for my mother, education, as the means to achieving independence, was what mattered. These are all good things, although for me, being neither particularly brave nor academically a high achiever, they were not so easy. I am also a middle child, so I learned to watch and wait. In different ways my siblings were both difficult children and so I learned how to read others so that I could placate where necessary to get my own way. I also learned the value of honesty, in that telling my parents what I was doing yielded better results than one sibling's attempts (which usually failed) to get their own way through deception or the other's attempts to express feelings through withdrawal and/or anger.

Because I had unrecognised learning difficulties, my siblings often mocked me for not knowing or remembering things, so I learned to pretend I did, either by saying little or by downright lies, which usually got exposed pretty quickly. It was some time before I developed enough humility and confidence to admit when I did not know something.

It was not until much later in life that I began to think about all of this and to develop a true sense of who I am without unconsciously reacting to childhood experiences. Later still I realised that I had developed a moral code of my own, in which integrity loomed large.

> How did you learn your own moral qualities?
> How did you develop these as you grew older?

Courage

Courage is defined as doing something that is frightening.

Aristotle (quoted in Goud, 2005) suggested that when facing fears, people have three choices: courage, cowardice or impulsiveness/foolhardiness. The truly courageous person does not take unnecessary risks but thinks through the options first. The impulsive person, on the other hand, might say or do something without thinking through the consequences, and the cowardly person will do nothing, out of fear of the consequences.

In psychotherapy we are talking about emotional or moral courage rather than physical risks. An emotional risk might be defined as a step into the unknown: saying something that has emotional weight. The unknown is the uncertainty of how others might respond to what has been said. However, without facing this fear, growth (as in personal development) is unlikely to occur, and indeed it is an important issue to model for clients who will themselves be struggling with their vulnerabilities. So, within the therapeutic relationship, courage may be defined as being able to bear difficulties or vulnerabilities in others.

The PD group is a particularly good place to practice this as it involves being vulnerable in front of one's peers, and often in front of someone who may be in a position to pass or fail work. Examples of therapeutic courage may be: sharing difficult or painful feelings; admitting to having made mistakes; telling a client that time is up even when they are displaying strong feelings; being willing to work at the edges of competency. Another example may be owning up or revealing the above to a supervisor or group leader.

> Can you think of a time when you have taken a risk in telling someone something?
> What happened?
> What did you learn from the experience?

Humility

Through the ages in literature and popular culture, from Enid Blyton to Harry Potter, from Shakespeare to EastEnders, it is always the villain who has the least humility. Voldemort, the villain of J.K. Rowling's Harry Potter stories, becomes powerful through too much pride and is ultimately punished for this by a boy whose humility is his chief virtue. It is an excess of pride and thwarted ambition that is the undoing of both Macbeth and Lady Macbeth. In TV soaps, the character with excessive pride always finds themselves thwarted or dead.

We may recognise a lack of humility when we see it but it can be hard to define. There are various definitions, but one of my favourites is this one: 'Humility is knowing you are smart, but not all-knowing. It is accepting that you have personal power but are not omnipotent' (Templeton, 1997, quoted in Tangney, 2000, p. 72). Bond (2010, p. 4) defines it as 'the ability to assess accurately and acknowledge one's own strengths and weaknesses' whereas Dale (2010) defines it as 'being open to the new: to seeking help when necessary'.

What all these definitions have in common is that they suggest humility is the opposite of arrogance but not of self-confidence. The quality of humility suggests being open to new ideas and new suggestions.

Another way of describing humility might be to say that it involves a recognition of one's own strengths and that with strengths, inevitably, come weaknesses. Students and newly qualified therapists can be especially at risk here as, while conscious of flexing their newly developed muscles, they may not always remember that strength needs building. So it is with all skills: they need to be consciously learned and practised. Humility is remembering that there is always more to be learned.

Integrity

Integrity tends to have two meanings: one is to do with honesty, having principles and upholding them, and the other meaning is to do with honesty and accuracy in everyday life. This is to do with applied ethics and the quotation at the beginning of this chapter which points us to thinking of ethical behaviour as how we behave in life as well as how we behave with clients.

It is this second definition that is perhaps the more difficult and the one that can be developed through practice and interactions. It could be thought of in the same light as Rogers' (1951) congruence or genuineness; that is, being who you are, both in the therapy room and in everyday life. This, as with so many issues, is harder in practice than in theory. Most people like to think of themselves as having morals but living up to them in ordinary life can be more problematic.

Have you ever...

- Taken a day off work when you don't really need to, e.g., blaming ill health or the weather when you could have gone in?
- Used work internet for personal reasons (assuming you are not supposed to do this)?
- Asked someone to say you are not there when not wanting to take a phone call?
- Been undercharged in a shop or restaurant and not returned the money?

In its very simplest form, integrity, as applied to therapy, might be defined as demonstrating honesty and moral principles in an everyday way. To put this in a very simple and crude form, integrity might be defined as doing what you say you will do. So, if you have told a client that you will see them at a certain time, for a certain length of time that is what you do.

The therapeutic contract also involves, whether said overtly or not, an agreement that the therapist gives their full attention to the client during their time together, and not doing so may be seen as a lack of integrity.

Acting with integrity includes 'playing by the rules' so, for example, understanding any organisational rules, which includes those of the PD group as well as the code of conduct of your training and placements institutions.

Examples of integrity could include being honest about your training and qualifications: this can pose an interesting dilemma for students on placement who are often advised not to tell clients that they are in training unless specifically asked. That in itself is not a lack of integrity, but denying student status if asked would demonstrate a lack of integrity.

A dilemma can occur when personal values supersede organisational values. If a training placement specifically instructs their trainees not to admit their status but a client asks the question, how would you respond?

Wisdom

The *Cambridge International Dictionary* defines wisdom as 'the ability to use your knowledge and experience to make good decisions and judgements' (Cambridge University Press, 2008). This definition makes it clear that wisdom is not innate, but something learned through knowledge and experience. As I say above, in some ways it is akin to the quality known as 'common sense', as that too is a quality that is developed through knowledge, practice and experience. It is not, however, a quality that a new-born baby will have much of.

If you have begun, what have you learned about yourself through the PD group?

How will you apply this to working with clients?

In terms of therapy, let us consider what wisdom may be. It is about understanding what the job is and not crossing boundaries. It is not responding to or making calls to clients outside working hours, as this blurs the boundaries between a professional and a personal relationship. In some ways wisdom is about knowing what those boundaries are and remembering that clients bring their vulnerabilities and need to be treated with care.

Activity

Now, thinking more generally about PMQs, can you write down which ones seemed most valued by your parents or caretakers when you were a child? Did this change as you got older?

Now consider the case study below in relation to the PMQs that have been considered in this chapter, i.e., courage, humility, integrity and wisdom.

Case study: Melinda

Melinda is coming to the end of her first year of her counselling training. She is enjoying it on the whole and is looking forward to her second year. She has become good friends with some of her colleagues but struggles with one or two other members of the course, particularly in the PD group. In particular, she is concerned about Bernie, who often gets very angry in the group, and who Melinda does not think is ready to be seeing clients. She and her friends have often discussed Bernie and are considering whether or not to say something to their lecturers. However, they have held back so far, not sure what their responsibility is in this.

During one group, when Melinda is disclosing something very personal to her, she experiences Bernie's reaction as hostile and unsympathetic. When she says this, Bernie responds by accusing Melinda of 'playing the victim card' and being unable to take constructive criticism. Melinda does not believe this is true of her, but the hostility from Bernie does take her aback and she is quiet for the rest of the group. Later, when she has had a chance to consider what has happened, she becomes upset and angry. She discusses what happened with friends on the course, some of whom were in the group, with her partner, and also with her counsellor and her supervisor, all of whom are sympathetic to her. Both her counsellor and supervisor suggest that she should bring it up in the next group meeting.

Melinda does do this, despite feeling anxious about how Bernie will deal with what she has to say. She explains that she is acting on advice from others who she has confided in. At this Bernie gets very angry and shouts that Melinda has broken the group rule of confidentiality, which says that what is said in the group should stay in the group and not be discussed elsewhere. The facilitator appears to agree with Bernie, telling Melinda that she should not have discussed group issues outside the group. Melinda is shocked and upset. It had not occurred to her that she could not talk about the group with her friends and family, nor that there were restrictions on what she could say to her counsellor or her supervisor. Indeed, it is common practice among her friends on the course to discuss what has happened in the group during breaks. However, no one supports her and she is left feeling very distressed and isolated.

What PMQs are relevant to the case study?

Let's analyse this case study, in relation to PMQs.

Courage

Remember that this has been defined as doing something frightening, or to put it another way, within counselling, bearing someone else's difficult feelings or vulner-abilities. Melinda showed courage in challenging a fellow group member, who she experienced as angry, on their behaviour in the group. It might have been easier for her to do or say nothing, but she decided to take a risk and speak up. This was a brave thing for her to do, and the group members might have noticed this and applauded her courage (but did not). On the other hand, she has perhaps fallen short in bearing someone else's difficult feelings and seeing them for what they are. Neither did Melinda have the courage to talk to her lecturers or tutors about her concerns, although she does discuss them with colleagues. It might be argued that this is not fair to Bernie, and that it would be better, and braver, if Melinda had a private conversation with Bernie about her concerns before discussing them with anyone else. Learning for Melinda, through the PD group, is to do with how hard it is to be courageous, but particularly hard when there is no external validation, i.e., when the courage is not recognised as such by others.

Humility

This is defined as understanding one's own strengths and weaknesses but also being open to others and their ways of working. Again, it is instructive to see where Melinda both showed humility and where she did not. A lack of humility can be seen in that she and some of her colleagues assumed that Bernie's behaviour would go unnoticed by the group leader and by the other lecturers. It may be that the course leaders were well aware of what was happening and had come to their own conclusions. Melinda would not have been privy to these discussions, but it is likely that they happened. In this instance, Melinda thought that she had information that was not held by them, which is possible but unlikely. On the other hand, in talking issues over with other people, it could be said that Melinda did demonstrate humility in that she looked to others for advice and support before acting. In particular in talking issues over with her counsellor and supervisor she demonstrates that she understands the principle of humility. Unfortunately, this was not recognised in the PD group any more than courage was.

It is also worth considering that, as a trainee, Melinda is still learning what her strengths and weaknesses are. She has not had time to work out what she is good at and what needs more work, in part because at this stage of her learning everything is so very new. Later, toward the end of her second year, perhaps, she will have had the time and experience to know what she needs to do but not yet. She is at the stage of trying out everything and learning more from mistakes than from when things go right.

Integrity

This is defined as having principles, in particular honesty, and being able to uphold them in everyday life.

Melinda would normally consider herself a reasonably honest and principled person. In this case, she was aware that the group rules stated that members should not discuss what happened in the group outside of group time. It could be argued that in doing so when she had agreed not to, Melinda did not demonstrate much integrity. However, it appears that this was common practice, at least among her colleagues in the group. In this case, her human need to debrief after a difficult session overrode the need to maintain confidentiality. What is less clear from the case study is whether or not she had remembered the group rule and chosen to ignore it, or whether she had simply forgotten it. If she had remembered the group rules and chosen to ignore them she may be showing a lack of principled behaviour.

On the other hand, it is an interesting point as to whether the group rules should apply to personal counselling or to clinical supervision. I would argue that they should not, as the client needs to be allowed to discuss anything they like in a neutral setting. If this has not been made clear in your own PD group it may be worth bringing it up and exploring it, remembering that counselling and supervision both offer safe and confidential places for trainees to discuss important issues in their life.

Wisdom

Whatever else happened, Melinda did not show very much wisdom. But looking again at the definition of wisdom, it is clear that while this may be an innate quality it also needs to develop through experience and knowledge. Melinda is new to the profession and had not fully taken on the meaning of group confidentiality nor has she had time to develop wisdom or courage within the context of her new profession. Let's consider the ways in which she was not wise. She was not wise in that she did not pay more attention, or remember, that the group rules forbade discussing group issues outside the group. If she was aware of the group rules but believed that somehow they could be discounted, she again showed a lack of wisdom. However, it appears that most other group members also discussed issues outside the group so perhaps there was learning for everyone here, including the group facilitator. Melinda was possibly not wise in challenging Bernie in the first place, as she was aware of the possibility of an angry response that she would not be able to process within the group. Later, with training, she would hopefully have developed the patience and resilience to hold her feelings until the next meeting.

Wisdom, in this case may be defined as knowing the limits of your own resilience and knowing where and when to go for help.

> What would you have done in Melinda's position?
> Which would show less integrity: Melinda having forgotten the rules completely or remembering the rule and deciding to ignore it anyway? Can you justify your response, using the PMQs?
> If you had been the facilitator of the group, how do you think you might have handled the situation between Melinda and Bernie?

PMQs and the PD group

Earlier in this chapter I quoted Tim Bond (2015) as saying that values should be consciously examined from time to time. In training the PD group is the place individual value systems can be examined and better understood. It is the place where our PMQs can be honed so that we become more aware of times when we fail to reach our own standards and can consciously consider doing better. Within counselling, values and PMQs need to fit within organisational codes.

This may seem a daunting task at first, as speaking one's truths in front of peers and assessors is difficult and demanding work. However, if it is seen as a skill like any other, it becomes easier. Think back to learning to read. At first this seems a difficult, perhaps almost impossible task. Later with practice, it becomes automatic. So it is with personal moral qualities. The first step is to be able to name them. The second step is to understand what they each mean, and what this means in practice and in particular what they mean for counsellors.

For example, humility can be practised through listening to others who have different opinions and accepting that their point of view is valid. For Melinda, a hard lesson may have been to accept that she did break the boundaries, and she may want to consider that later. She may also have to take on that Bernie has as much right to a viewpoint as she does, even if their views are fundamentally opposed.

Integrity, within the PD group is practised through attending psychologically as well as physically. It is not enough to be merely present in the group, but members need to be actively listening and thinking as well. Integrity also involves keeping to the rules of the group, or stating that they will not be kept to. While most people would claim to be honest, practising integrity at this more complex level is a hard task but can be at least aspired to.

Wisdom within the PD group may be learning what to say and what to withhold, which is trickier than it seems. It may also be about learning when to intervene and when to hold a silence and see what happens next. It may be that Melinda should have stayed quieter longer.

Last of all courage is about emotional risk-taking, which covers all kinds of risks, which may include disclosing difficult personal material or may include not doing so. Examples of courage may include challenging those who break group boundaries, or just disclosing uncomfortable feelings in the group as they occur.

Conclusion

As you have read through this chapter you may have noticed that the four primary qualities discussed are all interrelated. There is a connection between humility and wisdom, for example, as both involve a willingness to listen and to act on advice from others. Courage too, involves wisdom: the knowledge that it can take more courage, sometimes, to sit back and say nothing is a form of wisdom. Integrity, which sounds so easy in theory, is in fact more difficult to grasp within therapy as it involves a clear understanding of self, which can only develop as a result of deep and conscious personal development leading to increased self-knowledge. So integrity too needs the wisdom that only comes with knowledge.

I suggest that, in order to be ethical practitioners, it is important that relevant PMQs are at the heart of the would-be counsellor's value system and are seen as values to be aspired to, despite sometimes, as we all do, falling short of our expectations of ourselves.

In essence, PMQs are necessary qualities in would-be counsellors, and they also need to be honed and developed in order to become part of the mature counsellor's personality.

However, during counselling training, it may be that values or qualities that have, until that point, been unconscious are brought into awareness. This is the not-so-subtle difference: unconscious qualities need to be consciously and consistently applied when working with clients, as in the examples given above. As counsellors we also need to be consciously checking that we are doing this: for me, that means constant self-examination, not just with self-talk but also with others. This is because self-talk, while useful, does not offer the same level of dialogue as speaking out loud. While training, there are many opportunities to practice: with peers, in counselling or supervision and of course, within the PD group. This group is an opportunity to take risks; to have the courage to say hard truths and to listen and learn from how others perceive us.

Most people would want to lay claim to a moral code, and to moral qualities, but therapists have an especial responsibility to be consciously aware of the ethical component of their work. However, because there is such a lack of understanding of what PMQs involve they are often not applied or examined consistently. Once thoroughly understood they are easier to apply in practice.

Melinda, in the case study, did have courage, humility, integrity and some wisdom, but she was not at the point where she could apply them within the PD group. Her learning from this will be hard but hopefully important to her work with clients.

I began this chapter with a discussion on whether PMQs are innate or learned. I have concluded by saying that whether or not they are innate, they need to be applied, consciously, by therapists and would-be therapists. Ultimately each of us must decide this question for ourselves but I hope that reading this chapter has made you consider your own answer, and more importantly, allowed you to consider your own growth and development and how that may be enhanced by the PD group.

References

BACP (2018) *Ethical Framework for the Counselling Professions.* Lutterworth: BACP.

Bond, T. (2010) *Standards and Ethics for Counselling in Action.* London: Sage.

Bond, T. (2015) *Standards and Ethics for Counselling in Action.* London: Sage.

Cambridge University Press (2008) *Cambridge International Dictionary.* Available from: https://dictionary.cambridge.org/dictionary/english/wisdom (accessed 30 June 2019).

Dale, H (2010) Can ethics be sexy? *The Independent Practitioner*, p. 11.

Goud, N.H. (2005) Courage: Its nature and development. *The Journal of Humanistic Counseling, Education and Development*, 44(1), pp. 102–116.

Hamilton, M. B. (2009) *Online Survey Response Rates and Times: Background and Guidance for Industry.* Cambridge, MA: Tencent Inc.

Mearns, D. and Cooper, M. (2005) *Working at Relational Depth in Counselling and Psychotherapy.* London: Sage.

Palmer Barnes, F. and Murdin, L. (2001) *Values and Ethics in the Practice of Psychotherapy and Counselling.* Buckingham: Open University Press.

Richardson, J., Sheean, L. and Bambling, M. (2009) Becoming a therapist or counsellor: A survey of psychotherapy and counselling trainers. *Psychotherapy in Australia*, 16(1), pp. 70–80.

Rogers, C. (1951) *Client-Centered Therapy: Its Current Practice, Implications and Theory.* London: Constable.

Tangney, J. (2000) Humility: Theoretical perspectives, empirical findings and directions for future research. *Journal of Social and Clinical Psychology*, 19(1), pp. 70–82.

Chapter 11

Attachment styles and relational patterns

Tracy Hitchcock

But for those first affections, those shadowy recollections, which, be they what they may, are yet the fountain light of all our day

(Wordsworth, 1807)

Introduction

When two strangers are placed together in a room for the first time, it is not surprising if a degree of anxiety is present. Let's imagine a therapist and client meeting for the first time. For the client it could be a myriad of thoughts and emotions: 'Can I trust this person?', 'Will they understand me and my concerns?', 'Will what I say be confidential?', 'Will I be safe?'

For the therapist, it could be such concerns as: 'Am I able to help this person?', 'Will they be able to get what they need from me and from therapy?', 'Will I be able to do a good job?', 'Will I be good enough?'

In this intimate space, emotions, thoughts and physical experiences are paramount and each is asked to drop their guard and draw on their resources to cope, to protect themselves in this new, strange situation. The degree to which these inner resources are available is dependent on the relationship that both had with their own primary carers in the early stages of their life. It may be the lack of resources and coping strategies that has driven the client to therapy in the first place. The therapist is also trawling their psychological reserves to find a way of being physically and psychologically present in the relationship. Both are vulnerable and open and present to possibilities and whatever may arise in any given moment in this strange and unfamiliar place. What resurfaces for the therapist in this situation is dependent on their own experience of early attachment and how this manifests in their relational patterns.

When I talk about attachment theory to students, I am sometimes surprised by the strong emotions it can evoke. Familiarity with the process has led me to keep reminding myself that people may be hearing this for the first time. Behaviours or relational patterns that are entrenched in the person are suddenly being highlighted and brought into the person's conscious awareness. For some it may be a lightbulb moment, 'Oh, that's why I keep responding in that way'. I have even heard in a distressed panic, 'Oh God, what have I been doing to my children?' Whatever the person's reaction to the theory may be, it is an essential part of training to have a clear awareness of how much impact our attachment styles have on our relational patterns.

An essential feature of personal development groups is that they provide an arena for the expression and exploration of old patterns of behaviour that are remnants from our past and derived from our attachment styles which are being played out in our current relationships. It is only by taking them out and examining them carefully and congruently that we can develop an awareness about choosing different relational patterns that may facilitate healthy relationships.

In this chapter I will:

* highlight the importance of attachment;
* identify attachment styles;
* illustrate different attachment styles with case study examples;
* explore how they feed into our relational patterns;
* show how we can increase our awareness by recognising them as they arise;
* look at Menninger's two triangles.

Attachment styles

Infants are born into a network of relationships. This may include parents, caregivers, siblings or a variety of other people. What they experience then will have an impact on all future relationships.

The psychologist, John Bowlby (1988) coined the term, 'internal working model' or template. He says that we use this consciously or unconsciously as a blueprint for how we relate to others in our environment. His collaboration with Mary Ainsworth, led to the development of three attachment styles (Ainsworth and Bowlby, 1991).

Secure attachment is characterised by the primary caregiver being readily available, responsive and able to contain the child's emotions. The parent or carer is available both physically and psychologically for the infant. From birth, this person has been a constant source of comfort and security, helping the infant to contain his/her anxieties and frustration.

In Winnicott's words, the carer is 'the facilitating environment' (1965). S/he understands that the world is a strange and frightening place for the infant and that it is their job to knit together the physical and psychological parts of the infant so that they begin to experience a sense of coherence and togetherness. S/he understands that when they are absent (if only for a small fraction of time) that the infant will begin to experience, at an unconscious level, a disintegration of its bodily parts and a terror of falling apart psychologically. By being physically held and soothed, the infant is able to relax and enjoy the comfort of containment knowing that the parent or carer is both constant and consistent and 'there' for them physically and emotionally.

The child learns that they can express their rage and their anxiety and it will be acknowledged and accepted. The child has experienced that the world on the whole is a safe place. They have realised that any expression of feelings is acceptable and they will not be overwhelmed by them. They feel mirrored by the mother, father or caregiver, who gives love and protection to their child. The child accepts that the parent or carer provides a safe, protective space and will be there for them when they are feeling anxious and frightened. The child internalises this pattern of behaviour and will seek this in other relationships in their life. They can thus begin to experience a feeling of relatedness which is the beginnings of the sense of self.

Case study: Aswar

Aswar had warm supportive parents, therefore he expects authority figures to be warm and supportive towards him. He behaves towards them in ways that are likely to bring this attitude about by being open, warm, polite and friendly. This would be representative of his relationship with his parents.

Aswar has a securely attached relational style, which he brings into all his relationships with others. He is both empathic and interactive in the PD group and other group members warm to him as he is so friendly and open.

The *insecure ambivalent attachment* tends to develop if the main carer is inconsistent with the child. This may be because the carer is themselves insecure and therefore tries to meet their own needs through the child. The child's needs become second to the carer's. The child is confused as sometimes the carer is available to them and sometimes not. In some cases the carer may try to live vicariously through their child and push them to achieve goals in life that they were not able to attain for themselves. The child is in a state of constant anxiety and aims to be responsive to their carer's needs, thus sacrificing their own. Their needs become unimportant and it is vital to keep the carer on side as their very survival depends on it. Because their needs have been ignored the child may not be able to distinguish their own needs from those of their carer.

The infant has to stop *being* and developing naturally and start *doing* in order to survive. In other words, they develop a 'false self', Winnicott (1965) because the foundations have not been laid to facilitate a true self. This can cause extreme distress and confusion that can last throughout life. Those who have an insecure attachment style may need to attain a quick mind and be on the alert because they believe that security offered by others is unavailable, temporary or not real and they struggle to find a sense of identity, in the way that, as children, their own identities merged with their primary carer. Their relationships in later life may be fraught and marked by anxiety and confusion. They desperately try to find security in their relationships but their relational patterns prevent this and they may push away or reject partners.

Case study: Lisa

A typical scenario of someone with an ambivalent attachment pattern may be Lisa. She believed her partner was having an affair. She did not have any clear proof of this but she distorted events around her so that her expectations matched her beliefs. Every time Lisa saw her partner around attractive women, she believed that there was something going on.

She argued with him for giving other women his attention and did not believe him when he said he was only interested in her. He hated these arguments and became secretive if he bumped into anyone they both knew. She asked him why he didn't tell her he saw so and so. He became cagey, thus reinforcing her suspicions that he was being unfaithful. Eventually, he left her.

As a child, Lisa's mother was afraid of being betrayed by her father, which led her to become controlling. The father turned to Lisa for support, which made the child, Lisa feel very important. However, she felt emotionally abandoned at such times when the relationship between her parents was smooth.

Lisa's father eventually left the family. Lisa felt bereft and betrayed. Her mother then leant on Lisa berating her father and telling her that, 'All men are bastards. They use you, abuse you and end up leaving you.' Lisa took this fully on board and denied her own distress at the absence of her father to take care of her mother. This experience stayed with her and unconsciously she re-enacted the scenario in her own relationships with men by imitating her mother and mistrusting her male relationships.

In her forties, Lisa began counsellor training. In the PD group she brought in her beliefs about men and her relational patterns. For example, she imagined her male facilitator to have 'favourite' students who were given more time and attention than her. She withdrew physically and psychologically from the group, because she expected the facilitator and other group members to reject, abandon or betray her. The group facilitator came to represent everyone who had let Lisa down in the past.

When others showed empathy she initially felt accepted but then wondered if what they were saying was 'really' sincere and whether she could truly trust them or believe what they said to her.

Eventually, her anxiety became too great for her to bear and for a time she did not attend the group. She was feeling overwhelmed by what was going on for her.

According to Ainsworth et al. (1978), in an *insecure avoidant attachment* style, the carer may be distant and unresponsive to signs of vulnerability or need in the child. As a result, the child may in time give up expecting any response from the carer. Thrown back on their limited resources the child may withdraw into their own world in order to feel safe and present a face of invulnerability to the world. In adulthood, those with this attachment style may be living in a state of constant anxiety, perhaps fearing rejection and judgement from others. They may become cut off from their feelings or even feel cut off from life itself. Relationships could be fragmented and temporary.

Case study: George

George is somebody with an insecure avoidant attachment style. He finds it hard to fit in and relate to people. However, he is empathic and seen as a good listener but he is afraid to show his emotions, preferring to keep a distance to protect himself. About five years ago his wife left him for another man after George lost his job as a music teacher in a school after an emotional breakdown. He spent a period of unemployment just drinking and staring at the wall. George is the fourth son of five children. He has three older brothers and one younger sister. His father left his mother for another woman when George was just three years of age. He remembers the baby getting more attention than him. His memories of his mother are that she was always very busy and spent most of her time in tears, 'trying to cope with it all'.

When he first had to enter the PD group in his training, he was terrified, because he did not know what could happen to him. When he began to experience empathy from the group facilitator and other group members, he revealed to the group that he suffered from depression.

As he relaxed and opened up in the personal development group George began to feel less depressed and appreciated being with a group of people who seemed to understand what he had been through. Even though he found it hard, being in the PD group and personal therapy has helped him to understand himself better and he is now thinking about training as a music therapist after he has completed his diploma course.

It is clear that George needs time in the personal development group and his own personal therapy to feel safe and secure in the group. This enables him to open up and share his fears and discomfort.

Activity: Exploring behavioural and relational patterns

Can you identify any behavioural patterns of your own?
What kind of attachment patterns would you say you have?
How did you learn these?
How would you describe your relational patterns?

Consider how these relational patterns manifest themselves in different situations:

- Work
- Social events
- Personal relationships
- Intimate relationships

How do you think these might manifest themselves in the PD group?

We interpret current relationships in the light of our relationship history, on which our belief systems are based. The following is another example of how somebody may present in a personal development group with an avoidant attachment pattern.

Case study: Millie

Millie had a father who was cold, critical and humiliating. She expects male authority figures to react in a similar way. She behaves as if her expectation is the truth. She tries to protect herself from criticism and humiliation by being closed and secretive.

She behaves defensively in the personal development group whenever anybody challenges her. She also appears lacking in confidence and being hard on herself.

She is self-critical and puts herself down, e.g., get in there before anyone else does. She is defensive about constructive feedback, in much the same way she had learned to be with her father. She often defensively puts the other person down before they can do it to her, a pattern of behaviour learnt from her father.

These behaviours further increase the probability that she will receive the cold, critical humiliating response she fears and expects but does not want.

The other students in the PD group struggle with Millie. They want to accept her and be empathic towards her but they find it uncomfortable when she keeps pushing them away. The personal development facilitator is also aware of the tensions in the group and also how they may be perceived and experienced by Millie when she is in a state of anxiety.

You will see that early attachment styles lead to people repeating the same issues in relationships over and over again. This is often because these repetitive behaviours are unconscious. On the whole, we are all seeking security and empathy in our relationships but our behaviour may push away the very people we most want to offer this to us. Once we become aware of what we are doing, perhaps in the PD group or in therapy, change becomes more possible, although still not easy.

Triangles of conflict and persons

Karl Menninger (1958) identified two triangles (see Diagram 11.1). They are known as, 'the triangle of conflict' and the 'triangle of persons'. The point of the triangle of conflict is to help us understand what our coping mechanisms are for the times when we become anxious. The triangle of persons helps us to understand how we developed these defences or coping mechanisms through our early experiences. Both triangles may be useful in helping us to understand unconscious and/or real behaviours which are no longer useful.

Triangle of conflict

In the first diagram below, the triangle of conflict, each point of the triangle illustrates three possible links between the person's defensive strategy, their anxiety and their hidden feeling or impulse. The defence and anxiety lead to the hidden feeling/impulse.

Triangle of persons

In the second, triangle of persons, we can see that the person's feelings towards others come from their relationship with their parents or main carers. The defence or defences are ways that the person has learnt to protect themselves in the past from psychological attack. The anxiety is the leftover dread that the person carries with them into their relationships with others and the hidden feeling or impulse is the initial trauma that the person is struggling to defend.

The purpose of these triangles is to demonstrate the different ways we act out past unmet needs, the thwarted wants, the frustrations and all that was denied to us 'back

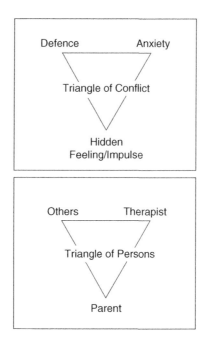

Diagram 11.1 Triangles of conflict and persons
Source: Adapted from Menninger (1958)

then' when strong attachments were being formed or not taking place. What we learn then, we take into relationships later in life, including within the PD group.

If we explore how this could be applied to the case study of Lisa, this may illustrate a possible way of highlighting Lisa's ambivalent attachment style and how it is impacting her relational patterns. It is significant that archaic forms of relating in the past are always carried through to the present.

Case study: Lisa and the PD group

Lisa took a break from the PD group to work on her issues in her personal therapy. After a short while she was able to return and discuss her issues in the group. She was now able to present her difficulty, saying that she had lost trust in her relationships with men. They always left her or she pushed them away and she didn't understand why this kept happening to her. This inability to feel or develop a trusting relationship with men could be seen to be a 'defence' which Lisa presented to the group.

As Lisa talked about her past relationships and her relationships with her parents it became apparent that her inability to feel and lack of trust had to do with her 'anxiety' back then about her father physically leaving her and her parent or carer being unavailable emotionally. Through further exploration it was revealed that the 'hidden feeling' was an overwhelming feeling of terror about being abandoned, isolated and not being able to fend for herself.

Clarity enabled Lisa to understand her anxiety and the origin of that anxiety, which was also linked to dark periods of depression that she now realised stemmed from the fear of abandonment. This also served to highlight what was going on with the personal development group facilitator in the group and why she has trust issues and particularly cannot stand breaks and holidays.

Although her issues were deep-rooted, as Lisa became more aware of what was going on and how her attachment styles impacted on her relational patterns, she was able to start making some changes in her life in how she related to other people.

The identification of relational patterns in the PD group and the realisation of attachment styles may enable you to learn and gain awareness at an emotional level that which may have only been explored cognitively. You would also learn to appreciate your strengths and weaknesses and gain awareness of your shadow side and the past relational patterns that are triggered by others. This in turn could enable you to avoid being tripped up by your clients and enmeshed in over-identification and collusion with your clients' attachment styles and relational patterns.

Conclusion

In this chapter we have explored how attachment styles have a significant impact on our relational patterns. The importance of early attachment styles has been highlighted and we have looked at case studies to illustrate these and how they manifest themselves in social situations. This should help increase awareness of hidden aspects of the self.

We have identified how we may be tripped up by our relational patterns if we are not consistently aware of our own processes. We can gain greater awareness of these through engaging in personal therapy and by also taking risks through exploring aspects of our self in the personal development group. This enables us to monitor our interactions with others and receive feedback for reflection and change.

Through exploration of a case study and the application of the triangle of conflict and the triangle of persons, we have seen how we can trace our relational patterns back to their origin. It is important to be aware of our anxieties and defences and the origins of these and how they impact our relational patterns.

Through expression and exploration of these aspects in the personal development group we can bring the hidden areas of ourselves into conscious awareness and through doing so, activate change. This means we have more choice in how we relate to others either personally or professionally in the counselling relationship.

References

Ainsworth, M.D.S. and Bowlby, J. (1991) An ethological approach to personality development. *American Psychologist*, 46(4), pp. 333–341.

Ainsworth, M.D.S, Behar, M., Waters, E. and Wall, S. (1978) *Patterns of Attachment: A Psychological Study of the Strange Situation*. Hillsdale, NJ: Lawrence Eribaum Associates.

Bowlby, J. (1988) *A Secure Base: Parent–Child Attachment and Healthy Human Development.* New York: Basic Books.

Menninger, K. (1958) The theory of psychoanalytic technique. In D. Malan (1979), *Individual Psychotherapy and the Science of Psychodynamics.* London: Butterworth & Co.

Winnicott, D.W. (1965) *The Maturational Process and the Facilitating Environment: Studies in the Theory of Emotional Development.* New York: International Universities Press.

Wordsworth, W. (1807) *Ode on Intimations of Immortality from Recollections of Early Childhood.* London: Macmillan.

Chapter 12

Identity and the counselling relationship

Who do you think you are?

Tara Fox and Jayne Godward

Introduction

This chapter focuses on how culture, background and worldview has an impact on your work as a counsellor. In our experience students tend to be more conscious of who their clients are rather than how their own personal identities may affect their client work. This chapter encourages you to really look at who you are and how your age, gender, class, sexuality, ethnicity, etc. may manifest in the counselling relationship. Exercises and questions will be used to explore your identity and raise awareness.

In this chapter we will help you to explore:

*   what identity is;
*   the importance of this for personal development and counselling work;
*   how the PD group helps you to become more aware of your identity including how it can impact on others;
*   how the group prepares you for working with clients who are different from yourself.

So what is identity and what do we mean by it?

Identity is about our sense of self and who we are. This shapes our worldview and perceptions of reality, but it is also about the groups we belong to and the people we do/don't identify with. Identity is not fixed but fluid. It is not about an 'it' but a 'they' as we don't just have one all-encompassing identity but multiple identities that make us who we are. In the next two sections we will explore these ideas more.

> Each of us is embedded in a structural, cultural and political existence, the groups to which we belong, and each aspect of our identity, has a structural, cultural and political significance. Who we are is never socially neutral.
>
> (McFarlane, 2008, p. 171)

Activity

Think about the different groups you belong to.
List all of the things that make you who you are.

Do the different aspects of you have any priority over another?
Does this depend on who you are with or where you are?

The concept of 'salience' (Sellers et al., 1998) has been presented in the literature on racial identity as an explanation of how we may choose one aspect of identity as more significant than another. This concept takes into account the different groups we may identify with and how these may fluctuate in importance to us depending on the context we find ourselves in. It suggests an element of choice over which groups we may identify with and emphasises the fluid characteristics of identity.

Salience suggests fluidity where different groups we identify with may be more or less important to us depending on how salient it is at any given time, e.g., our age, gender, race, sexuality, belief, etc. If we were to face the end of our lives, some of us may choose our spiritual identity as salient over other aspects of our identity.

Fatima Adam (2016) writes about being a British Asian, being a Muslim, female, divorcee, lone parent, a daughter, sister, friend and therapist. She looks at how people relate to her based on their expectations of her depending on which group they are from and the difficulty she has had knowing where she fits in. So, the impact of her different identities changed over time depending on the context she was in.

How we develop our identity

Although identity development has been associated with adolescence (Erikson, 1950, 1968), it is a process that continues throughout adulthood as we navigate life's transitions, e.g., leaving home, starting a new career, becoming a parent and, not forgetting, becoming a counsellor. As we face each transition, we renegotiate our identity to adapt to our changing environments and social context.

Historically, linear models of identity development such as Erikson's psychosocial stages (Erikson, 1950) and Freud's psychosexual stages (Freud 1986 [1905]) imply conflicts need to be resolved before a person's identity may be realised. Modern thinking on identity celebrates the fluidity of ourselves. A narrative view of identity development (McAdams, 2001) is particularly relevant to counselling for trainee counsellors and clients alike. This concept of 'narrative identity' (Singer, 2004) is a life-story model that helps people to communicate with themselves regarding who they are and who they want to be in the future. The 'I' is the narrator and the 'me' is the 'self-concept' created by us, the storytellers. The stories may change over time and represent a renegotiation of how we think about ourselves. This depends on who we are with or the new knowledge and hindsight we have gained. In the PD group you may strengthen who you are through hearing other's stories that shed the light on some of the episodes of your own life. This impacts the way you relay your own story to others.

> How would you tell the story of your first day at your upper/senior school?
> Do you think you may have told a slightly different story at the time?
> Can you think of other times when you have retold a story with an altered narrative over time?

We all belong to cultural groups which shape our identities. Some of these are linked to the families we are born into, e.g., class, race, religion, etc. We are socialised by our parents and significant others to conform to these cultures, while others are chosen or thrust on to us as we grow up and develop our identities. Later we may be able to make choices as to what we accept or what we reject, see Jayne's account below.

Case study: A personal view

I was born into a white British, working-class family with strong Christian beliefs. As a female child I realise now that I was socialised to behave in a way that befitted my female gender; I was expected to get married and have children and go into a caring profession. Putting other people first and caring for others were strong values instilled into me. The family attitudes and norms were typical of the time and as a working-class person, university education was not a norm and professional people were looked up to and seen as above us or authority figures.

It was only as a young adult that I started to question some of the norms of my culture. For example, after starting my social science degree and studying Marx and feminism, I began to question the value of marriage and no longer followed the strict religious rules of my upbringing.

Although I had followed my mother's implicit wishes and went into nursing at 18, I realised it did not really fit with who I was and following this left to go and study for a degree, and eventually started teaching, something that had felt a natural choice for me since a child. I still chose to identify as a woman but was not overly feminine.

I am still proud of my northern working-class heritage, while belonging to the professions of lecturer/tutor and counsellor, which may be seen as middle-class occupations.

Developing our professional counselling identity

Part of becoming a counsellor is about learning the values and beliefs which help us take on this role and identity. We are subscribing to a certain philosophy and set of values that will inform how we relate to others and we are starting to belong to a group who also ascribe to these (Gazzola et al., 2011).

This new identity will affect how people relate to you and how you relate to others. When you began your professional counselling training you may have felt like you had stepped outside of the expected parameters of your social class. Your social class status may have impacted on your identity development according to Nelson, Englar-Carlson and Tierney (2006). For example, more students are coming into counselling training from working-class backgrounds as access to further and higher education has widened. Taking on a more professional and what would be traditionally a middle-class role in society may have its challenges. In our experience, those affected by this shift struggle between meeting the expectations of the family circle and embracing the new relationships arising from professional counselling settings. The PD group is a place where students can share their thoughts and feelings about this struggle and this exploration helps to make sense of how they have an impact on others as well as how others impact on them.

Importance of identity awareness for personal development and counselling

One of the biggest factors in effective counselling is the relationship between the counsellor and the client. A review of the research by Paul and Haugh (2008) found this to be the most important in-therapy factor when compared to other factors such as client variables, techniques and the therapeutic model.

As therapists we are entering into a relationship with another and need to be aware of what we are taking into this venture. Whether we like it or not we are taking our whole selves in there, including our different actual identities (who we are and how we see ourselves) and our perceived identities (how we are seen by others). Interestingly clients will see a part of us that others don't normally see, as counselling is a special relationship unlike any other we have.

Activity

Ask yourself:

How do you present to your clients? What do you think they see?
Are there aspects of your identity which you would like to hide?
Or are there aspects other people would like you to hide?
Are there any aspects that you deliberately reveal?

What is important here is your self-awareness and ability to recognise the possible impact you may have on your clients due to your actual or perceived identities. You also need to be aware of how you are seeing them. Being aware of the differences between you is also necessary as well as the similarities and how this affects your attitudes and behaviour.

In his article 'You're a white therapist: have you noticed?' Lago (2005) discusses the idea of white males having an invisible rucksack of privilege, which brings with it lots of advantages usually denied to non-white clients. He says being white is a racial position and the power it brings with it is often ignored. Similarly, we have found that being male brings advantages of privilege. Male assumptions and values are often seen as more valid than female ideas and attitudes as in the statement below:

Since I changed gender I have blended in much better. My lack of subservience is normal for a man.

Men are more likely to listen to me than before, to consider what I say, and to challenge it or agree with it. Before they simply ignored it, talked over me, told me I didn't know what I was talking about, or changed the subject.

Women are more likely to listen to me than before, and to listen to what I say as if it matters, which it may or may not. It is interesting that women often do not challenge me, which I would welcome, but I understand why they do not if they are anticipating the kind of reaction I used to get before from men when I looked female.

This is a trans male student writing after a session discussing diversity.

The same principle of power and authority being attached to aspects of identity could be applied to other aspects of identity; for example, being able-bodied as opposed to having a disability, being heterosexual rather than having another type of sexuality.

Spirituality and religion

Our worldview and spiritual beliefs also have an impact on the counselling relationship.

Research into a therapist's spirituality stressed the need for therapists to pay keen attention to the possible importance of their own and the client's spirituality in counselling (Blair, 2015). So if the trainee counsellor identifies and owns their own spiritual perspective prior to working with clients, they become aware of their blind spots, assumptions and prejudices, which are potential empathy-blockers.

In a study of Christian counsellors, it was recognised that working with different values and beliefs was challenging (Scott, 2013). The process involves these therapists rejecting some of the values they held strongly, and moving towards being more psychologically minded, eventually developing an ability to integrate their Christian beliefs with the psychological perspectives they were studying.

Although this is a study of Christian counsellors, the same kind of attention needs to be applied to the value base of students from other religions and spiritual beliefs.

In her recent unpublished research, Tara found that counsellors who identified as spiritual felt that their spirituality was a part of them that could not be separated out from the person they are in the therapy room. However, participants also felt their spirituality ought to be kept outside of the therapy room for fear of being judged either in supervision or by their clients. Trainees could benefit from communicating about their spiritual beliefs/experiences during training to normalise and better prepare therapists for experiencing spirituality in therapy (Fox, 2018).

Interestingly, even if you are from the same racial or cultural orientation as your client, because counsellor training has its roots in a Eurocentric and American philosophy, you will be bringing this into the counselling room (Shafi, 1998). As an example, if you are a Muslim woman counselling a Muslim woman, you may still bring Western values to your work that may be alien to the client's culture. Your professional counselling identity might be in the forefront while your religious and cultural identity is in the background.

Pieterse et al. (2013) suggest that when students become more aware of their self-identity, it gives them more control over their reactions to clients and an ability to use these reactions to facilitate the therapeutic relationship. We can look at how far the facets of our identity can intersect and interact with those of our clients. This may help develop an empathic bridge between ourselves and others.

For example, Jayne noticed recently that she was using her professional academic identity and her working-class background identity to relate to her client who is academically successful but finds that his working-class roots affect his self-worth. Understanding these two identities and their influence helped her empathise more with her client and this in turn helped strengthen the relationship.

How can the PD group help?

In this section we will ask you to imagine a fictitious PD group which contains (among others) four characters, Naomie, Jon, Lucy and Dave. This is based on our experiences of how identities manifest in the PD group and interplay together.

> ### Case study: Naomie
>
> Naomie is the only non-white woman in this group. Her heart sinks as she worries that this is going to be a repeat of previous group situations where she felt in a minority and did not feel able to speak up.
>
> In her previous counselling course group no one, including the tutor, had acknowledged that she was from a different culture. As usual she had merged into the background and pretended, she was the same as anyone else.
>
> She is dreading going on placement as she knows that not all clients will ignore her difference and some may be downright racist or insulting with their stereotypes. She does not feel able to talk about this in the group or the supervision group as this will set her apart and accentuate her difference.

Often in PD groups there is a strong cultural norm for people to try to be the same and not acknowledge differences. Dwight Turner (2016) discusses the tendency for people to sacrifice their identity to fit in with others.

How easy is it for you to be yourself in your PD group? Students often find it difficult to share their hidden identities, e.g., faith, occupation, previous history, sexuality, etc. As time goes by and trust develops, more sharing will occur. Try the following exercise when you have started to get to know your peers.

> ### Activity
>
> Thinking about your PD group colleagues or any other group you might be in, identify as many differences in the group including factors that make up people's identities. Some of these things may be aspects you know about people which are not visible but are about beliefs, values, culture and worldview, while others will be more visible.
>
> Which people were you drawn to or are you drawn to? How does this link to how you see yourself and your identity?
>
> Which people did you particularly not feel drawn to? How were they different to you?

Interestingly Turner says: 'we identify our self not just by who we are but also by who we are not' (2016, p. 16). So, when you are looking around or thinking about your colleagues then you are becoming more aware of who you are and who you think you aren't. He goes on to say:

we are moulded into being by the rules of these groups, so another group with different rules is therefore seen as alien to us, and threatening. Yet it often holds aspects of our sense of self that we cannot own, due to our membership of the original group.

(Turner, 2016, p. 18)

So, although we may appear to be very different from some of our colleagues, there will be aspects of that person that we can recognise at some level but cannot accept because we don't belong to that group. We will also be able to identify with some of their experience of being different or 'the other'.

Case study: Jon and Lucy

Jon has come from a strict evangelical working-class Christian background where homosexuality is not seen as an option and is even condemned as being sinful. In this PD group there is also a lesbian, Lucy, who is open about her relationship with her partner and her sexuality.

At the beginning Jon had a strong reaction to Lucy and could not stand to hear her talk in the group. He found what she was saying an affront to him. As time went by and he became more self-aware and understood his background more, he came to recognise aspects of himself in what she was saying regarding feeling different and being bullied at school. He had felt he did not fit in when growing up and had been picked on for his religious views. What he had found hard to bear was the pain and the sense of difference, which was really more his experience rather than Lucy's.

This is an example of the 'shadow', aspect of ourselves which we see in others but we do not own (Jung, 1938; Turner, 2016).

Identity exploration can be stressful and the PD group is often the place where you may begin to explore who you are, just as clients do in the therapy room. If you take some time through your training to think about your identity formation then you will be more able to support clients through this exploration. As counsellors we aim to help clients develop a sense of self that feels genuine for them and authentic. Likewise, in the PD group you may begin to notice more of who you are through being with others.

Sometimes the whole PD experience and what we see as its expectations might conflict with our cultural backgrounds and identities. This can be very difficult but can lead to learning and development as in this example:

I felt pressured to speak about my feelings because of the fear of not being included and fitting in. I also had a lot of assumptions and beliefs related to myself and the idea of sharing emotions. For example, I felt it was selfish to talk about myself and I felt extremely uncomfortable doing so.

(Shanaya, see Chapter 4)

Case study: Dave

Dave is white, male, married with three children and he appears to be very professional and middle-class, being a university lecturer. Jon sees Dave as an educated, well-spoken individual who is too intelligent for him to get along with. Lucy sees him as a straight male, obviously middle-class, who might judge her as others have done previously, and Naomie sees him as a privileged white male who has never had to face the barriers she has had of being black and a woman.

What happens next to members of this group will depend on the factors discussed in Chapter 6, i.e., it really depends on how the group develops and the facilitation of this. There will have to be high levels of trust and honesty made possible by the group feeling safe, as emphasised by the study looked at earlier (Robson and Robson, 2008).

We have found that students usually feel a little exposed and vulnerable when they begin the PD group. They may be self-conscious and self-questioning. It is not uncommon for people to feel as if they have nothing to contribute or anything worth saying. This might particularly apply if you have come from a background where you have suffered disadvantage and this difference has been highlighted in previous groups. When your sense of self-importance is low, it can be very difficult to speak up in a group, particularly if it is on the large size.

As people start to trust others, they will begin to share experiences and more personal aspects of themselves. The group acts as a big mirror where what you see in someone else is what you see in yourself and you start to learn more about yourself. We often look for similarities in others but we also see differences. By listening to others, we can develop our empathy, which means that we are going to be more receptive to clients with similar issues and backgrounds in the future.

The PD group is, hopefully, a safe place to ask questions of others about their experiences and also to explore reactions to the other person.

Case study: The group process

Our imaginary group has been meeting for several months. People have formed their own impressions of different group members and, as we have seen, have had various reactions to others. The facilitator is encouraging people to look at difference and to be more open about how they see other members. This process takes place over several weeks and is simplified here.

Dave asks people how he is perceived, as he is aware that sometimes he dominates the group. When people start to share their responses to him, it becomes apparent that Jon, Lucy and Naomie, among others, are prejudiced against the way he is, e.g., his middle-class presentation, his educated manner. They have reached a conclusion that life has been easy for him and that he does not understand what it is to struggle.

When these views are expressed, Dave reveals that he came from a financially poor background with a single-parent mother who suffered from chronic mental ill-health. To reach his present position in life had been a struggle but with determination he had achieved this. This is a big lesson for some of the group members about not making presumptions about others.

Dave starts to understand the impact he has on people due to this presentation of himself and also to recognise the differences in the room rather than thinking that treating everyone the same is the same as treating people equally. Through the sharing and some challenge from others, Dave realises that he could be seen to be in a privileged position and realises he needs to temper down this appearance of privilege, for example, by using simpler language rather than always talking in complex ways. This may be useful when relating to certain clients.

Jon starts to share what he has been looking at in personal therapy. He now recognises he is prejudiced and homophobic due to his upbringing and that being a heterosexual is not the only type of life, but also he recognises that he is afraid of his feelings of identification with Lucy as it is painful to remember the discrimination and bullying he suffered due to his beliefs. He is now more likely to own more of himself and to question his prejudices and values.

Lucy is shocked by Jon's disclosure and they are able to discuss this. She starts to realise that sometimes she dominates conversations and that her blatant sexuality can be a struggle for others from different backgrounds. She also recognises the need to be softer in her approach to others and more sensitive rather than attacking people as a form of defence.

Naomie, starts to share how she feels about the group and her previous experiences of prejudice as a black woman. She expresses her concern and anger about the colour-blind attitude of the group, where there seemed to be a pretence that it does not matter what colour or race or gender you are, we are all equal. She also recognises her bias against white males due to previous experiences as a child, when her family were discriminated against by older white men as hers was the only black family in a white working-class area.

Over time the group members continue to explore their identities and recognise their prejudices.

Personal change continued with the support of the group and there may be a positive effect on client work; the self-awareness gained gives the participants more choice in how they present to their clients, making them more approachable.

By encountering different identities in the PD group and hearing people's experiences, these students are more able to work with diversity in the counselling room as they can empathise more with people who are different from them.

Above we have used a simplified example of what can happen usually over a period of time when people share their impressions of other people's identities and look at their reactions to perceived difference. Being an active member of a PD group means you take risks. The invitation is there to share but it takes courage to share more of yourself as you cannot predict what the reactions might be. It also puts you under the spotlight. The beauty of the PD group is, once one person has shared, this may trigger thoughts and feelings in others to share their experiences so that personal awareness is increased. There is a lot of learning to be gained from being in a room with a diverse group of peers who give you the insight into their lived experience and how they see their identities.

Conclusion

In this chapter we have explored the meaning and significance of your identity for personal development and counselling work. Rather than talking about 'identity' as one thing, we have seen that we all have multiple identities that form who we are. The importance of these different aspects is often context-related.

We have considered how the PD group plays a part in helping you to become more aware of your different identities, including how these can impact on others. This increased self-awareness can be beneficial for client work where we can relate to our clients better by using our identities to build a rapport with them or to help us understand their experiences.

The extended case study of a peer group and some of its members represented typical occurrences in a PD group, where judgements are made on perceived identities and where having the space to be congruent and give feedback to each other helps break down barriers and increases self-awareness. This illustrated both the journey of getting to know who you are in relation to others and also how trainees start to recognise how they react to others with different identities due to previous experiences.

Although this chapter is not specifically about diversity issues, we have shown that being aware of our identity and how we are seen and how we see others helps us to recognise difference more. This may prevent us from overlooking (deliberately or not) the differences that exist when we are working one-to-one with clients. Just as this is not to be smoothed over in the PD group, it is important to address this in the counselling room or in our supervision where appropriate.

References

Adam, F. (2016) Who am I and what makes me who I am? *Therapy Today*, 27(3), pp. 20–23.

Blair, L.J. (2015) The influence of therapists' spirituality on their practice: A grounded theory exploration. *Counselling & Psychotherapy Research*, 15(3), pp. 161–170.

Erikson, E.H. (1950) *Childhood and Society*. New York: W.W. Norton.

Erikson, E.H. (1968) *Identity: Youth and Crisis*. New York: W.W. Norton.

Fox, T. (2018) *An Exploration of Spirituality in Counselling and Psychotherapy*. Unpublished MA thesis, Leeds Beckett University Repository.

Freud, S. (1986) Three essays on the theory of sexuality. In J. Strachey (ed. and trans.), *The Standard Edition of the Complete Psychological Works of Sigmund Freud*, Vol. 7. London: Hogarth Press (original work published 1905).

Gazzola, N., De Stefano, J., Audet, C. and Theriault, A. (2011) Professional identity among counselling psychology doctoral students: A qualitative investigation. *Counselling Psychology Quarterly*, 24(4), pp. 257–275.

Jung, C.G. (1938) *Psychology and Religion, Collected Works Volume 11: Psychology and Religion: West and East*. London: Routledge and Kegan Paul.

Lago, C. (2005) *Race, Culture and Counselling: The Ongoing Challenge*, 2nd edition. Milton Keynes: Open University Press.

McAdams, D.P. (2001) The psychology of life stories. *Review of General Psychology*, 5(2), pp. 100–122.

McFarlane, K. (2008) Interconnections between privilege and oppression. In S. Haugh and S. Paul (eds.), *The Therapeutic Relationship: Perspectives and Themes*. Ross on Wye: PCCS Books Ltd., pp. 168–180.

Nelson, M.L., Englar-Carlson, M. and Tierney, S.C. (2006) Class jumping into academia: Multiple identities for counseling academics. *Journal of Counseling Psychology*, 53(1), pp. 1–14.

Paul, S. and Haugh, S. (2008) The relationship, not the therapy. In S. Haugh and S. Paul (eds.), *The Therapeutic Relationship; Perspectives and Themes*. Ross-on-Wye: PCCS Books Ltd., pp. 9–22.

Pieterse, A.L., Lee, M., Ritmeester, A. and Collins, N.M. (2013) Towards a model of self-awareness development for counselling and psychotherapy training. *Counselling Psychology Quarterly*, 26(2), pp. 190–207.

Robson, M. and Robson, J. (2008) Exploration of participants' experiences of a personal development group held as part of a counselling psychology training group: Is it safe here? *Counselling Psychology Quarterly*, 21(4), pp. 371–382.

Scott, A. (2013) An exploration of the experience of Christian counsellors in their work with both Christian and non-Christian clients, with particular reference to aspects of cultural transition. *Counselling and Psychotherapy Research*, 13(4), pp. 272–281.

Sellers, R.M., Smith, M.A., Shelton, J.N., Rowley, S.A., and Chavous, T.M. (1998) Multidimensional model of racial identity: A reconceptualization of African American racial identity. *Personality and Social Psychology Review*, 2, pp. 18–39.

Shafi, S. (1998) A study of Muslim Asian women's experiences of counselling and the necessity for a racially similar counsellor. *Counselling Psychology Quarterly*, 11(3), pp. 301–314.

Singer, J.A. (2004) Narrative identity and meaning making across the adult lifespan: An introduction. *Journal of Personality*, 72(3), pp. 437–459.

Turner, D. (2016) We are all of us other. *Therapy Today*, 27(5), pp. 16–19.

Section D

Other aspects of personal development

Chapter 13

Personal therapy in counsellor training

Heather Dale, Jayne Godward and Carole Smith

Most professional therapy organisations, such as the BACP and the UKCP, rightly insist on a certain level of self-awareness and psychological understanding of self before trainees can join. This is because therapists need a high level of self-awareness and self-knowledge in order to be able to separate their own issues from those of their clients. In therapy jargon this would be referred to as 'staying clean'.

The question we are debating in this chapter is this: in order to achieve that level of self-awareness, should personal therapy be mandatory for trainees or can it be gained in other ways?

However, before continuing it might be helpful to define what personal therapy is when compared to personal development. Generally speaking, it is claimed that personal counselling gives clients an opportunity to look at the underlying issues behind current problems. Personal development, on the other hand, is described as developing a better understanding of self. There is some overlap here as a better understanding of self can and could also be achieved through therapy and underlying issues may also come out of work done in the PD group.

In this chapter we will:

- give an overview of the research into personal therapy in counsellor training (Carole);
- debate the pros and cons of mandatory personal counselling in training (Jayne and Heather);
- draw conclusions from this discussion (Carole).

Existing research

Personal therapy in counselling training has been discussed for many years; Freud believed that trainees should not expect their clients to enter conscious or unconscious places that the therapist had not explored herself (Freud, 1915). Freud (1937, p. 246) believed that 'the ideal qualifications' for engaging with clients were in self-analysis. However, there is still little evidence base for the requirement of personal therapy to be enforced.

Conversely, my own research on PD groups has illuminated the challenges faced by trainees in their PD groups – participants talked about emotional disturbance, trauma and the need to have resilience and tolerance to process some of the emotions triggered in PD groups. Many of them named personal therapy as a 'lifesaver'.

Most participants in Rizq and Target's study (2008, p. 29) 'felt that personal therapy should remain an obligatory part of the training curriculum, [but] they were ambivalent about specifying its aims or evaluating its outcomes'. Nine participants took part in interviews to ascertain their views on the meaning and significance of therapy in training. Responses ranged from awareness of the intensity of a relationship with a therapist, learning about attachment patterns, safety and using the therapist as a role model for professional role modelling. Some talked about using therapy as a buffer against very challenging work with clients. All participants recognised the need for personal therapy but also acknowledged the financial burden it placed upon them. The most interesting aspect of this study was the way in which participants felt ambivalent towards therapy being mandatory in training. This could have related to the financial implications, of course. In their analysis of responses, Rizq and Target (2008) used the term 'going through the hoops' as opposed to investing emotional work in therapy. They concluded that an insistence on personal therapy is no guarantee of the authenticity of the experience (2008, p. 40).

Murphy (2008), Atkinson (2006), Kumari (2011) all found in small studies, that personal therapy was of benefit and contributed to the process of training in counselling/psychotherapy, although it can also contribute to trainees' levels of stress. Murphy (2008) also acknowledged his growing awareness of the differences between personal growth and personal development, the latter being likened to professional development in which the mandatory personal therapy is a required element to 'tick the box'.

These views have been previously challenged (Clark, 1986; Macran and Shapiro, 1998; Lambert, 2003; Chaturvedi, 2013), and questions posed as to whether the requirement for personal therapy has any effect at all on client outcomes.

Of course, the logical argument against personal therapy would be – what if therapy raises problems for the trainee that he/she was previously unaware of? Or what if the trainee decides or is unable, for whatever reason to focus on their important personal issues?

Orlinsky et al. (2011) go further in raising the question of whether the number of therapists undertaking personal therapy may be due to the potential issue of us entering training with 'wounded healer' traits or that we are above averagely psychologically unhealthy or suffer from emotional distress. However, they are quick to repudiate this with a reminder that applicants to training courses are intensively screened.

King's (2011) small-scale research study showed that there were a number of dilemmas such as boundary issues when supervision and therapy were 'in house'. Other uncertainties arose around confidentiality and fitness to practice as well as concerns and poor motivation and reluctance to engage on the part of trainees.

Similarly, Moller et al.'s study (2009) even found that trainees may become preoccupied with their own troubles at the cost of their client work, although McMahon (2018) reviewed other studies yielding only positive results, and indicating that personal therapy is one of the three top influences on professional development with the other two being clinical supervision and working with clients, (Grimmer and Tribe, 2001; Orlinsky et al., 2005, 2011; Bike et al., 2009; Geller, 2011; McMahon and Hevey, 2017; Murphy, 2008). These findings are not at all surprising, but they also illustrate personal therapy enhancing empathy and emotional resilience. Conversely, there were only a small number of reports of negative experiences within these studies, which included financial stress.

McMahon's (2018) comprehensive review and debate highlight the pros and cons against a backdrop of personal therapy mandated by the Psychological Society of Ireland. Interestingly, she points out that despite the BACP removing the requirement, over 50 per cent of BACP accredited courses still require personal therapy during training.

The pros and cons of mandatory personal therapy in training

In this next section, Jayne Godward argues why she believes that students should have personal therapy during counsellor training and uses the views of some of her students on the benefits of this, while Heather Dale, argues against these points. Having read our discussion, you can make up your mind as to whether personal therapy should be compulsory on counsellor training.

Jayne: I would like to argue in favour of personal therapy being mandatory on counsellor training courses. This is based on my experience as a personal tutor and course leader and is backed up by feedback given to me by students currently studying on our courses.

Heather: I am going to debate with Jayne. My experience, both from anecdotal evidence and evidence-based research, suggests that while therapy is important, mandatory therapy can sometimes do nothing to encourage self-development and/or self-analysis.

Jayne: My first reason is that it is very useful for students to experience the role of the client and to have a first-hand understanding of how counselling works in practice. Unless you have counselling yourself, you do not realise the vulnerability and uncertainty that a client experiences when they first begin counselling. You don't recognise the importance of the counselling relationship and the pain and emotional side of uncovering experiences or feelings that were buried or too difficult to look at.
Is it fair to expect our clients to go to these deep dark places, if we aren't prepared to go there ourselves or are avoiding these?
Many of my students would not have gone for personal therapy had it not been a course requirement.

> I feel that I have more understanding of how clients will feel attending their first counselling session, it can make you feel nervous and unsure. I also have a better understanding of endings and how clients may feel when it is time to end. Overall, I feel that I can be more empathic and understanding towards clients.
>
> (Year 1 diploma student)

Heather: This is what I call one of the great myths of mandatory or compulsory personal therapy for trainees. It is the myth that having had the same experience as someone else increases empathy. It does not. What increases empathy is the ability to use one's own experience/imagination to relate the feelings to someone else's completely different experience. As an example, I have never experienced the grief of losing a child. However, I have experienced other forms of both grief and bereavements. I have also read and spoken with many people, both women and men, who have lost a child. This has given me enough understanding to be able to empathise with that grief, and to offer a place to explore the feelings of anguish that losing a child brings.

Jayne uses anecdotal evidence (evidence from one person's story rather than evidence taken from a research trial) to make her point. Of course, for some trainees, therapy will be a great help, but for some it will be positively damaging. As Carole says in her introduction to this chapter, there is little or no evidential research that demonstrates mandatory therapy is of benefit or that it equals being a better therapist (Chaturvedi, 2013). This is one of the reasons that, in 2011, BACP dropped their requirement for members to have had personal therapy. Given these two facts, it would be interesting to know why many or most training organisations currently insist on trainees having some personal therapy, usually between ten and 70 hours depending on the provider (Chaturvedi, 2013).

We also need to bear in mind the first of Rogers' (1957) 'necessary and sufficient conditions', which states that clients should be in a vulnerable and anxious state. On these grounds alone, it is hard to justify trainees going into therapy merely for the sake of the experience. Trainees who are not ready to go into therapy may be wasting both their time and money.

Jayne: In their study Rizq and Target (2008) identify that some students can use their therapist as a role model. I learned a lot from how my therapist worked, as well as how I would not want to work. Counselling is a very isolated profession; it is very rare for us to observe a counsellor at work. Attending your own therapy is a way of learning how to practice while undergoing this yourself. My students have found this useful. It may be a way of learning about managing boundaries and about how to be professional. One student said:

> I had not had counselling before the course, so for me it was a new experience, I am learning from my personal therapist, watching how she is with me, thinking about how I do things with my clients, I challenge myself, I think it has been very beneficial and given me an understanding of how my clients feel.

Heather: First, we need to consider the point of personal therapy. It is to help the client move toward change and/or to explore blind spots. It is hard and painful work and needs total commitment from client and therapist.

While I agree with Jayne's point that there is a lot to be said for observing experienced counsellors at work, personal therapy is not the space for this. If trainees are watching how their own therapist works, they are not allowing themselves to be truly immersed in the process of their own therapy. In this way they are doing themselves a disservice rather than gaining self-knowledge from the process. It is not the point of personal therapy for the therapist to demonstrate their techniques but rather for the client to be helped to explore their own issues.

As a trainer, I make sure there is plenty of space for students to watch tutors working with each other as counsellor and client, or to watch videos of professionals working. This is true of most counselling courses and gives the opportunity to discuss the issues later. Again most, if not all, courses have their students work in threes, where one student takes on the role of the observer. This gives time to consider and reflect on each other's ways of working. So, my argument is that this this can and should be done within the training. This is because trainees can sit back and observe rather than be expected to be focusing inwards on themselves

Jayne: The obvious benefit of having personal therapy is so that you can really look at yourself and increase your self-awareness, looking at past events, relationships and how these have impacted on your personality. This increased awareness may prevent harm to clients in that if you are aware of what you are doing and the motives for your actions you will be able to spot when you are over-identifying with a client or when you are being biased or prejudiced due to your own values and beliefs. So, chances of discrimination or unfair practice can be reduced.

Often students are not aware that they have personal issues before beginning therapy, as with a student who said:

> I have found that I have been able to discuss personal issues with my counsellor that I did not even realise were affecting me and my personal life. I have found that I have 'unfinished business' regarding my previous job and how I was treated, and I didn't realise how it was affecting me and my personal and professional life until I took it to my therapy sessions. This has really helped me to better understand myself and how I have been acting and feeling and dealing with difficult situations in my current life.

Also, becoming more self-aware through therapy might help students recognise wounded healer traits or other traits that might lead to them being sucked in to an unhealthy relationship with a client. With a wounded healer trait, you may be using your counselling work to help heal yourself and the best interests of the client may not be paramount. Often students have a strong 'please others' driver, which would mean they collude with clients rather than challenge unhelpful behaviour. Those with strong rescuer tendencies may be tempted to cross boundaries in a wish to help their client. Being more self-aware through therapy can help you protect yourself and keep your personal boundaries, enhancing self-care.

One student said the benefits of personal therapy were 'increased self-awareness and ability to understand one's personal process which in turn protects the counsellor and client alike from the intrusion of the counsellor's own personal issues into the client's process'.

Heather: This is what I call the second great myth of mandatory therapy for trainees. It may be true, as Wosket (1999) so neatly puts it, that personal development and personal therapy can be compared to gardening: in the first the weeds are pulled out but will soon grow again but in the second they are dug out and eradicated. Actually, while this is a lovely metaphor, it is no truer in therapy than in gardening: weeds, however carefully dug out, do generally return each year and in the same way, however well we understand ourselves we will still sometimes behave as if we are still the child we once were. For some, personal therapy is all-important on the journey to becoming a therapist, but for others, alternative forms of personal development may lead to an equal amount of self-knowledge and self-analysis. The PD group may be one example of much of their personal development.

This myth leaves out another important fact: that people who don't want therapy don't use it properly.

Not everyone who wants to be a therapist is a 'wounded healer'. This means not everyone will have undergone and come through severe or medium trauma, and as a result, have decided to train as a therapist in order to help others. Some may have other motivations for coming into the profession and wanting to help people heal.

As an example of trainees who are not motivated to engage in therapy, I once had a client, a trainee, who came to me for his compulsory 25 sessions of therapy. Although he undoubtedly had issues that he could have worked with, he was so angry about having been made to come that he did very little work in those sessions. However, when he returned on his own terms some two years later, having suffered from some life-changing events, he did some wonderful work and made great progress in understanding himself better.

The therapist who works with this kind of trainee client puts themselves in a double bind: they are taking money from someone who does not want to be there (the first rule of therapy is that it does not work if the client does not want to be there) but they also know if they don't, the next therapist might.

What was your motivation for beginning counsellor training?

If your training provider insists on personal therapy, what are your thoughts on this?

Jayne: Having personal therapy during training means that there is support available when students hit personal difficulties when working with clients or when covering material on their courses. Sometimes client issues really resonate with our own material and we need somewhere to take this. To an extent this can be done in supervision but sometimes it is beyond the remit of supervision. The personal therapy is also a big support for issues that arise in the PD group and gives students a private space to explore material which they can then share in their groups.

Heather: Again, I agree with Jayne that personal therapy can be helpful. In particular it can be a space to discuss difficult issues that arise in the PD group (although the PD group needs a clear rule that this is acceptable practice). However, this will not be the case for all students and thus I maintain my position that personal therapy should be encouraged but not be made mandatory. This would make a much more flexible system rather than imposing ten or 20 sessions on students, which can become just a tick-box exercise.

Jayne: I would like to argue that having personal therapy makes you a more effective counsellor. If you have done personal exploration and know yourself more, you can use yourself more in the counselling relationship. This might mean that you are more aware of how you are being, how you are reacting and when to share of yourself or self-disclose.

Having personal therapy can increase self-confidence and self-esteem, which will help in the work and also give you confidence in the counselling process.

If you are more emotionally mature, it seems to make it easier for students to work with emotions in their clients. Many students I work with start off being afraid of their emotions or ashamed of them and do not feel comfortable with showing them. I think if you are comfortable with different emotions and their expression, you will be comfortable working with them. Usually you would only become aware of this through personal therapy. I have found that students who have not started personal therapy tend to work in less depth during their skills sessions than those who have done a lot of personal exploration and are more in touch with their feelings.

Students who are being defensive and are protecting themselves and their emotions are likely to want to make things better for clients, e.g., emphasising the positives or avoiding negative emotions altogether.

Heather: These are all good points, but they do not make the argument for mandatory personal therapy. I totally agree that counselling training needs to incorporate a high level of personal development including the ability to understand and express emotions (what might be called emotional literacy). Personal therapy, if used well, will certainly help in achieving these ends. However, it is not the only way, nor is it necessarily the most appropriate way for all students. The PD group, while not a therapy group, does offer the chance for personal development, as do many other activities within the courses.

Conclusion

Jayne: It has been interesting discussing these issues with Heather and I do agree with some of her points; however, I am still of the opinion that students do benefit from personal therapy and most would not go for this if it was not stipulated for on counselling courses due to the expense and the extra commitment. Personally, I would probably have not gone for therapy if I had not been required to do so and I would have missed out on all the learning I gained from this and the individual and confidential support of my counsellor. I would have also missed out on having a model in my counsellor in the way she approached her work. I was not deliberately looking at what she was doing but just as we learn from experiences with people we are close to, e.g., parents, partners, friends, we learn from our therapists.

My previous experience working with different groups and hearing their contributions in PD groups give evidence for the value of personal therapy for development. The students who have not used their personal therapy or have not found it valuable have been in the minority not the general majority.

Heather: I too have enjoyed this exchange. During the writing of it I have become more and more convinced that while I agree, as I have said consistently, personal therapy is a useful adjunct to any would-be therapist, there is no evidence that mandatory therapy works for everyone. When therapy is just a tick-box to complete coursework, its value is sorely diminished. The PD group, at its best, offers a huge opportunity for personal development (provided that the facilitator is outside the teaching group) and maybe that should be considered good enough. Not everyone who wants to be a therapist is also a 'wounded healer'.

Jayne and Heather have offered two contradictory views on the pros and cons of mandatory therapy.

Having read these arguments for and against this, what is your view?

Overall conclusion

It can be seen from this debate that the subject of personal therapy in counselling training elicits strong feelings on both sides, and it is important to draw the distinction between optional and course-led mandatory personal therapy. Jayne's argument is based on her personal experience as a trainer and her belief that *counsellors should have an in depth understanding themselves which can only be achieved through personal therapy*. As Rizq and Target's (2008) study showed, having personal therapy was helpful in learning through role modelling. Jayne's conviction that we need to 'go to these deep dark places', in order to understand and be able to support clients in their own depths of emotion is perhaps based on an assumption that there will necessarily be an assimilation of learning about ourselves and others, which will help in client work. In many cases, this may be absolutely right and is borne out by Jayne's survey of her own students. It is also supported through outcomes in my own PhD research in which many of the participants talked about how personal therapy sustained and helped them to process their own personal development.

However, as Heather points out, this assumption is not and should not be a 'go to' for our learning about ourselves and clients. There are many ways we learn about ourselves in relation to clients, not least in working at the coal-face with them and making mistakes which can be managed through clinical supervision. In fact, conversely, as Moller et al. (2009) showed, trainees can get preoccupied with their own issues at the cost of the client work.

As Cooper (2008) demonstrated, in order to benefit most from counselling, the time has to be right and the client motivated. Enforcing personal therapy may have the opposite effect on trainees resulting in demotivation and resentment. My own experience in my psychotherapy training, which required me to be in therapy for the duration of training, led me to initially 'pay lip service' to it as I was not ready to explore myself in depth. However, sometime later, I realised the benefits of personal exploration and was more able to take on the support of my therapist when I became a more 'mature' trainee. Indeed, I am still motivated to access therapy now and again to help support me in difficult personal and professional situations and can absolutely learn things from differing styles, techniques and approaches to help me in my own work.

Although Heather's use of the gardening metaphor is useful, if we deal with weeds thoroughly enough we can bring about change and difference in the particular patch we are tending. So, even if we go to therapy as part of a course requirement, we must not assume that the individual will self-reflect and learn from it; there is no checklist that can be ticked off in relation to 'necessary items learned about ourselves'. It is only if the gardener is careful and motivated enough to deal with the weeds completely, that any transformation will occur.

Jayne's point about the avoidance of personal therapy is a good one. My own experience of working with students generally is that a perceived unpleasant task will be forestalled or side-stepped completely – this is human nature after all. However, there is an ethical consideration that supports Jayne's argument here; that the client should have a right to the 'best possible' care from a personally developed, self-aware counsellor according to the principles of non-maleficence and beneficence (McMahon, 2018) to reduce the possibility of harm. However, there is no evidence, as Heather points out, that the client experience is enhanced by counsellors having had their own therapy.

Perhaps clinical supervision could be used more effectively in the identification of issues that arise in the trainee's client work or personal domains, with the supervisor helping her/him to identify a time when counselling is needed. Similarly, course trainers could do the same through personal development groups on a regular basis.

On the whole, there seems to be little doubt that personal therapy is beneficial to both counsellors and trainees, if used effectively and if the individual is motivated. The caveat, of course, is whether this should be enforced or just advocated at some point in training.

To sum up, in the words of Hughes, Kinder and Cooper (2018, p. 255):

> In resilience terms, personal and professional development is concerned with acquiring skills and competencies to enhance our knowledge and understanding, and in so doing become better adept and resourced to tackle all the tasks, demands, challenges and stresses which life throws at us.

The question remains, is mandatory personal therapy within counselling training the best way to do this?

References

Atkinson, P. (2006) Personal therapy in the training of therapists. *European Journal of Psychotherapy & Counselling*, 8(4), pp. 407–410.

Bike, D.H., Norcross, J.C. and Schatz, D.M. (2009) Processes and outcomes of psychotherapists' personal therapy: Replication and extension 20 years later. *Psychotherapy: Theory, Research, Practice, Training*, 46(1), pp. 19–31.

Chaturvedi, S. (2013) Mandatory personal therapy: Does the evidence justify the practice? In debate. *British Journal of Guidance and Counselling*, 41(4), pp. 454–460.

Clark, M.M. (1986) Personal therapy: A review of empirical research. *Professional Psychology: Research and Practice*, 17(6), pp. 541–543.

Cooper, M. (2008) *Essential Research Findings in Counselling and Psychotherapy: The Facts are Friendly*. London: Sage.

Geller, J. D. (2011) The psychotherapy of psychotherapists. *Journal of Clinical Psychology*, 67(8), pp. 759–765.

Grimmer, A. and Tribe, R. (2001) Counselling psychologists' perceptions of the impact of mandatory personal therapy on professional development – an exploratory study. *Counselling Psychology Quarterly*, 14(4), pp. 287–301.

Hughes, R., Kinder, A. and Cooper, C.L. (2018) *The Wellbeing Workout*. London: Palgrave Macmillan.

King, G. (2011) Psychodynamic therapists' dilemmas in providing personal therapy to therapists in training: An exploratory study. *Counselling and Psychotherapy Research*, 11(3), pp. 186–195.

Kumari, N. (2011) Personal therapy as a mandatory requirement for counselling psychologists in training: A qualitative study of the impact of therapy on trainees' personal and professional development. *Counselling Psychology Quarterly*, 24(93), pp. 211–232.

Macran, S. and Shapiro, D.A. (1998) The role of personal therapy for therapists: A review. *British Journal of Medical Psychology*, 71(1), pp. 13–25.

McMahon, A. (2018) Irish clinical and counselling psychologists' experiences and views of mandatory personal therapy during training: A polarisation of ethical concerns. *Clinical Psychology & Psychotherapy*, 25(3), pp. 415–426.

McMahon, A. and Hevey, D. (2017) 'It has taken me a long time to get to this point of quiet confidence': What contributes to therapeutic confidence for clinical psychologists? *Clinical Psychologist*, 21, pp. 195–205.

Moller, N.P., Timms, J. and Alilovic, K. (2009) Risky business or safety net? Trainee perceptions of personal therapy: a qualitative thematic analysis. *European Journal of Psychotherapy & Counselling*, 11(4), pp. 369–384.

Murphy, D. (2008) A qualitative study into the experience of mandatory personal therapy during training. *Counselling and Psychotherapy Research*, 5(1), pp. 27–32.

Orlinksy, D., Norcross, J., Ronnestad, M. and Wiseman, H. (2005) Outcomes and impacts of the psychotherapist's own psychotherapy: A research review. In J. Geller, J. Norcross and D. Orlinksy (eds.), *The Psychotherapist's Own Psychotherapy*. New York: Oxford University Press, pp. 214–230.

Orlinsky, D.E., Schofield, M.J., Schroder, T. and Kazantzis, N. (2011) Utilization of personal therapy by psychotherapists: A practice-friendly review and a new study. *Journal of Clinical Psychology*, 67(8), pp. 828–842.

Rizq, R. and Target, M. (2008) 'Not a little Mickey Mouse thing': How experienced counselling psychologists describe the meaning and significance of personal therapy in clinical practice. *Counselling Psychology Quarterly*, 21(1), pp. 29–48.

Rogers, C. (1957) The necessary and sufficient conditions of therapeutic personality change. *Journal of Consulting Psychology*, 21(2), pp. 95–203.

Wosket, V. (1999) *The Therapeutic Use of Self: Counselling Practice, Research and Supervision*. London: Routledge.

Chapter 14

Supervision and personal development

Heather Dale and Jayne Godward

Introduction

The aim of this chapter is to explore how supervision helps us to become more aware of our blind spots and develop personally. Although supervision is often seen as being only about professional practice, it also allows us to become more aware of areas for personal development. This is because time will be spent exploring our responses to clients and the dynamics of the counselling relationship. We can also learn more about ourselves by examining the process in the supervision relationship itself.

We will use case examples and our own experiences as supervisors to make our points clear. Research will also be drawn upon to discuss this interesting area. So, in this chapter we will look at:

- what supervision is and why it matters;
- choosing a supervisor and what this says about our wants and needs;
- personal learning from the process and dynamics of the supervisory counselling relationship and its development;
- the role of the supervisor in helping trainees become more aware of areas for personal development through exploring responses to clients;
- the personal development effects of being in a positive or negative supervisory relationship;
- how our personal history affects the supervisory relationship.

What is supervision?

Therapy is an odd profession in that it is the only one that we are aware of in which trainees are not overseen in their work. This is because of the confidential nature of the work with clients. So, supervision is not synchronous (done at the same time) as the client work, but takes place later, usually once a fortnight for trainees.

All reputable therapists, however experienced, will have a supervisor who they talk to regularly and who offers a safe place to discuss client work, to offload when necessary and who offers support and advice.

But what is supervision? BACP defines it as:

> A specialised form of professional mentoring provided for practitioners responsible for undertaking challenging work with people. Supervision is provided to ensure

standards, enhance quality, stimulate creativity and support the sustainability and resilience of the work being undertaken.

(BACP, 2018)

If we break this down a little, it becomes clear that supervision involves a high level of experience and knowledge and is also a key activity for all therapists as the supervisor is the person who will have the best idea of how client work is going and how trainee and qualified therapists can progress.

Given that many trainees consider supervision to be the pivotal experience of their training, the importance of supervision cannot be exaggerated (Kozlowski et al., 2014).

It is also the place where we can become aware of implicit processes that are going on for us when we are working with clients. Or it can highlight when we need to do more personal development work on ourselves. This extra knowledge allows us to be more effective in our work with clients, often by being able to be clearer about what belongs to us and what belongs to the client.

Case study: Tracy

Tracy is a first-year diploma student. She was struggling with a client, Amy, who was very stuck. Amy had had 15 sessions with Tracy after her marriage break-down but did not seem to be moving on at all. Amy seemed defensive and Tracy felt a failure. She was new to counselling and doubted her abilities. She eventually shared with her supervisor what her interventions were in the sessions and her supervisor discovered that Tracy was trying to problem-solve the situation rather than listen to her client's experiences.

When her supervisor made this observation, Tracy realised that she needed her client to be happy as she had been through a comparable situation and was finding it hard to hear her client's story. Instead of giving Amy the chance to explore and express her feelings Tracy was pushing her to move on with her life before she was ready.

Through supervision Tracy also realised that her client felt a failure for not making her marriage work and Tracy was feeling a failure for not helping her client, so there was a parallel process going on.

The above is an example of how supervision can make us aware of our blind spots and the areas that we struggle to work with due to our own life experiences. Becoming more aware of these meant Tracy could work more effectively and was able to listen to her client more.

The strange relationship: The process and dynamics of supervision

The supervisory relationship is a slightly odd relationship in that while the supervisor is independent of the training establishment and of the placement, they would normally be required to write at least one report. These reports go to the training organisation and may be a deciding factor in whether or not the supervisee succeeds in their training. This is known as an *evaluative function*. Part of this function will be to work with the trainee regarding their professional and ethical behaviour. It is worth remembering that for most trainees, such as members of the BACP or the British Psychological Society, the supervisor may hold the ultimate responsibility for the well-being of the trainee's clients, so they have a fair amount invested in the process themselves.

Therefore, the supervisor is in a position of authority, not only in terms of their experience and knowledge but also in terms of having some say in the student's final result. As the final arbiter on the student's ability to work independently as a therapist they may be perceived as having much power. This can bring up old issues of dealing with authority figures. Expecting our supervisors to behave in the way that, say, our parents or teachers did, can be positive, if our early experiences of authority were mostly good, or can be negative, if early experiences were mostly negative. This is a process known as transference, which is defined as is a redirection of feelings about one individual to another individual (Short and Thomas, 2015).

Given that our responses to perceived authority figures are likely to be consistent, an examination of the relationship between group facilitator and trainee within the PD group might also be useful. This is because the facilitator may also be perceived as a powerful authority figure and the same issues as mentioned above may surface. These issues may well be replicated within the supervisory processes, so it can be a good idea to consider them early in the training process.

Activity

Consider your early experiences of authority figures such as your parents or teachers:

How do you consider you were treated? How did you respond?
Do you respond in the same way to the PD facilitator? Course tutors?
If so, can you link this back to past experiences?

Choosing a supervisor – what does this say about your wants and needs?

As you get closer to starting a placement, where you will be seeing 'real' clients, you need to find a supervisor to help steer you through the challenges and difficulties you might face. The PD group can offer some support in helping you explore what you want from supervision and the best ways of getting your needs met. The case studies in this chapter give examples of how the PD group, discussed earlier, might be used in this way.

Right from the moment of choosing a supervisor it is possible to learn about your own unconscious processes. Sometimes it is not the supervisor themselves that is important but other factors entirely. For example, one student said that she did not want to work with a certain supervisor because when she visited their home where they had their work room, there were shoes everywhere in the hallway and she felt that the environment was rather chaotic. Another felt as if his supervisor's room was in a garden shed. A third person did not like going upstairs in her male supervisor's house as it felt too intimate being taken past bedrooms.

These comments are likely to be the outward expression of the student's own concerns and worries rather than necessarily anything about the supervisor or where they practise. For example, the student who complains about shoes everywhere may be expressing a fear of her own chaos, or a fear of running from the process; the student who is concerned about passing bedrooms (how did the student know they were bedrooms?) is expressing her own fears, possibly of intimacy or perhaps of attraction to the supervisor, and the garden shed issue may be a student who is anxious that he will not be taken seriously.

These sorts of issues can be usefully brought to and explored in the PD group. It may be that for some people working with a supervisor who initially does not seem a good match but who will take the supervisee outside their comfort zone is useful and worth having. Whereas for less confident individuals, their first supervisor might need to be someone with whom they feel comfortable with right from the beginning.

Raising therapist self-awareness leads to increased confidence and congruence which makes client work more effective (Vallance, 2005). Supervision is also useful in highlighting blind spots, such as strongly held views, stereotypes and prejudices.

For example, an issue that often comes up in supervision is about age; students may have rigid views about older people. This may lead them to treating clients differently because of their numerical age or making assumptions about their abilities.

At the other end of the spectrum, older students with younger clients can easily slip into a parenting role as they may be comparing their clients with their own children and may want to 'mother' the person rather than seeing them as a young independent adult. Supervision can be a time to consider these aspects.

What kind of supervisor do you want?

There are different modes of supervision but basically it comes down to the supervisor who is 'case-centred' and encourages a focus on the client work, or the 'therapist-centred' approach, which focuses on the therapist's feelings and concerns, or a hybrid of both those two.

Another way of describing this is to say that supervision has three functions normative, formative and restorative (Proctor, 1986; Henderson et al., 2014). In this scenario, normative is a managerial function, relating to accountability in terms of ethical, legal and professional issues; the formative process relates to the supervisee developing their professional identity, through the learning of skills development; and the restorative function offers emotional and professional support. Parker, Suetani and Motamarri (2017, p. 625) describe this rather neatly as 'as a balance between the supervisor "looking after" and "looking over" the supervisee'.

It is worth thinking about what you are expecting from supervision in terms of these tasks, as there should be elements of all these occurring when working with your supervisor. For example, if you just want a cosy place to go to talk about client work and gain support with no challenge, you may be being unrealistic and may be feeling very insecure about your work and abilities. The same would apply if you want to go and learn from your supervisor but not look at what is going on for you or not wanting to be challenged on how you are working. There may be aspects of yourself that you are trying to avoid or wanting to hide.

The case study below shows what can happen when there is not a balance between the supervisory functions.

Case study: Janet

Janet has 50 hours of client hours She has supervision from Tam, who she finds very supportive and encouraging. As far as she can see there are no issues with her client work and everything is going well. She has to submit a tape of her client work for her final piece of work and brings it to Tam for them to discuss together. As always Tam is nothing but encouraging.

However, Janet's course tutors disagree, telling her that they can see no evidence of change in her client, and that she must resubmit. Janet takes this back to Tam asking why she has been so encouraging. Tam explains that she does not see her job as offering criticism but to offer a space for reflection and emotional support.

In this scenario, Tam has offered a restorative model of supervision. She had given Janet a safe place to talk about her clients but has not encouraged Janet to think about her working styles and develop as a therapist. In order to do this, the supervisor needs to offer some challenges as well as encouragement. Ultimately, this has been detrimental for Janet.

The role of the supervisor in your personal development

As supervisors who work with trainees, we see our roles as nurturing and being supportive to the student who is just starting placement. We aim to provide a secure base so that they can come to talk to us about their work, fears and anxieties about beginning placement and working with clients. Sometimes there are issues about working in an agency where they might struggle with being a student among experienced and qualified practitioners. We also want to encourage our trainees to value the work they are doing and to share their achievements. Early work with supervisees might involve helping them build self-confidence and help value the skills they bring to the work.

Trainees at the beginning often focus on the client and what they are bringing and their narratives. We see our roles as encouraging our supervisees to look at their process and how this affects the client. By process we mean what happens for the counsellor on hearing the client's story, how they see and experience the client and how they react to the client internally, resulting in external behaviours and interventions.

Supervision is about the whole of the supervisee's professional development, so as well as providing this safe space we are also always mindful of our obligations to help students become more aware of legal and ethical issues, as well as their personal issues. This will help them to develop their burgeoning skills.

In the following example the supervisor would need to be aware of the ethical issues while working with the counsellor's personal process and needs.

Case study: Glenn

Glenn is a second-year trainee who has been working with his client, Nina, for several sessions. They appear to have built a good relationship where she has shared a lot about her relationship break-up, her life and her frustrations. Glenn has found that she has similar hobbies and interests to himself and feels really on the same wavelength with her. To add to this, she is very striking in appearance and he finds her extremely attractive.

He admires the life she leads, going to music festivals and appearing to have many friends and contacts. This was what Glenn used to do before he married and had his three children. What Nina represents to him is the life he has lost, which is in stark contrast to the existence has he working full-time.

When he sees his supervisor, he trusts her enough to disclose that his counselling relationship is becoming more personal and that he would like to move it on a stage, as he is really drawn to his client.

What does Glenn need to look at here in his supervision in terms of his blind spots and also the ethical issues involved?

This is not an uncommon situation, but the role of the supervisor is to help the trainee look below the surface of what is going on. Here the supervisee was able to share what was happening because he trusted his supervisor, even though potentially this could have led to condemnation. What the supervisor has to do here is balance the supportive/restorative elements of her work with the normative aspects related to working ethically (Henderson et al., 2014).

Our experience as supervisees

On the other side of the coin, we have found our own supervision invaluable in keeping an eye on what is happening to us in terms of our fitness to practice and in terms of our resilience.

As trainees, we both had to bring transcripts and recordings of sessions to supervision on a regular basis. Although it is hard to have your work so exposed and writing a transcript takes a long time, it does help to develop work. This is because listening to a tape over and over again means that you can notice, for example, when you are saying too much, or not allowing pauses, or interrupting the client, It also gives you a chance to think about your use of skills: to ask yourself what you meant with each intervention and to look at whether or not it was therapeutically useful.

Both of us encourage students to bring recorded client sessions, as tone and expressions are so important and cannot necessarily be judged from reported conversations. It can feel a difficult experience as a recorded session is so 'in your face' but it is also a great learning experience. It allows the listener to reflect on their interventions: and in particular where their own agenda or issues might have come into play. This is called attending to the process of counselling, and helps us to notice our own issues, as for instance when the need to be helpful means we are giving advice.

Often, we are drawn to areas of client work that are too close to our own experiences and our motives for choosing these are not obvious. Jayne chose to go into cancer support because of her personal experience but did not realise how she was losing her empathy and was becoming burnt-out by the work. Supervision was essential for challenging her to look at her responses and attitudes to her clients and her work. The work was of an existential nature and also helped Jayne look at her beliefs and views on life generally (Godward, 2007).

Supervision as in this example can also help highlight the need for personal therapy on unresolved issues.

The development of the supervisory relationship

At first, the challenge of telling someone about what is happening between you and your clients may seem rather frightening. However, a relationship of trust should develop, in which both can feel comfortable enough to challenge and be challenged. We have seen the importance of this in the previous section. Supervision is a place to obtain reflection and feedback, which is not something that can be achieved through client work alone (Wilson et al., 2015).

Within supervision, while the focus is always on encouraging the supervisee to be more effective in helping clients reach desired outcomes, there are other issues apart from the actual client work that can emerge. For example, a student may have a client with an issue that mirrors their own. This could be almost anything but examples could include: the early loss of a parent or close family member; a client with a history of abuse that also applies to the trainee; or a client who struggles with mental health issues. This can sometimes lead to inappropriate techniques used in the counselling process and it can take some teasing out within supervision to discover what the underlying issues may be.

Case study: Ola

Ola has just begun the second year of his training. He has also just started his placement at an organisation that offers up to 12 sessions of therapy. He talks very positively about it to his supervisor, Cathy. He tells her how much he is enjoying the work and how much progress his clients are making. He explains how much they benefit from all the good advice he gives them. Cathy questions him about the advice-giving and Ola explains that he is responding to questions he is asked. Cathy suggests that this may not be appropriate. Feeling criticised and misunderstood, Ola stops telling Cathy everything that is happening with his clients.

After a couple of months Cathy comments that she has noticed that Ola never appears to bring problems with his work and she wonders why this is. They look together at his caseload and she notices how many DNAs (Did Not Attend) there are and comments that this is not something he has mentioned. He says that this is because there is no point – if someone does not come back after one session, they are clearly not ready for therapy. Cathy asks him if he has ever considered that there may be something in his approach that causes this. Ola is not willing to look at this and leaves feeling very angry with Cathy for suggesting, as he sees it, that his work is anything less than perfect.

He brings it up in the PD group where, to his surprise, he is given feedback that while he is a useful member of the group, he does seem to see his role as the 'wise man' of the group, offering help and advice where none has been asked for.

Within the group, where he feels safe, Ola is more able to consider this feedback and takes it back to Cathy where they discuss it, both in terms of the client work and also in terms of their developing relationship.

As the supervisory relationship continues it will hopefully deepen. It should become the place where issues and dilemmas can be brought and discussed openly in a safe space. However, sometimes the relationship becomes unsatisfactory for the trainee. It may have become too cosy, and the student may no longer feel that they are developing, or too confrontational, or – in some cases that we have known – sexualised.

In any of these cases, the PD group may be a better place than personal therapy to explore what is happening, although both may be useful and may throw up different issues to be considered in each. In the same way that the PD group is not a personal therapy group, nor is it a supervision group, it can be a place to reflect and get feedback for professional development.

Case study: Sadiq

Sadiq, a first-year trainee, has been seeing his supervisor for a few months. He chose him because he was a male, lived in his area and had a lot of experience. The first session went well, with them discussing things generally and agreeing a contract together, but as the sessions progressed he felt that his supervisor was challenging him too much and questioning his interventions with the client.

Sadiq got to a stage where he was feeling criticised rather than supported. In his head he kept saying to himself, 'Man up! This person is trying to help you improve your work – if you cannot take criticism what sort of man are you?'

He eventually shared his thoughts and feelings in the PD group. By hearing other people's views and reflections he realised that his confidence was being knocked, but another part of him was saying he should be able to take this, which linked to his culture's norms about being a strong male.

He also realised that his supervisor reminded him of an elderly relative who always seemed disapproving. He unpicked all of this in his group and as a result was able to discuss openly what he wanted from supervision in their next session

---

In this scenario Sadiq learned about his own processes by stepping back and looking at what was going on for him as a result of his interactions with his supervisor. He realised how much his upbringing and previous relationships impacted on his work and his patterns of relating in the present. It also made it clearer what actions he needed to take to change his relationship with his supervisor so that his needs were met more fully.

Another example of what can happen in supervision that is brought into PD groups is when a student loses faith in their supervisor.

Case study: Loss of trust

In a PD group, Jess said that she did not want to share her work with her supervisor, Ray, because she had lost trust in him. Their relationship had started well but her supervisor always seemed to be in a rush and did not seem prepared for their sessions. Jess did not feel he was trustworthy and reliable, and this had created a block for her. She discussed this further in her group and found that it took her back to partners she had had who had let her down or were not really interested in her. She was seeing her supervisor in the same light.

What became apparent was that her expectations of men were very low and because on a couple of sessions Ray seemed a bit flustered or had confused a couple of her clients, she had jumped to the conclusion that he was not wanting to work with her and was not interested.

The group helped her to check the reality of her beliefs and also accept that supervisors are human and make mistakes. They also highlighted a wish she had for a 'perfect' supervisor, which was unrealistic.

As a result of this Jess was able to discuss how she felt with her supervisor and this led to him apologising for any minor mistakes he had made, but also the relationship deepened and her trust built again due to the new honesty between them.

Conclusion

In this chapter we have explained what supervision is and why it is important within therapy. We have looked at the role of the supervisor, stressing that supervision is about the whole of the therapist's professional and personal development, and not just about client work. We have examined some of the processes of choosing a supervisor and explained how sometimes this can be driven by childhood patterns of behaviour. Taking the time to learn to understand these patterns will enhance personal development and therefore client work. Reflecting on these patterns can best be done within the supervision itself, within personal therapy or within the PD group.

We have included several case studies that we hope you will be able to reread and learn from as you continue your training. You will see from the case studies that the PD group can help students see situations more clearly and empower them to take action, which can lead to more professional and ethical practice.

We have also shared some of own experiences, both as trainees ourselves and later as supervisors of trainees. In writing this section, we reminded ourselves how useful we found recording our early work, which is why we encourage trainees to bring both transcripts and audio recordings to supervision whenever possible, despite the effort involved.

We have mentioned the PD group as a useful place for support and learning, although we have stressed that the PD group is not instead of personal therapy, nor instead of supervision, but rather as a source of peer support and a place to take a fresh approach to issues that have occurred.

References

BACP (2018) *Ethical Framework: Glossary*. Lutterworth: BACP.

Godward, J. (2007) Cancerland. *Therapy Today*, 18(3), pp. 18–20.

Henderson, P., Holloway, J. and Millar, A. (2014) *Practical Supervision*. London: Jessica Kingsley Publishers.

Kozlowski, J.M., Pruitt, N.T., DeWalt, T.A. and Knox, S. (2014) Can boundary crossings in clinical supervision be beneficial? *Counselling Psychology Quarterly*, 27(2), pp. 109–126.

Parker, S., Suetani, S. and Motamarri, B. (2017) On being supervised: Getting value from a clinical supervisor and making the relationship work when it is not. *Australasian Psychiatry*, 25(6), pp. 625–629.

Proctor, B. (1986) Supervision: A co-operative exercise in accountability. In M. Marken and M. Payne (eds.), *Enabling and Ensuring: Supervision in Practice*. Leicester: National Youth Bureau and Council for Education and Training in Youth and Community Work, pp. 21–23.

Short, F. and Thomas, P. (2015) *Core Approaches in Counselling and Psychotherapy*. London: Routledge.

Vallance, K. (2005) Exploring counsellor perceptions of the impact of counselling supervision on clients. *Counselling and Psychotherapy Research*, 5(2), pp. 107–110.

Wilson, H., Davies, J. and Weatherhead, S. (2015) Trainee therapists' experiences of supervision during training: A meta-synthesis. *Clinical Psychology & Psychotherapy*, 23(4), pp. 340–351.

Chapter 15

Self-care and support for trainee counsellors

Heather Dale

No [one] is an island alone, entire of itself.

John Donne (1572–1631)

Introduction

Although it is a hugely rewarding profession, there is no doubt that being a therapist can also be difficult, demanding and lonely. This is in part due to the confidential nature of the service, which means that, unlike most professions, the daily work cannot be discussed outside of supervision. Therefore, the training needs to be rigorous and challenging.

A writer called April Kaeding suggests that students are at particular risk of emotional stress (Kaeding et al., 2017). Trainee therapists have additional stresses, in that they are engaged in their own personal therapy and supervision and also, by the second year, are likely to start seeing clients. Unlike other professions, within therapy training, the biggest stress may be the need for relentless self-analysis and personal development, much of which takes place in the PD group. In addition, many, if not most, students may be working full- or part-time, and/or have personal or professional commitments that have to be balanced with their studies. These are considerable issues to deal with.

All this means that it is easy to become so involved in the course and the new learning that taking good care of one's own emotional and physical needs can easily be forgotten. However, paying attention to both physical and emotional health matters is important for all of us, but especially for therapists. This is because holding clients' emotions and distress can easily become overwhelming and in the worst-case scenarios leads to a breaching of boundaries such as good timekeeping. Looking after ourselves helps aid resilience and makes the holding and maintaining of boundaries easier. It is worth noting here that self-care is important not just for trainees but for all therapists whatever their level of experience.

Therefore, this chapter takes a long look at exactly what self-care is, and how it can be implemented. As self-care and resilience are inextricably linked, I will also define and write about resilience.

In this chapter I will:

- define and explain self-care;
- define and explain resilience;

- explain the connection between resilience and self-care;
- explain what burnout is and what causes it;
- relate the above to the challenges of the PD group;
- give some techniques for increasing self-care;
- encourage the reader to develop a self-care plan to see them through their training.

What is self-care?

Before you read on, do take a look at the quotation at the top of this chapter. John Donne was a British poet who lived in the sixteenth century. The poem reminds us that we are all involved with each other, and all have an impact on each other.

One way of understanding what Donne means is by remembering that self-care does not mean exactly what it says: no one can completely care for themselves without external support. Everyone, to some extent, must rely on external validation for a sense of self or for self-esteem. This means that part of self-care involves having or developing a robust system that involves having other people in our lives, who can be turned to for help and support (and who will also be helped and supported in their turn), but also people who are available to have fun and relax with. Self-care also means building in enough time during the week for solitary time (sometimes this is called spiritual time). This might include socialising, making time for hobbies or having time to spend quietly alone. Whatever it is that is required to recharge batteries needs to be done on a regular basis.

This may sound obvious but, in fact, making time for self-care when also involved in day-to-day living as well as a demanding course can be very hard. It is well-known that that under stress immune systems may lower, and this includes our emotional immune systems. Consequently, it is important to pay close attention to our own needs and make sure that we are in tip top emotional health in order to give full attention to clients.

Self-care involves a certain amount of thoughtful work, starting with an inventory of what is needed. In short, self-care means developing and applying activities that allow us to function well despite professional and personal stressors (Barnett et al., 2009).

What happens without self-care?

Although not an exhaustive list, here are some of the things that can go wrong when therapists have not been taking care of themselves, both physically and psychologically:

- Becoming confused about times of appointments and turning up late or not at all for clients or forgetting which client is due.
- Being unable to hold information forgetting from one week to the next what clients have said.
- Forgetting or deciding not to write up notes in a timely manner.
- Losing or becoming confused about simple boundary issues; for example, not starting or finishing sessions on time.
- Forgetting which issues or emotions belong with the therapist and which belongs with the client; for example, wanting the client to talk about an issue that is really yours.

- Using client time to talk about own issues often under the guise of giving an example.

Remember that therapy is a tiring business and takes energy. If you recognise that any of the above is currently true of you, do consider what steps you might take.

Resilience

One of the most important qualities needed for a therapist is that of resilience. It is often associated with self-care as it is a quality that can enhance and be enhanced by good emotional care.

There is some debate about whether resilience is innate or learned, but there is no debate that it can be developed. I would argue that part of the point of counsellor training is to encourage the development of resilience and, as you will read later, this can be an important learning point within the PD group.

One way of understanding resilience is to see it as having two distinct, but overlapping, meanings:

- the quality of being able to bounce back after a difficulty has arisen;
- the ability to be able to resist being damaged in the first place by being able to put distress to one side and concentrate on the next issue needing to be dealt with (Harms et al., 2018).

Let's take these issues one at a time and see how they relate to therapy.

The ability to bounce back after a difficulty

Therapist training, as I have said, is hard work, and will often throw up difficulties between people. This might be particularly true of the PD group. This is because while the PD group should offer a safe and holding place where students can give each other feedback, which is usually intended to be helpful, it can also be experienced as challenging or confrontational. In this way, it mirrors some of the issues that may be brought up when working with clients. Those with more resilience will be able to deal with difficult feedback more easily than those who have less resilience. This is not to say that it is not normal to feel a little shocked or disappointed if given feedback that is negative. However, if it then feels impossible to return to the group, then that may be a sign that resilience is an area to be worked on.

The ability to resist being damaged in the first place

This is particularly relevant to therapists because we work with clients' distressing issues. Inevitably these will sometimes touch on the therapist's own issues. An example of this might be a therapist who themselves has recently suffered loss or bereavement when that is the issue that the client is bringing. Having enough resilience to hear the client's story without being damaged by own issues is hugely important. In the case of the PD group, resilience is the ability to hear criticism or challenges as observations, whether justified or not, without loss of self-esteem.

Resilience in this case also means being able to 'hold' clients' distressing stories without being emotionally affected outside of the client hour. This can take practice.

In either case, the PD group should be a good place to practise and develop the quality of resilience, as, if the group is working well, members should be challenging each other in a way that may sometimes pick on vulnerable areas. For example, if one group member seems excessively concerned about a particular client, the group may be able to pick that up and offer support or challenge as appropriate. If a group member discusses a client without protecting that client's identity, then hopefully the group would pick up on that.

Burnout

The term *burnout* has become increasingly used to describe those who have become exhausted from day-to-day living.

It is what happens when resilience is depleted, usually due to taking on too much, either personally, professionally or, commonly, from a mixture of the two. Again, there are particular risks here for trainee therapists due to the nature of the training and, later, the work of a therapist. Given that counselling trainees are all adult learners, there may be particular stresses involved, both in terms of time-management and in terms of the emotional hard work of being expected to examine one's self deeply. Before we go further, let's look at a definition of burnout relating to studying:

> Burnout in the study context can be defined as a syndrome of emotional exhaustion that is an outcome of high perceived study demands, the development of a cynical and detached attitude towards one's studies and feelings of inadequacy.
>
> (Salmela-Aro and Read, 2017, p. 21)

A simpler way of saying this is to repeat that burnout is the term used for someone suffering from mental and/or physical exhaustion. Symptoms of exhaustion may include: feeling emotionally exhausted, feelings of low achievement, loss or enthusiasm and so forth (Lawson, 2007). Other symptoms may include a change in sleep patterns (not sleeping as much as normal or sleeping much more than normal) or eating patterns (again, eating much more or less than normal), feeling alone in the world, becoming unusually irritated with small things and other such changes.

Burnout can be seen as having three main components, which are emotional exhaustion, increased cynicism and inefficacy (Callahan et al., 2018).

Emotional exhaustion means a lack of energy for others, and feelings that life and the universe have become too much. Cynicism can be recognised as a feeling that the course, the people in it and the job themselves have become worthless or lack meaning. The trainee who finds themselves saying or thinking that all client problems are beginning to sound similar or that the course itself is useless and they cannot wait to finish may be approaching burnout. Another symptom of cynicism may be compassion fatigue – when the therapist just cannot cope with any more emotional stress from their clients.

Lastly, there is ineffectiveness, particularly for trainees, which can be especially difficult to acknowledge. Utilising good supervision can be of enormous benefit here. It is incredibly important that the trainee trust their supervisor to challenge appropriately and safely and is willing to tell them when/if a client or client work has become too much. It is only through reflection and discussion that any issues in terms of the trainee effectiveness will come to be understood.

Different therapists will have different triggers for burnout: as an example, for some trainees three clients a week will be quite enough, while others are able to see six to eight clients without their resilience being lowered. To some extent this will be down to personality, but it may also be down to the client group. Working in a college setting with a six-session limit for clients may be experienced as less draining that working in an open-ended way with sexually abused clients. Or the opposite may be true.

Burnout and the PD group

While PD groups are notoriously difficult and challenging, they are challenging because they involve not only looking at oneself but also looking at interpersonal styles. This can be hard to hear, especially as the feedback is commonly given within the group setting. The feedback is not necessarily given in the most tactful way and can be experienced, however unintentionally meant, as hurtful. In addition, there is often a requirement to submit a piece of work concerning the group experience that may be graded, although often it is simply assessed as pass or fail. Ironically, this part of the course, however stressful, can also be the place where it is easiest to learn about and to develop resilience. Many students comment that although the group has been hard work, it is also where most learning has occurred.

Quite often, the time when burnout is most likely to occur is at the beginning of the second year. This is because this is the time when extra demands are being made in terms of collecting hours of therapy, work to be handed in and signed off, and the other small issues that go to completing a course. However, the end of the course is still not in sight, so these extra pressures can feel very hard.

At this stage, two things might happen in the group: participants might find excuses not to come as in saying, for example, 'this group does not work', or they become increasingly aggressive. If this happens it is often an exercise in cynicism and suggests that at least some of the participants are burnt out. Notice if this is happening in your group, either to yourself or someone else, as it might be a sign of increased stress that needs dealing with.

How self-care relates to PD groups: asking for help

Those who are themselves in, or entering, the caring professions are notably diffident about asking for help for themselves. I suspect this is because, at least in part, people training to be helpers prefer to help than be helped. However, once again, please read the quotation at the top of this chapter. No one can be completely independent of others, and having a healthy support system is an essential element of being a good and useful therapist. Asking for help is a strength rather than a weakness.

People get support from many sources such as friends and family, pets, neighbourhood, religious or political communities, but because this book is mainly concerned with PD groups, let's look at what support can come from the members of the PD group. Obviously, the PD group cannot meet every need, but it can be a place to start to notice that, when a healthy amount of stress is becoming unbearable, it may be to begin to look at other support systems outside the course.

Given that everyone will be struggling with the same issues, group members are in a good place to support each other through the challenges of the course. However, in order to access that support, members have to be prepared to take the risk of asking for support and that can be the hardest thing of all. If that particular barrier can be overcome, much support can be gained. Listening to each other's issues and difficulties with all aspects of the course can be very comforting, as it allows individuals to realise that they are not alone in their feelings and they will (probably) pass, in time. The stressful issues will still be there, but they can be borne more easily. Asking for and receiving support, whether from the PD group or outside of it, is a good way of building resilience.

Eric Berne (1910–1970), the founder of a theory known as Transactional Analysis, was interested in the different ways in which people organise their time and in particular, how they related to each other. He developed a theory that says there are six basic ways of structuring time (Berne, 1961). I have adapted them here to fit with the PD group:

Withdrawal: Spending time out of contact with others, whether or not they are present. If you are withdrawing within the PD group you are not likely to be listening to others, and just thinking about, for example, what you will do when the group is over.

Rituals: Interacting with other people but in a structured way, as in saying good morning to a bus driver or passer-by. Within the PD group this may happen in the first moments of the group, while you are settling in. It is a good way of starting the group, but notice if you are doing this all the time; for example, saying everything is fine, and asking others how they are, rather than admitting to vulnerabilities, etc.

Pastimes: Also known as 'small talk'. This is what you might have with colleagues at work or at a party. Within the group this might take the form of chatting about the course rather than really exploring how you feel and what needs to change. Watch out for this in the group as it is a form of avoidance but also a form of safety.

Activities: Defined as an activity that has a clearly defined goal: this might be on your own, in a study context or involvement in a joint project. In some ways the whole course is a shared activity. Within the PD group this might be when you and the rest of the group begin discussing how to structure a forthcoming assignment rather than how you feel about this. Discussing the assignment, although useful in itself, may be a way of withdrawing from the real work of the PD group. The PD group could be defined as an activity because it has a goal of each person developing their self-awareness, but it is important to bear that goal in mind. The group facilitator should be helpful here.

Psychological game-playing: This could be defined as the acting out of unconscious patterns learnt in childhood. Psychological games always end up with all players having familiar but uncomfortable feelings that can be hard to deal with. If this happens to you in the PD group, it may mean that you need to explore this in more depth in your personal therapy rather than the PD group.

Intimacy: Defined as shared moments of honesty and trust. These come when your self-esteem is strong enough to say your truth without fear of the responses. As the PD group develops, more and more of you should be able to share at a deeper level.

There are two important issues to recognise here: one is that the ways of structuring time that involve other people are much more supportive than activities undertaken alone. Make sure that you build in time for family and friends. The second point is that it is worth noting your own part in playing psychological games as this can be useful if you are willing to take the time to deal with the underlying issues.

Case study: Mo

Mo considers himself to be a person who takes reasonable care of himself. He is outgoing and friendly. He is single but has friends and is involved in a running club. Since leaving education ten years ago, he has been working for a public relations company, which he enjoyed at first but no longer finds satisfying. He wanted to change career and to work in a role where he could help people and feel that he was contributing to overall health.

He therefore decided to retrain as a therapist, in part because friends and family constantly told him what a good listener he was and turned to him for advice. Needing an income, he continued to work full-time. He quickly became popular in the course, making a name for himself as the class joker in that he would often lighten a difficult atmosphere.

Toward the end of the first year, he was doing well academically, and had passed all the written assignments. However, he noticed that he was frequently unusually tired and was struggling to do the required reading as well as to concentrate at his paid work. Toward the end of the course, the members of the PD group were asked to give each other feedback. Mo was assuming that his would be mainly positive. However, several people commented that his jokes were no longer funny but appeared to be rather bitter and cutting. Other members agreed that they had noticed his declining enthusiasm and lack of energy in the group.

Mo was devastated by this despite the fact that he had recognised his high stress levels. He had hoped that he was keeping this covered up and had not realised he had changed in a way that was clear to others. He became quite angry, to the point of considering leaving the course.

However, over the summer break, he discussed the issues with his supervisor and therapist. His therapist encouraged him to consider what had happened. They discovered that his need to please everyone had led him to over-working and over-pleasing.

The therapist encouraged him to consider other ways of getting his needs and especially to look at how he cared for himself.

His supervisor, working from a different angle, asked him to look at the impact this might have on clients when he started his placement. She asked if he was in danger of trying to placate or rescue clients, or colluding with them to try to make them feel better rather than allowing the process of therapy to take its course. Both therapist and supervisor encouraged Mo to build a support system so that he could become more resilient and also encouraged him to discuss the issues in the PD group in his second year

Mo did do this and was able to discuss his feeling about needing help, and also to ask the group to let him know if he appeared to be making too many jokes or, on the other hand, was appearing unusually irritable. He decided to look at all the ways he accessed support (see below).

Mo's support system

Step one: Making a list of everyone in his network, including family, friends, work colleagues and college network.

Step two: Considering different needs for support, such as: eating and sleeping well; taking regular breaks; making regular time for work commitments; building in time for fun, and for being alone as necessary; and, perhaps most importantly, confirmation that he was liked and approved of. In doing this step, Mo became aware of several issues. He noted that his running gave him enough exercise, but that his social life tended to be geared around groups of friends who had fun together but where there was little chance of having serious talks or of offering each other much individual support.

Step three: Putting the two lists together and looking at the different kinds of support each person can offer. For example, in order to eat well, Mo agreed with a friend that they would each cook for one another a couple of times a week. Mo also noted that his alcohol consumption had recently gone up. He was using it as a crutch to get through his stress – this is sometimes known as 'self-medicating'. He decided to limit himself to a couple of drinks on weekend nights but not to drink alcohol at all during the week. Because he was drinking less and eating better he found that his sleeping improved too, which was an added bonus. He also decided to use the PD group as a place where he might include some external validation. He began to ask for positive feedback each week and this quickly became a slot in the group, with others also asking for the same thing.

Developing a self-care plan

Part of developing a self-care plan can involve an understanding of your own flash points. This means noticing times where you feel overwhelmed or stressed. An easy way of doing this is to note changes in behaviour; for example, if eating habits change, so that you are eating more or less than usual. The same applies to sleeping – noticing that you are sleeping much more or less than usual can be a sign of stress. Being more irritable than usual, or being more restless than usual may all be signs of increased stress. Having noticed those signs, consider what your plan of action is and use it. Mo's plan, above, is one way to develop a self-care plan and here is another.

Activity

First of all, think of what you have done this week and note how much time you spend in each of the following categories:

Physical self-care: e.g., taking exercise; healthy eating; sleep.

Psychological self-care: e.g., recognising strengths and weaknesses; talking about my problems in the PD group or elsewhere.

Social self-care: e.g., making time for family and friends.

Study self-care: e.g., good planning and taking breaks or 'buddying up' with other people on the course.

Spiritual self-care: e.g., going for a walk; admiring the sunset or sunrise; meditation.

Now, using the information above, make a table as below that shows your activities each week with as many categories as you like.

Then, decide which ones you would like more of, less of, or what you would like to stay the same. Then write yourself a plan of how you will achieve your goals. This should include a final column of when this change will start from.

Table 15.1 Self-care

	More of	Less of	Stay the same	How to change (add your own thoughts)
Psychological self-care	x			
Physical self-care	x			
Study self-care			x	
Social self-care			x	
Spirituality self-care	x			
Work–life–study balance		x		

(adapted from TherapistAid.com, 2018)

Conclusion

In this chapter, I have pointed out that trainee therapists do suffer particular stresses. This is not something to be ashamed of, but to be noted as something that can be discussed within the PD group (and out of it too) as it is likely that many of you will find yourselves in the same position. It really helps to know that others are feeling the same way. Remember too that self-care involves other people – all of us need external validation to keep us motivated and moving forward in our lives. Sometimes this can be from family and friends but sometimes, for various reasons, this may not be sufficient.

In order to avoid burnout, a comprehensive self-care plan can really help, so do use the ideas you have read above. I have offered a couple of variations of self- care plans and it may be that, in your reading, you come across others that work better for you.

There are quite a few exercises for you to try out in this chapter. Not all of them will work for everyone, so don't be put off if some of them are not appropriate for your particular needs. Pick and choose, or work out a plan that fits best for you and in particular remember that while the PD group may contain particular stresses it can also, used well, offer comfort and support. Use it well but don't rely on it, or any one other person, to meet all your needs.

References

Barnett, J.E., Cooper, N. and College, L. (2009) Creating a culture of self-care. *Clinical Psychology: Science and Practice*, 16, pp. 16–20.

Berne, E. (1961) *Transactional Analysis in Psychotherapy*. New York: Grove Press.

Callahan, K., Christman, G. and Maltby, L. (2018) Battling burnout strategies for promoting physician wellness. *Advances in Pediatrics*, 65(1), pp. 1–17.

Harms, P.D., Brady, L., Wood, D. and Silard, A. (2018) Resilience and well-being. In E. Diener, S. Oishi and L. Tay (eds.), *Handbook of Well-Being*. Salt Lake City, UT: DEF Publishers.

Kaeding, A., Sougleris, C., Reid, C., van Vreeswijk, M.F., Hayes, C., Dorrian, J. and Simpson, S. (2017) Professional burnout, early maladaptive schemas, and physical health in clinical and counselling psychology trainees. *Journal of Clinical Psychology*, 73(12), pp. 1782–1796.

Lawson, G. (2007) Counselor wellness and impairment. *Journal of Humanistic Counseling, Education and Development*, 46(1), pp. 20–34.

Lawson, G. and Myers, J. (2011) Wellness, professional quality of life, and career-sustaining behaviors: What keeps us well? *Journal of Counseling and Development*, 89, pp. 163–171.

Salmela-Aro, K. and Read, S. (2017) Study engagement and burnout profiles among Finnish higher education students. *Burnout Research*, 7, pp. 21–28.

Therapistaid at www.therapistaid.com

Chapter 16

Mindfulness and self-compassion

Tara Fox

Introduction

This chapter draws from my significant experience of running personal development groups during counselling training. It attempts to demystify the meaning of the 'here and now' by presenting mindfulness as a helpful practical tool. There are many benefits of practising mindfulness including increased self-compassion and compassion for others. Through my experience as a personal development (PD) group facilitator I have witnessed how counsellors may have a lot of compassion for others but lack any for themselves.

In this chapter I will:

- explore mindfulness;
- discuss how the present moment can be a gift and a personal challenge;
- explain the Seven Pillars of Mindfulness;
- explain how to break habits and shift out of 'automatic pilot mode';
- discuss compassion and self-compassion;
- explain how to recognise when we are in the automatic pilot mode;
- explore visiting the now;
- use exercises to prompt awareness and discussion/engagement with the material.

What is mindfulness?

Mindfulness is often misunderstood as being 'mindful' (or 'mind-full') when in fact it is about choosing to be aware of this moment in time and of ourselves in the moment without judgement. It is in contrast with self-consciousness, which is about thinking and analysing the self by comparing the self to others. Jon Kabat-Zinn describes mindfulness as 'the awareness that emerges through paying attention on purpose, in the moment, and non-judgementally to the unfolding of experience moment by moment' (Kabat-Zinn, 2003, p. 145). Another way to describe mindfulness is to become awake to our whole self as a 'human being' rather than a 'human doing' and is therefore a shift from 'doing mode' to 'being mode' as described by Hick and Bien (2008). In this sense we move away from living life through habit (automatic pilot mode) to living life with more awareness of ourselves and of what is around us. Being still helps us to notice more, which may be one of the reasons why the PD group can feel challenging. At the same time, the more we slow down to notice, the more we may see of the joy in the world around us.

The present moment as a gift and personal challenge

The personal development group is a place where you are asked to sit down in an open circle for a length of time. This can generate anxiety for students who are used to striving towards achieving something or those that are used to being busy. They often feel frustrated at the group not going anywhere or feeling as if they want to drive the group to achieve a task. Being asked to 'be here' is a challenge and yet a large part of counsellor training tells you about the importance of the 'here and now'.

Your course may provide theoretical models to assist in understanding patterns of relating such as the drive to strive and achieve. Your training offers you the opportunity to be in the here and now through skills practice and the provision of PD groups. It may not explore ways to help you to be present in the here and now.

Activity

Have you ever wondered what is the here and now?
What does this mean to me?
Can I be in the here and now?

Make a list here of your responses to these questions, e.g.,

The here and now...............

Now consider the following case study.

Case study: Gael

Gael did not like being in the PD group. Her mind raced as each person shared something that she could relate to. The silences revealed to her that she has a hectic mind. She began to plan a supermarket shop to distract herself from the discomfort of being in the here and now.

Reacting by fighting against these thoughts can lead to an increase of them. It would help Gael if she shares what is going on for her with the group. Others may relate and some may offer helpful suggestions for the value of being here in the group. Either way, a reaction such as this is telling Gael that something needs her attention. Gael could take this to supervision or therapy if she does not feel able to share it in the here and now of the group. This could be an opportunity to discover a lot about her patterns of relating if she responds to this awareness in her journal, therapy and PD group.

Various studies have shown how mindfulness-based interventions (MBIs) such as the eight-week Mindfulness Based Stress Reduction course (Kabat-Zinn, 1992) and eight-week Mindfulness Based Cognitive Therapy (MBCT) course (Segal et al., 2002) reduce levels of stress, anxiety and rumination along with an increase in self-compassion (Cohen and Miller, 2009; Moore, 2008; Rimes and Wingrove, 2011; Shapiro et al., 2007). Trainee therapists have found MBIs to increase counsellor presence (enhanced attention to the present moment) in therapy and the ability to stay more with a client-induced silence. The ability to concentrate and focus on the client's experience was also experienced as increasing after MBIs.

Often trainee therapists have a strong sense of compassion for others and this inspires and motivates them to seek a professional career in therapeutic work. I find many students really struggle with finding self-compassion, as they often struggle with feeling that it is selfish to consider oneself. Self-compassion can help guard against compassion fatigue and burnout if you can overcome this restricting attitude and there is scope for this to be shifted in the group. Kristen Neff (2015) in her book *Self-Compassion: The Proven Power of Being Kind to Yourself* defines this stance as one that focuses on common humanity, a recognition that we all suffer and have similar problems. This can parallel the PD group, where students may experience and nurture 'a connected mind-set that feels more inclusive of others' (Germer & Neff, 2013, p. 857). As people share vulnerabilities in the group a 'common humanity' is felt and others can support and challenge self-destructive attitudes and thinking that can block progress. 'Self-compassion is relevant when considering personal inadequacies, mistakes, and failures as well as when confronting painful life situations that are outside our control' (Germer & Neff, 2013, p.856).

Mindfulness meditation leads to the activation of brain pathways that are associated with empathy (Siegel, 2010) and therapists who have a mindfulness practice have been found to have increased empathy in several studies (Aggs and Bambling, 2010; Bruce et al., 2010; Davis and Hayes, 2011; Schure et al., 2008; Keane, 2013).

In addition, a quantitative and qualitative study of 11 trainee clinical psychologists who completed an eight-week MBCT course found empirical evidence for changes in empathy. The analysis of the data revealed two themes, one relating to an 'altered therapy experience', such as less performance anxiety, increased empathy and less personal rumination of the client's material (Hopkins and Poeve, 2013).

The other theme relates to changes in the therapist's response to stress. A non-reactivity was reported along with an increase in awareness and resilience. This piece of research claims that mindfulness training can improve the therapeutic skills that are mentioned as significant 'common factors' contributing to an improvement of client outcomes. Germer et al. (2013) claim there is a theoretical link between client outcomes and mindfulness, given that mindfulness appears to activate brain pathways that are associated with regulation and attunement (Siegel, 2010).

The PD group provides the opportunity for you to get in touch with the here and now.

This is a gift when you use the time to notice what is going on for you moment by moment in the group. Here you may notice irritations, admirations, jealously, even rage, as well as joy and peace. The range of emotions you may experience as a group member is immense. It may be that you will never experience such an intense range of emotions and racing thoughts as you do in the PD group. However, this may be difficult when there is so much going on for you, so monitoring your emotional and bodily reactions may help.

Once your responses become conscious to you, they can actually be helpful to you. You may notice, for example, a strong reaction to a group member if you allow yourself to tune in to yourself in the here and now. This can then be shared in the group or taken to therapy and any insights then shared back to the group. When this happens it also helps others in the group who may not be as in touch with their own responses in the here and now. It can help others to see that they too are having a reaction to a group member. In the example below, it is unlikely that Kate is the only person in the room that is feeling this way.

Case study: Kate

Kate was feeling increasingly self-deprecatory. Each time Jo, a highly educated woman spoke eloquently in the room about her self-awareness it triggered a feeling of inadequacy and shame in Kate. Slowing down and noticing this in the here and now allowed Kate to take this to personal therapy. She was embarrassed but knew that her response to Jo needed to be explored rather than ignored.

The therapist helped Kate explore where these feelings were coming from. Kate had always felt below average at school. Her school report had said 'must try harder'. Jo had represented all that Kate felt she was not – intelligent, articulate, seemingly superior, a high achiever.

However, at the same time Kate noted Jo had disclosed a feeling of not being in control of her life, of being bullied at school for being an outsider. The therapist reflected this incongruence of experience back to Kate who realised she had projected her insecurities onto Jo. She chose to share this insight in the group even though this felt risky. Both Jo and Kate were able to clear this up and see each other clearly and non-defensively.

Kate was comparing herself to others. A mindful approach to the above encounter would involve noticing the comparing and accepting that this is happening rather than battling with the thought and following its pull into a negative spiral of self-criticism.

The Seven Pillars of Mindfulness

Mindfulness is an attitude rather than a skill. These pillars of mindfulness are attitudinal foundations (Kabat-Zin, 2004) of a mindfulness practice:

- **Non-judging:** Being with yourself requires self-kindness The PD group can encourage you to be gentle with yourself by offering the core conditions and you can also do the same for others. In the group you can recognise that we all suffer and this should help us to have more self-compassion and self-kindness. Carl Rogers believed that a group possesses its own kind of life and that this needs to be trusted. Presence is the group's wisdom, 'the wisdom of the organism, exhibited at every level from cell to group' (1970, p.44).
- **Patience:** Your mind has a life of its own and you can practise accepting this during mediation by returning to the breath or another anchor such as a sound. 'To be patient is simply to be completely in each moment, accepting it in its fullness' (Kabat-Zin, 2004, p. 35).

- **Beginner's mind:** What we know can prevent us from seeing things as they really are. Noticing aspects of life as if for the first time helps to build this.
- **Trust:** Releasing the 'inner critic' and instead learning to accept your own inner experience, feelings and intuition.
- **Non-striving:** 'Almost everything we do, we do for a purpose, to get something or somewhere. But in meditation, this attitude can be a real obstacle' (Kabat-Zin, 2004, p. 37). This also applies to being in a PD group as was illustrated by the student Gael in the case study mentioned above.
- **Acceptance:** 'You have to accept yourself as you are, before you can really change' (Kabat-Zin, 2004, p. 38).
- **Letting go:** This may also be called 'non-attachment' and it is challenging to neither wish to hold onto, nor to reject experience.

Breaking habits and shifting out of automatic pilot mode

However busy you are, you will notice the benefits if you regularly build in short five-minute mindful awareness exercises into your daily life. Routine and everyday experiences once again can be viewed with fresh eyes. This does require practice and some discipline.

Shifting out of 'thinking mode' in everyday life involves shifting to a noticing, describing mode rather than a thinking mode.

Thinking, analysing, self-reflection and evaluation can become tiresome and heavy on our hearts and this may peak during counsellor training. Everything comes under scrutiny. It is essential to take regular breaks from this as introspection can become exhausting. There are different types of thinking:

- **Active thoughts:** Planning, doing, researching.
- **Flowing thoughts:** Thoughts occur but are not judged or followed.
- **Automatic thoughts:** Often unhelpful thinking. Not usually based on reality and may include predictions about the future or ruminating on the past (Segal et al., 2002).

You may wonder how you can shift out of thinking mode. One way is to use VAKGO to help you, as outlined in the box below.

Activity

Shifting out of your thinking mode – use VAKGO.

Visual: What do I see around me?
Auditory: What do I hear around me?
Kinaesthetic: What do I feel?
Gustatory: What do I taste?
Olfactory: What can I smell?

In everyday life we can foster a 'beginner's mind' through paying attention to our senses. You will be amazed at what you have never noticed before once you start to do this on a regular basis. Why stand at the station/wait at the traffic lights chuntering and huffing and puffing? Try shifting to your VAKGO.

What do I see? Birds, moving trees, light reflecting on windows, clouds shaped like animals, puddles with rainbow colours.
What else can I see? Look up.
What do I hear? Rustling leaves, children's voices, beeps from the pedestrian crossing...
What can I feel? The cold on my feet, the feel of the socks on my legs, the coat on my arms...
What can I smell? Depending on the smell it may be not be worth staying with this one and as for taste this may not be relevant if you are standing outside and therefore not eating, but the seeing, hearing and feeling are the main ones that will be of use to you in shifting out of thinking and moving into a noticing mode.

This is called informal mindfulness practice and is relatively straightforward to do because it does not require you to give up any time. You can easily introduce mindful walking by labelling what you notice as you walk slowly along.

Do one thing at a time

I hear women say they are fantastic at multitasking as opposed to men, who are criticised for not being able to do this. Doing things at the same time is impossible. Multitasking really means shifting your attention rapidly from one job to another and can be exhausting. To shift from task to task is a sign of being in the 'automatic pilot' mode, where you are working towards various jobs mindlessly (Williams and Penman, 2011). Try to focus on one job at a time; for example, if you are making lunch, do not look for other jobs to do. Instead use the few seconds of thinking time to come back to your breath as opposed to thinking/beginning another task.

This meditation of breath awareness helps us to stop thinking and be in the here and now. When I first learnt this meditation, I found it easy to remember to do while waiting for the kettle to boil before making a cup of tea. The key to learning this is to choose an everyday activity and to do it mindfully, noticing the moment as if it is the first time you have seen it.

Activity

It's OK to just be! Who said you had to be always doing something all the time? You are a 'human being' not a 'human doing'. Try the 15-minute challenge:
I challenge you to sit and read a magazine for 15 minutes without checking your phone, watching TV or anything else.

What was easy about this? What was difficult?
When you try this again what might you do to help?

Compassion and self-compassion

Being in the present moment involves 'being with yourself'. Having a relationship with yourself may be something you have not thought about before. Whether you have thought about it or not, you do have a relationship with yourself. This includes how you talk to yourself, the internal voice that speaks sweetly or harshly to you. Throughout the day you will be constantly communicating with yourself, rallying yourself along, reassuring yourself, criticising yourself, doubting yourself. Be aware – whatever you are saying to yourself affects how you move throughout the day, what you do and how you feel.

When you first began training in counselling it was likely you were introduced to the core conditions for the counselling relationship. Commonly through counsellor training you will have been challenged to develop these through various activities. During the giving of feedback to others you are challenged to be congruent. You are also directed to focus on your developing congruence in your personal journal and later in personal therapy. As a skills user you are challenged to have empathy for others, to not judge others harshly but to respect their human errors and to have compassion, unconditional positive regard. As a client and as a member of a PD group you are developing a sense of congruence too and becoming aware of perhaps how incongruent you are.

Activity

How about having the core conditions for yourself:

Empathy for yourself?
Unconditional positive regard (UPR) for yourself?
Treating yourself with respect?
Attending to yourself?
Having compassion for yourself?
Forgiving yourself?

Gilbert (2005) tells us that the ability to care for yourself is related to the ability to be compassionate towards yourself. In my experience, trainee counsellors often struggle to care for themselves. It was certainly something I struggled to understand, and I am still learning ways of looking after myself as well as others. Trainees are expected to look after themselves as well as others, but little attention is placed on how to do this.

It may upset you to realise you don't have empathy for yourself. However, noticing is the first step to changing something. Your family upbringing instilled a set of values and rules for living that can get in the way of taking care of yourself. Chapter 15 on self-care looks at this in more depth.

In addition, your therapist can help you to explore the barriers you have put in place that prevent you from having self-compassion and self-care, but sharing them in the group helps you and others to challenge themselves.

Activity

Consider here your rules for living as absorbed from your family when you were growing up, e.g., complete all work before playing, do not cry, always do your best, etc.

How have these affected your life?
What are the costs and benefits of having these rules for living?

The PD group can also help you explore self-imposed limitations such as these. The main point is for you to take an accepting attitude of yourself, a compassionate, non-judgemental stance for your misgivings rather than a critical one. Paul Gilbert (2005) considers our painful experiences in childhood of not feeling loved are linked to a person's difficulty in having self-compassion. In my experience, the compassion felt from the group can greatly assist in students finding more self-compassion. If you do not feel this in the group then your therapist and supervisor are there to support you with finding self-compassion.

Recognising when I am in 'automatic pilot' mode

Practising mindfulness can help you to notice more of your life. When we inevitably reconnect to the treadmill of the autopilot, remember you can choose to step off and experience daily actions with a joyful beginner's mind.

Case study: Claire, part 1

Claire, an experienced business coach, had been finding the work increasingly demanding this year and had been leaving the office in a rush to get to her professional counselling training course. She consequently felt unsettled and breathless when she arrived in the PD group and could barely concentrate on what people were sharing in the group.

This left her questioning herself and wondering if she had made the wrong choice in retraining at her age. She was criticising herself for not keeping up with what was being shared in the group and began to feel vulnerable. She kept quiet in the group and felt like an outsider who did not belong.

In this scenario Claire's critical inner dialogue sent her into a downward spiral of negativity leading to feelings of vulnerability and rejection. These are self-imposed thoughts. Claire is responsible for creating her own negative experiences. If she could shift to noticing what she is doing here it could help to distance her from the thoughts.

What evidence do I have to tell me that I am functioning in a 'doing mode'?

> ### Case study: Claire, part 2
>
> Claire shared in the PD group how she really wishes she had told her family she wouldn't come to the meal on Saturday. She says she should have said 'no' this time, but she would like to go next time when she had more free time. She called herself an idiot, a fool. She explains how the consequences of her agreement to attend are now going to impact on her family time/time on her assignments.
>
> She begins to question herself and her decision judging her choice as inferior to what ideally should have happened. The group picks up on this and someone points out that she is beating herself up a lot, using a lot of 'shoulds' and comparing herself to an 'ideal'. She has no self-compassion.

Notice how Claire is effectively attacking herself with critical thoughts. She is revisiting how she feels over and over again and retelling the story. This is typical of the mind in 'doing mode'. When you notice yourself engaging in self-criticism, you are functioning in an automatic pilot and a *doing* mode rather than *being*.

In the PD group you can help each other to notice when you are in a *doing* rather than *being* mode by looking out for signs of yourself and peers engaging in self-criticisms/beating yourself up/reliving and rehearsing stories. The course is deigned to engender reflexivity, analysis and self-evaluation skills as well as critical thinking. However, it is just as important to learn how to *be*. Participating in a PD group reminds us of how challenging and rewarding it is to just *be*, to 'be here' and 'just now' in 'this moment'

Take the time to visit the now

When you are counselling you will certainly experience the *now*. This is when you are unaware of the time passing. You are 'in the zone', completely absorbed in what you are doing. Notice how enjoyable this is. To be absorbed in an activity has been described as 'flow' by Hungarian researcher Mihaly Csikszentmihalyi (1990) and is said to be when humans are at their happiest.

Practice visiting the now...

In your mind's eye, take the journey through the front door of the building where you are training, or perhaps your placement entrance. Write down what you can remember. The next time you enter look again look to see what else you notice that you may have missed before. Practise developing more of a sense of your home environment. Can you remember what is under your kitchen cupboard? You can practise noticing more of what is around you at home, more of what you see when you come to work and study. This is a simple way of visiting the now.

In the PD group, trainees who struggle to 'be here now' often experience a racing of thoughts that either takes them to the past, where they can relive painful feelings or replay mistakes, or takes their mind to the future, to anxieties. The PD group provides the opportunity to be here now, to attend to others, to notice our reactions to others, to notice our own feelings and memories that other people trigger.

Shifting into 'being mode' means directing your attention to observing what is happening in the present moment. This involves noticing and accepting the thought but not following it or joining in with the content. You are cultivating a gentle awareness. This is self-compassion as opposed to self-criticism. Being neutral about our own thoughts and feelings or preoccupations helps us to be here with ourselves.

Preparing to be in the group

Consider preparing for being here on the course/in the PD group by settling yourself down and checking in with how you are in the current moment. Notice what you notice and agree with yourself to pay attention to and to act on this later if necessary.

If at all possible, arrive early so you do not bring a sense of being rushed with you into the room. This parallels the counselling relationship, where equally you and the client will benefit from a settled and relaxed you.

To help you to feel more grounded for the day, consider how you might introduce a 'Three-Minute Breathing Space' (Segal et al., 2002). You would need to look down/close your eyes to prevent you from becoming distracted by your surroundings.

Activity: The Three-Minute Breathing Space

I am just stopping and pausing. Bringing myself into the present moment by noticing what is happening now in my thoughts… in my mind… and in the body. Just noticing what's there without having to change or alter it in anyway…

And now moving my attention to the breath as it enters and leaves my body…. the in breath and the out breath… Just noticing the breathing itself… This is a body that is already breathing, and I am just joining in with it. The in breath and the out breath…

And now moving my attention to the whole of my body including posture and facial expression, the room I am sitting in. I will open my eyes when I am ready. I thank myself for giving this time to reconnect with how I am.

Conclusion

This chapter has drawn your attention to the benefits of being in the present moment, celebrating the here and now as both a gift and challenge. I hope you can see the ways in which you may move out of the automatic pilot mode and into a state of awareness.

Cultivating mindfulness can help you in being fully present in client work, and in the PD group to notice more of how you feel and respond. As such it can increase your ability to make choices about what you respond to as well as helping you to develop what Carl Rogers called 'presence' (1951). Developing more self-compassion can greatly assist with the challenges of training and working as a therapist. The group provides an opportunity to discover and be, to recognise that we all suffer, to offer and experience kindness and compassion, and it is a place to be a 'human being' rather than a 'human doing'.

References

Aggs, C. and Bambling, M. (2010) Teaching mindfulness to psychotherapists in clinical practice: The mindful therapy programme. *Counselling and Psychotherapy Research*, 10(4), pp. 278–286.

Bruce, N.G., Manber, R., Shapiro, S.L. and Constantino, M.J. (2010) Psychotherapist mindfulness and the psychotherapist's process. *Psychotherapy Theory Research Practice Training*, 47, pp. 83–97.

Cohen, J.S. and Miller, L.J. (2009) Interpersonal mindfulness training for well-being: A pilot study with psychology graduate students. *Teachers College Record*, 111, pp. 2760–2774.

Csikszentmihalyi, M. (1990) *Flow: The Psychology of Optimal Experience*. New York: HarperCollins.

Davis, D.M. and Hayes, J.A (2011) What are the benefits of mindfulness? A practice review of psychotherapy related research. *Psychotherapy*, 48, pp. 198–208.

Germer, C.K. and Neff, K.D. (2013) Self compassion in clinical practice. *Journal of Clinical Psychology*, 69(8), pp. 856–867.

Germer, C.K., Siegel, R.D. and Fulton, P.R., eds. (2013) *Mindfulness and Psychotherapy*. New York: Guildford Press.

Gilbert, P. (2005) Compassion and cruelty: A biopsychosocial approach. In P. Gilbert (ed.), *Compassion, Conceptualisations, Research and Use in Psychotherapy*. New York: Routledge.

Hick, L. and Bien, T. (2008) *Mindfulness and the Therapeutic Relationship*. New York: Guildford Press.

Hopkins, A. and Poeve, M. (2013) Teaching mindfulness based cognitive therapy to trainee psychologists: Qualitative and quantitative effects. *Counselling Psychology Quarterly*, 26(2), pp. 115–130.

Kabat-Zinn, J. (1992) Effectiveness of a meditation-based stress reduction program in the treatment of anxiety disorders. *The American Journal of Psychiatry*, 149, pp. 936–943.

Kabat-Zinn, J. (2003) Mindfulness-based interventions in context: Past, present and future. *Clinical Psychology: Science and Practice*, 10(20), pp. 144–156.

Kabat-Zinn, J. (2004) *Wherever You Go There You Are: Mindfulness for Everyday Life*. London: Piaktus Books.

Keane, A. (2013) The influence of therapist mindfulness practice on psychotherapeutic work: A mixed methods study. *Mindfulness*, 5, pp. 689–703.

Moore, P. (2008) Introducing mindfulness to clinical psychologists in training: An experiential course of brief exercises. *Journal of Clinical Psychology in Medical Settings*, 15, pp. 331–337.

Neff, K. (2015) *Self-Compassion: The Proven Power of Being Kind to Yourself*. New York: HarperCollins.

Neff, K.D. and Germer, C.K. (2013) A pilot study and randomized controlled trial of the mindful self-compassion program. *Journal of Clinical Psychology*, 69, pp. 28–44.

Rimes, K.A. and Wingrove, J. (2011) Pilot study of mindfulness-based cognitive therapy for trainee clinical psychologists. *Behavioural and Cognitive Psychotherapy*, 39, pp. 235–241.

Rogers, C.R. (1951) *Client-Centred Therapy*. Boston: Houghton Mifflin.

Rogers, C.R. (1970) *Encounter Groups*. Harmondsworth: Penguin.

Schure, M.B., Christopher, J. and Christopher, S. (2008) Mind-body medicine and the art of self-care: Teaching mindfulness to counselling students through yoga, meditation and Qigong. *Journal of Counselling and Development*, 86(1), pp. 47–56.

Segal, Z.V., Williams, J.M. and Teasdale, J.D. (2002) *Mindfulness Based Cognitive Therapy for Depression: A New Approach to Preventing Relapse*. New York: Guilford Press.

Shapiro, S.L., Brown, K.W. and Biegel, G.M. (2007) Teaching self-care to caregivers: Effects of mindfulness-based stress reduction on the mental health of therapists in training. *Training and Education in Professional Psychology*, 1, pp. 105–115.

Siegel, D.J. (2010) *The Mindful Therapists: A Clinician's Guide to Mindsight and Neural Integration*. New York: W.W. Norton & Company.

Williams, M. and Penman, D. (2011) *Mindfulness: A Practical Guide to Finding Peace in a Frantic World*. London: Piatkus Books.

Chapter 17

Reflecting on and capturing your personal development

Study skills support

Heather Dale and Jayne Godward

Introduction

Throughout this book we have discussed different ways of developing your personal development, with an emphasis on getting the most out of your PD group.

In this short chapter we want to focus on reflecting on and capturing your personal development. This is because counselling courses often do assess this aspect of training and look at how trainees have developed an understanding of themselves both in and out of the PD group.

There are many and various ways in which you can capture your learning and development. In this chapter we will give you a few ideas and will look at:

- using a personal development journal;
- recording;
- client process notes as opposed to session notes;
- keeping comments and feedback from your peers and tutors so that you can refer to them later;
- using the PD group to reflect on self;
- creative ways of looking at your progress and personal development;
- using and reflecting on personal and professional development post-qualification.

Using a personal development journal

Many courses expect their students to keep a journal, learning review or diary of their personal development, which may or may not be assessed. In this section we are going to give two examples of ways of recording your experiences. One way is how you might have done this at the beginning of the course and the other way shows how your way of thinking may have changed over the time of the course.

These scenarios take you back to the Wednesday PD group (see Chapter 8).

Case study: The Wednesday PD group

The PD group is made up of ten individuals who are in their first year of counsellor training. One group member, Maria has missed several group meetings and often arrives a little late for the group. Rukhsana in particular, gets very angry.

One day Maria comes in ten minutes late, apologising as usual, Rukhsana loses her temper and says, very angrily, 'How come you are always late Maria? I thought we had a group contract regarding boundaries and timekeeping?' Maria cries and says it is not fair to be angry with her as she has such a lot on.

After the session Rukhsana writes the following reflection about the session.

Rukhsana's reflection: Take 1

Today I finally had enough of Maria always being late. She was ten minutes late again today and whinged and whined about what a hard life she has. The implication being that the rest of us have it easy, I suppose. Well it is not easy for me either but I still get here on time so why can't she? She complains about the bus being late but the PD group is at the end of the day and she should have been here all day anyway.

I got mad and had a real shout at her, reminding her about the boundaries and rules we agreed at the beginning of the group and she wailed some more and then of course everyone took her side. I don't think I should have been quite so angry as I was but really – she is such a victim!

In her reflections here, Rukhsana blames Maria for her own anger. She says that Maria is a victim, but in fact, in blaming someone else for her own behaviour, she is herself a victim, although an angry one. A useful piece of theory for both Maria and Rukhsana to read would be Karpman's Drama Triangle (Karpman, 1968).

Now let's imagine that Rukhsana has written a more reflective piece.

Rukhsana's reflection: Take 2

Today I finally had enough of Maria always being late. She was ten minutes late again today and whinged and whined about what a hard life she has. I became angry but afterwards I thought about what had made me angry. After all, what real difference does it make to me if Maria is late or not? She slips in like a little mouse and does not really disturb anyone. I suppose I get angry because I have a struggle getting here too but I have always managed it.

I think I rather pride myself on being tough and stoical and getting through things and that might make me rather unsympathetic to poor Maria sometimes. Or maybe I rather admire her for her rule-breaking because I know I would never dare. Oh dear. I started off wanting to say what a victim Maria is but now I think perhaps it is me who is the persecutor.

You can see that in this piece, Rukhsana accepts some responsibility for her own behaviour. She is writing about her own feelings and thoughts and realises that Maria coming late does not really affect her or the group. She wonders if she is angry with Maria because she would like to break rules and come late sometimes but lacks courage. This is a much more reflective piece of writing.

Now let's have a look at what Maria would say about the situation.

Maria's reflection: Take 1

Today I went to the PD group. As soon as I walked in Rukhsana started having a go at me. Asking why I am always late and why I can't get there on time when other people can. She pointed out the group contract and I felt like a two-year-old. Then the others started having a go at me. I felt upset and I just wanted to run out of the room, they were so nasty. The tutor let it go on for ages but finally started to ask people to calm down and then gave us all a chance to speak. It got better then as I did have chance to explain my situation. It is so hard for me at the moment being a single parent now Michael has left me. I have to take the kids to school before I set off and then it is a long way to travel to get to the course. I'm fed up and feel all alone.

How reflective is Maria being here?
What view is she taking of this situation?

Now have a look at a possible second reflection to this situation. How is this different?

Maria's reflection: Take 2

Today I was late again for the PD group, As soon as I walked in Rukhsana started asking me why I am always late and why I can't get there on time. She was obviously very annoyed with me. Initially I felt ashamed and upset. Then I realised that this took me back to being a child, when I always seemed to be in trouble and getting punished.

At first I started to cry and wanted to stamp my feet like I had as a child at the injustice of it. Then I realised that I was behaving as I had when I was a child and that I don't need to do that anymore. So I apologised to the group, and explained how drained I am, with everything that is going on in my life. Through talking about my situation I realised that I need to ask for help more; for example, I could ask a friend to take my two to school on a Wednesday so that I could catch the earlier bus.

I had not been brought up to ask for help. I always felt that I had to 'be strong' and not rely on others. This may have caused problems in my relationships as well as in the group.

As with Rukhsana, there is a qualitative difference here between Maria's two responses. In the first response, she is taking a defensive position, seeing herself as a victim of others. In the second reflection, she is more able to stand back and think about why she has behaved in the way that she has. Usefully, Maria was able to learn from this difficult situation and start to think about how she could change her situation. She made some links between her personal history and her current behavioural patterns that she will be able to use in the future.

Your journal should be a space where you can reflect in the way that Rukhsana and Maria do in the 'Take 2' examples above. It is not always easy to reflect on yourself in this way, but a journal can be a good way of taking stock. Some people like to write up journals after their therapy sessions or after the PD group, especially when either of these have been particularly challenging.

However, do remember that, in all likelihood you will have to hand in your journal at some stage and that it might be read by tutors and external examiners. It is also important to keep other people's names anonymised to protect their confidentiality.

Recording learning

Writing notes does not work for everyone. If this is true for you, you could record instead, or draw pictures, write poetry or music. Most smartphones or MP3 players have a recording app on them and you could use this to record your immediate reflections before you write them down. If you wish to record therapy sessions make sure you ask permission first. It would not normally be acceptable to record the PD group as there are too many other people talking who could be identified.

Consider your favourite way of capturing memories:

Do you draw, take photographs, keep a diary, or just rely on memories?
What other ways can you think of?

Client process notes

When students start counselling they are often encouraged to keep two sets of notes: one is the formal logging of what has occurred in the session and the other contains the thoughts and feelings of the counsellor in relation to the client. Process notes must be handwritten for the sake of data protection and the client must not be identifiable. Use a code for the client, such as A for the first client you meet with, B for the second one and so on. This can be a useful way of keeping your reflections alive, as they may change over time.

The beauty of process notes is that rather than looking at client issues, your focus is about what was going on for you. Some of the things you can focus on are your thoughts and feelings when you are with the client and how this affects the counselling relationship and your interventions. You can also reflect on whether some of your own personal issues are emerging in your client work. These reflections will help you prepare for supervision or personal therapy or you may be able to share personal responses in your PD group so long as this is not client material.

Keeping comments and feedback from your peers and tutors

During the length of your course, it is inevitable that you will be given feedback, both on your developing skills and how people see you as a person. Again whether or not you agree with it, remember that this is how you appear to that person or to that group and make a note of it to consider later.

There is a saying that we have come across, attributed to Fritz Perls, which goes like this: 'If only one person calls you an elephant you can ignore them, but if a whole bunch of people do, start eating peanuts.' So if in the PD group your feedback is that many people see you as being assertive and articulate, whereas you consider yourself shy and struggling for words, the chances are they are right. You may have a false impression of yourself and the real 'you' may be more confident and more articulate than you know. If you write this in your journal, you can come back to it when you need to.

Using the PD group to reflect on what you have done

By the time you have read this far you will, we hope, have realised what an essential place the PD group can be for exploring your learning and reflecting on insights you have gained into yourself. Students often use it as a way of giving and getting feedback. Sometimes this is in the form of structured peer feedback activities and sometimes it is naturally occurring. Your peers and tutors may be able to see changes which have occurred in you that you are not as aware of.

Creative ways of looking at your progress and personal development

As we have said, there are different ways of reviewing your progress as well as writing. One way is to visualise where you are. In Chapter 5, Jayne invited readers to imagine where they were in relation to an imaginary pool at the start of their course. You can also use the same metaphor as you progress in order to capture your learning and development so far.

Activity: Swimming pool

Where are you now and what are you doing in terms of your personal development? At different points during your course, you could visualise an imaginary pool and place yourself according to where you feel you are.

For example, are you in the shallow end, deep end, on the diving board, relaxing by the pool, swimming under water, floating etc.?
Swimming or wading? On the edge dangling your feet in? Or even sinking under the water?

If you record this in your journal, you can look back on this and review later.

Another way of capturing your personal development in a creative way is to draw a picture that represents your development.

Activity: Draw a picture that represents your 'journey' or development on the course.

This can use a lot of colour and be as abstract or as realistic as you want. To be effective you don't have to be an artist or artistic, but it can be a good way of getting in touch with yourself and to reflect on your personal growth.

Some people will draw it as a road and other people will draw it as a landscape or a picture story or even a tree.

On the picture try to represent:

- the highs and lows;
- the learning that has taken place for you personally;
- possible insights;
- how you see yourself now compared to when you started the course or 'journey'.

If you can share it with someone who you trust or possibly your personal therapist, this may be useful, as you could gain more depth by talking about it.

After the course

As this is the last chapter, we wanted to say a word about what happens after your course has finished and you are a qualified counsellor. Most therapy organisations expect members to accumulate a certain amount of continuous personal and professional development (CPPD) each year. This can take many forms. You may decide that you have enjoyed study so much that you would like to carry on to the next level. You may decide that you want to do some more specialist training.

Whatever you do for your continuing professional development (CPD) after the course, whether this involves short courses, conferences, networking groups, writing articles or joining committees, it is important to carry on reflecting on your processes and learning to ensure you are being a reflective practitioner and are applying your learning to yourself and your client work. Recording the important points in your journal or capturing these in general will help you remember.

Reading articles and books and reflecting on your learning is an important way of continuing your development.

Continuing to reflect on your supervision and personal therapy also will help you to develop further.

Conclusion

In this short chapter we have aimed to offer you tips on how to reflect and capture your personal development. This can take many different forms from straightforward journal writing to creative methods involving drawing, poetry and music.

We have stressed the importance of charting your progress and continuing to do so even when qualified, in whatever way works for you.

You can start right now, by recording your responses to the exercises and activities in this book

References

Karpman, S. (1968) Fairy tales and script drama analysis. *Transactional Analysis Bulletin*, 6(7), pp. 39–43.

Conclusion

Introduction

This book has covered a range of topics associated with personal development and the personal development group. We have aimed to give you a wide overview of the history of personal development and personal development type groups and a good knowledge of how PD groups work in practice. We have used personal experiences of both students and tutors to bring the subject alive and have looked at topics associated with personal development, e.g., attachment, mindfulness, ethics. In this conclusion we would like to highlight some of the themes which came out from this work.

Sections A and B: Understanding personal development and personal development groups

In these sections we set the scene. We explored the history behind PD groups, the research into their effectiveness, and also students wrote about their own experiences. We have explained where the PD group sits in terms of helping trainee counsellors develop their self-awareness.

We have taken some trouble to emphasise that, although there is, of course, a link between personal development and issues that need to be taken to personal therapy, these are different activities. However, we understand the line can get blurred from time to time.

A key issue is the importance of the PD group in helping students to be more effective with clients, due to the insights gained by trainees about themselves, which might have otherwise affected their client work positively or negatively.

Carole Smith's current research demonstrates that there is emotional learning to be had from the PD group that may not be found on other areas on the course and that qualified counsellors are still able to use that learning to help them work at relational depth with clients. She also highlights that all the participants in her research found the PD group meaningful and worthwhile in promoting sound and safe client outcomes.

We explained that conflicts and difficulties are often part of the PD group, and that great learning can come from the management of this. Storms and conflicts are inevitable in PD groups and may be essential for the group's progress, so preparing for these and managing these is an essential part of the group work rather than an added problem.

Section C: Developing self-awareness to enhance practice

In this section of the book, we moved on to consider other areas of self-development, with an emphasis on how these may play out in the PD group.

We looked at ethics and the importance of being aware of your personal ethics as well as professional ethics and how the PD group can be used to explore these. We also asked the reader to focus on personal moral qualities. Being aware of these is fundamental for client work and we hope that this chapter has helped you really look at what you bring to the counselling relationship. These aspects will underpin and inform who you are and how you operate in the world.

Another area explored in this book was to do with attachment styles. Attachment styles involve looking at how we relate to others, including those in the PD groups. These areas often come up in PD group discussions and an understanding of relational patterns and their origins may allow us to become more aware of how we relate to clients.

Similarly, looking at identity and who we are and the impact we have on others is another area for exploration in the PD group, where we are in a group of 'strangers' who we are reacting to and who are reacting to us. Being aware of difference and diversity is essential for counsellors and this chapter looks at how we will be seen by others depending on how we present and whether we appear similar or different from others.

Section D: Other aspects of personal development

The final section of this book explored activities that are intended to enhance personal awareness and development. Suggestions were made as to how these could link with PD group work.

The chapter on personal therapy did not begin originally as a debate between two opposing sides but we realised that having looked at published research, it would be useful to unpick the arguments for and against mandatory personal therapy. Many courses stipulate this but the research into its usefulness is mixed. We hope you found the arguments there stimulating and were able to reach your own conclusions

Chapter 14 looked at the essential area of supervision with a focus on the supervisee's personal development and self-awareness. Several case studies demonstrate the personal insights which might emerge in supervision or even in the choosing of a supervisor.

The next chapter discussed the need for self-care. It makes the point that counsellor training is a stressful endeavour. You will find exercises here to help you think about your own self-care and what you can do to look after yourself physically, psychologically and spiritually. The PD group can also offer support, of course.

We have included a chapter about mindfulness, another form of self-care that has become popular in recent years. If we can become more mindful generally and aware of what is going on we will be more present and effective in client work. Tara encourages us to be a 'human being' rather than a 'human doing'.

Finally, we offered some tips on how to capture your personal development and reflect on your learning. Here we stressed the importance of remembering and recording the learning about yourself and insights you gain, as you take part in your personal development work and PD group sessions.

We hope you have found this book useful and will be able to use it as a resource in the future.

Index

Printed in Great Britain
by Amazon

46811074R00110